UNEXPLAINED NATURAL PHENOMENA

Keith Tutt

First published in 1997 by Orion Media
An imprint of Orion Books Ltd
Orion House, 5 Upper St Martin's Lane, London WC2H 9EA

A CIP catalogue record for this book is available from the British Library.

ISBN 0–75281–216–5

Typeset by SetSystems Ltd, Saffron Walden, Essex
Printed and bound in Great Britain
by Clays Ltd, St Ives plc.

CONTENTS

CONTENTS

To Hannah, for your support throughout.

FOREWORD

'The most beautiful thing we can experience is the mysterious.
It is the source of all true art and science.'

Albert Einstein

We are all afraid of the unknown – it is programmed into our
very cells to be so. This instinctive fear is the reason we have
survived as a species: by being alert to new dangers, new
threats, new opportunities. We have needed this fear to keep
us safe – while our need to survive has been stronger and
more important than our need for truth. After all, who cares
how many planets fill the skies when the wolf is howling at
the cave mouth?

Many of us in the modern world are now fortunate to have
solved some of the basic problems of survival: when food is
short we can go shopping, not hunting; when water runs dry
we turn on a tap; when our fires go out, we can always
switch them back on. This, we understand, is called civilization. And if civilization brings anything worth having, it is
the opportunity to make the search for truth more important
than the desire for survival and comfort. It brings a hope that
we can find answers to our deepest and strangest questions
about our world, our universe, and the unexplained natural
phenomena that fill them.

Now we have a new, more interesting problem: the fact
that many things remain unexplained. Our choice is stark:
shall we fill our 'truth void' with easy answers, common
prejudices and received opinion, or shall we start the search –
not just for answers, but for truth?

This is not a book about easy answers. It is a book for those who want to do the searching for themselves – because, in the end, the real search for truth never stops. If we ever reach a point where we think we have reached the truth ... then we have just stopped looking. I don't know whether every word in this book is true. The phenomena described here are certainly real to the people who experienced and reported them. Just because we were not all there at the time, does not mean the experiences are not true. It also does not mean they *are* true. In the end it is for you to decide ... or not decide.

1

POWERS OF THE MIND

'We are both spectators and actors in the great drama of existence.'

Niels Bohr, physicist

The 20th century has been the century of the mind. Since the findings of Freud and Jung, we have learned that the relationship between mind and matter, between the inner world of perception and 'objective reality' is not what we previously believed. Science has gone on to confirm the strange nature of this relationship from the results of quantum physics. We must now ask: is our reality 'out there', or is it really happening 'in here', in the conscious, unconscious and superconscious parts of our minds? We seem to face two new and potentially contradictory ideas: first, that our minds are infinitely more powerful than we had thought; and second, that our potential for self-delusion may be limitless.

These advances in understanding mean that the *powers of the mind* are expanding. Some futurists believe that with the arrival of the new millennium we may expect to see great advances in our mental capacities, our creative abilities, our psychic powers. In areas like sport and business, it is the mind and its capacity to create, using vision, focus and concentration, that is now at the heart of things. In this section we look at those who have already explored the new possibilities of the mind – to affect matter, to communicate, to heal, to resist the elements, to see the future, to solve crime, even, it seems, to fly. When it comes to the mind, it looks as if *we* may get to decide where to set the limits, if there are any . . .

LEVITATION

On a dark London night in December 1868 an assembly of three important and influential members of London society were treated to a demonstration of levitation which is still the subject of controversy today.

Lord Adare, a former *Daily Telegraph* correspondent, his cousin Captain Charles Wynne and a gentleman named the Master of Lindsay were all present when D.D. Home – the world-renowned medium and psychic – apparently floated into the air, and was wafted out of one window, only to return through another. The Master of Lindsay described the events:

I was sitting on December 16 1868, in Lord Adare's rooms in Ashley Place, London, S.W., with Mr Home and Lord Adare and a cousin of his. During the sitting, Mr Home went into a trance, and in that state was carried out of the window in the room next to where we were, and was brought in at our window. The distance between the windows was about seven feet six inches, and there was not the slightest foothold between them, nor was there more than a 12 inch projection, which served as a ledge to put flowers on. We heard the window in the next room lifted up, and almost immediately after we saw Home floating in the air outside our window. The moon was shining full into the room; my back was to the light, and I saw the shadow on the wall of the window sill, and Home's feet about six inches above it. He remained in this position for a few seconds, then raised the window and glided into the room feet foremost and sat down.

Lord Adare then went into the next room to look at the window from which he had been carried. It was raised about 18 inches; and he expressed his wonder how Mr Home had been taken through so narrow an aperture head first, with the body rigid, and then returned quite quietly. The window is about 70 feet from the ground.

Daniel Dunglas Home was born in Scotland in 1833, but was taken to America at an early age, where his psychic abilities soon began to emerge. At 13 he had a vision of a friend named Edwin. From Edwin's gesturing Home intuited that his friend had been dead for three days. This turned out to be true. Later, when Home's mother, who had remained in Scotland, died, Home saw her 'spirit' before news of her death arrived.

In America's growing Spiritualist movement, Home's talents flourished. Nevertheless he eschewed the darkened seance rooms that had become the fashionable places for conversations with spirits. Instead he concentrated on concrete, tangible demonstrations of physical phenomena. In 1852, at a demonstration in the home of Connecticut businessman Ward Chency, Home's feats were closely watched by a local journalist, F.L. Barr:

> Suddenly, without any expectation on the part of the company, Home was taken up into the air. I had hold of his hand at the time and I felt his feet – they were lifted from the floor. He palpitated from head to foot with the contending emotions of joy and fear which choked his utterances. Again and again he was taken from the floor, and the third time he was carried to the ceiling of the apartment, with which his hands and feet came into gentle contact.

The fact that Home allowed such close contact with his audience contrasts starkly with the work of today's illusionists. Home described his own experiences in plain, but graphic language:

> I feel no hands supporting me, and since the first time, I have felt no fear; though should I have fallen from the ceiling of some rooms in which I have been raised, I could not have escaped serious injury. I am generally lifted up perpendicularly; my arms frequently become rigid, and are drawn above my

head, as if I were grasping the unseen power which slowly raises me from the floor.

Throughout his long career Home performed levitation feats in an impressive variety of places. Often Home had never seen or visited the location before the event. Indeed many demonstrations are supposed to have occurred spontaneously. This makes the potential for the setting up of illusions much less likely, though not wholly impossible.

Home was investigated by the rich and powerful of his day, many of whom became either supporters or detractors. In 1863 he was invited to 'perform' for the then French Emperor Napoleon III. Despite the Emperor's employment of conjurors and debunkers, eager to expose any fraud, Home's reputation remained unblemished. Yet when Home travelled to the holy city of Rome his work was declared satanic. He was asked to leave, never to return.

Home was scientifically investigaged by the physicist William Crookes, who later became president of the British Association for the Advancement of Science and was knighted for his contribution to science. In Crookes' study Home's abilities were listed to include: movement of furniture with no contact, levitation of furniture with no contact, alterations in the weight of objects (both heavier and lighter), rapping noises, and the spontaneous sounds of musical instruments. Also witnessed and investigated by Crookes were the manifestation of human faces and human hands. Crookes published his findings in the *Quarterly Journal of Science*, and neatly summarized the rational scientist's dilemma when faced with Home's wild talents:

> The phenomena I am prepared to attest to are so extraordinary and [so] directly oppose the most firmly-rooted articles of scientific belief – amongst others, the ubiquity and invariable action of the force of gravitation – that, even now, on recalling the details of what I witnessed, there is an antagonism in my mind between *reason*. which pronounces it to be scientifically

4

impossible, and the consciousness that my senses, both of touch and sight, are not lying witnesses.

There have, of course, been tales of levitation before and since. The modern Transcendental Meditation (TM) movement claims that we can all levitate if we learn to become expert meditators. This 'yogic flying' is, they say, a natural by-product of the calm and conscious state reached by the expert meditator. Some believe that such levitation can only be witnessed by other meditators in the privacy of TM events. The presence of those without faith in the process is thought to reduce flying ability. The sudden arrival of non-flyers is even believed to be the cause of crash landings.

The TM movement has strong roots in India, where its founder the Mahareshi Mahesh Yogi was born. In India the tradition of the wise yogi or guru is still strong, and the yogi will often prove his superior spiritual evolution by the per-formance of spectacular acts. Levitation is but one of these talents: surviving burial underground, lying on a bed of nails, passing nails through parts of the anatomy, living atop tall posts, and the manifestation of objects are all recognizably impressive acts. India is also the territory of the fakirs, who are part holy men, part magicians. Fakirs blur the distinctions between the holy and the magical, and there are known to be many who are either illusionists, or practised in inducing mass hypnotic effects.

One of the most convincing reports of levitation comes from southern India in 1936 and was given by P.T. Plunkett, a British tea planter who witnessed and took photographs of a fakir called Subbayah Pullavar:

The time was about 12.30pm and the sun directly above us so that shadows played no part in the performance ... Standing quietly by was Subbayah Pullavar, the performer, with long hair, a drooping moustache and a wild look in his eye. He salaamed to us and stood chatting for a while. He had been practising this particular branch of yoga for nearly 20 years (as had past generations of his family). We asked permission to take photographs of the performance and he gave it willingly, thus dispelling any doubt as to whether the whole thing was merely a hypnotic illusion.

Pullavar sprinkled some water around a small tent, which he then entered. When the tent was removed a few minutes later, the assembled crowd could see the yogi floating a few feet above the ground, apparently reclining. Plunkett then took photographs from all angles, and prodded the area under and around Pullavar with a stick. He concluded that there was 'no support whatsoever except for resting one hand lightly on a cloth-covered walking stick'. The yogi remained in this position for about four minutes, before the small tent was re-erected around him. Plunkett then viewed the yogi's descent through the thin fabric of the tent:

> After about a minute he appeared to sway and then very slowly to descend, still in a horizontal position. He took about five minutes to move from the top of the stick to the ground, a distance of about three feet ... When Subbayah was back on the ground his assistants carried him over to ... [us] and asked if we would try to bend his limbs. Even with assistance we were unable to do so.

Pullavar was then massaged and doused with cold water – apparently to bring him back to a more normal consciousness. Plunkett remained convinced that he had witnessed genuine levitation.

While mystics of the East have gathered a reputation for levitation, it is also a feat which has been used to identify and confirm saints of the Roman Catholic Church. Saint Teresa of Avila was a Carmelite nun in the 16th century. In her autobiography she described her rapturous states:

> I repeat it; you feel and see yourself carried away you know not whither. For though we feel how delicious it is, yet the

6

weakness of our nature makes us afraid at first ... so trying is it that I would very often resist and exert all my strength, particularly at those times when the rapture was coming on me in public. I did so, too, very often when I was alone, because I was afraid of delusions. Occasionally I was able, by great efforts, to make a slight resistance; but afterwards I was worn out, like a person who had been contending with a strong giant; at other times it was impossible to resist at all; my soul was carried away, and almost always my head with it – I had no power over it – and now and then the whole body as well, so that I was lifted up from the ground.

It seemed to me, when I tried to make some resistance, as if a great force beneath my feet lifted me up ... I confess that it threw me into a great fear, very great indeed at first; for when I saw my body thus lifted up from the earth, how could I help it? Though the spirit draws it upwards after itself, and that with great sweetness, if unresisted, the senses are not lost; at least, I was so much myself as to be able to see that I was being lifted up ... I have to say that when the rapture was over, my body seemed frequently to be buoyant, as if all the weight had departed from it; so much so that now and then I scarcely knew that my feet touched the ground.

Here Sister Teresa appears to be in a mystical state: many would argue that this makes her perceptions and experiences less reliable evidence. In Teresa's case, though, there were many eye witnesses who recorded their own accounts of her rapturous levitations. Sister Anne of the Incarnation, a fellow nun, waited until 13 years after Teresa's death in 1582 to provide sworn testimony:

On another occasion between one and two o'clock in the daytime I was in the choir waiting for the bell to ring when our holy Mother [Teresa] entered and knelt down for perhaps the half of a quarter of an hour. As I was looking on she was raised about half a yard from the ground without her feet touching it. At this I was terrified and she, for her part, was

7

trembling all over. So I moved to where she was and put my hands under her feet, over which I remained weeping for something like half an hour while the ecstasy lasted. Then, suddenly she sank down and rested on her feet and turning her head round to me she asked me who I was and whether I had been there all the while. I said yes, and then she ordered me under obedience to say nothing of what I had seen, and I have in fact said nothing until the present moment.

Saint Joseph of Cupertino was another Italian saint whose flying abilities brought him to beatification. Indeed there are so many descriptions of his levitation that it makes an assessment of his abilities very difficult: his life has taken on the image of a folk tale or myth. Nevertheless there still exist many signed and well-attested personal accounts of Saint Joseph's miraculous talents. Some accounts describe how, while at prayer in his chapel, Joseph would be transported through the air to the altar, where he would remain – unharmed by burning candles – until he made the return flight to his original place.

In the 1630s Joseph's levitation was witnessed by Pope Urban VIII, who was personally willing to testify to the reality of the event. Later Joseph was visited in Assisi by the Spanish ambassador to the papal court and his retinue. What followed was testified to under oath by many first-hand witnesses:

In point of fact no sooner had be entered the church than his eyes rested on a statue of Mary Immaculate which stood over the altar, and he at once flew about a dozen paces over the heads of those present to the foot of the statue. Then after paying homage there for some short space and uttering his familiar shrill cry he flew back again and straightway returned to his cell, leaving the Admiral, his wife and the large retinue which attended them speechless with astonishment.

During the last months of his life, Joseph underwent medical treatment at the hands of surgeon Francesco Pierpaoli. One day, while Pierpaoli was cauterizing the saint's leg, Joseph went into a rapture and remained floating some inches above the operating table while the treatment continued. Joseph of Cupertino died on 18 September 1663, and was canonized on 16 July 1767. He remains the world's most active flying saint.

PSYCHOKINESIS

In 1934 an American ex-botanist named Joseph Banks Rhine published the account of his early studies into the effects of mind over matter, or psychokinesis, entitled *Extra-Sensory Perception*. The book soon became a best seller, and secured J.B. Rhine his reputation as a pioneer in the new field of 'PK', as psychokinesis was soon called.

Just a few years earlier Rhine had abandoned a more orthodox academic career to establish the first university laboratory for the study of parapsychology at Duke University in North Carolina. During these first years of research, Rhine seemed to have struck it lucky when a young gambler approached him claiming that he used will-power to influence the outcome of dice throws at the gaming tables. He told Rhine that he could significantly increase the chances of getting the score he wanted and, equally importantly, that he could decrease the chances of his opponents winning. This was the starting point for years of experimentation in which Rhine and his associates tossed dice millions of times in the search for statistical evidence of psychokinesis. The information was collected and compared with the expected outcome of random chance.

When Rhine's formal, experimental results were published during the Second World War they were not well received. Apart from people's attention being firmly focused on winning the war, scientists were damning of Rhine's techniques. While the results initially appeared impressive, they were called into question when it was revealed that some trials had been carried out by volunteers in their own homes without the supervision of scientists. His methods were viewed as sloppy science, and there was a feeling that Rhine's own favouring of PK had an influence on the results. The other key factor was the failure of subsequent experimenters to replicate his results. 'The Duke experimenters seem to have fallen into pitfalls that an intelligent schoolboy should have avoided' was the final comment by one British sceptic.

Nevertheless Rhine defended his methods, claiming that they had not yet been perfected. His subsequent trials became more mechanized – machines were used to throw the dice – and increasingly imaginative in their scope: were small dice more suggestible than large dice? (Yes, apparently.) Did alcohol help? (No.) Did Coca-Cola help? (The stimulating effects of caffeine were thought to be beneficial.) Did faith help? (Divinity students and hardened gamblers scored well!) Children were also tested for their PK ability – with prizes on offer for successful PK effects!

For the study of PK, though, the die was already cast: psychokinesis had become a valid area of study, and there was encouragement for those who believed in the strange and unusual powers of the mind to come forward and be counted. Of the many who have submitted themselves to the public glare, one man has stood out for his persistent presence over 25 years, his name: Uri Geller.

No account of psychokinesis would now be complete without mention of Uri Geller, the Israeli psychic, metal bender and entertainer whose exploits first hit the news in 1973. So much has been written about him, his appearances have been so frequent, scientific studies so numerous, that the judgement on his powers, or lack of them, must surely be available for all to see. Yet it is not. There are still those who believe wholeheartedly in his psychokinetic powers, there are still those who think him a fraud, and there are still those whose judgement is suspended.

For all the scientists who have studied Geller in their laboratory and found in his favour, there are as many who remain to be convinced of his ability to create measurable effects. Nevertheless Geller is still alive and well, and earning a living from his 'powers': very few weeks go by without an appearance in a newspaper, a magazine, or on television. He has amassed a millionaire's fortune by working for oil and mineral companies – flying over sites under investigation and determining the likelihood of striking 'lucky'. Should we presume that companies would not employ him unless he were right more often than luck would suggest?

His attempts to galvanize the nation's psyches behind the English football team in the European Championships in 1994 were very publicly unsuccessful. Despite the television invitation to look into Geller's eyes, touch the television screen, and concentrate on England winning, the team were knocked out in the semi-finals. Some footballing observers pointed out that if England *had* won it would have been a miracle – even if Geller hadn't been involved. Either way it is unlikely that anyone would have accused Geller of a conjurer's sleight of hand – the charge that has dogged his entire psychokinetic career.

Since Geller's arrival on the psychic scene over 20 years ago, he has been tracked, attacked and vilified as a fraud and charlatan by one ultra-sceptic named James Randi. 'The Amazing Randi' is actually a magician and illusionist who claims to be able to replicate every single 'trick' that Geller can perform. In his own early days Randi himself claimed to be a psychic – successfully 'predicting' the outcome of the baseball world series as well as the number of visitors to Canada's 1950 National Exhibition. Since he 'came out' as an ordinary, non-paranormal magician, though, Randi has dogged Geller and other claimants to the paranormal crown of thorns. He even carries a signed, blank cheque to the value of $10,000 for the first person who can convince him of their genuine powers. Needless to say he has never relinquished the cheque.

Randi has gone to extraordinary lengths to prove his point that every person claiming to possess psychic or supernatural powers is, in fact, a fake. To prove his point he has been behind a number of radio and television stunts involving members of his psychic-busting team. Randi's psychic imposters go on radio and television programmes posing as the genuine article. In typical 'stings' they mimic Geller's technique of asking the audience to focus on the psychic's voice for a few minutes during a broadcast and then asking listeners or viewers to ring in to describe any extraordinary happenings that occurred during the focusing period. Even with fake psychics, hundreds of people would ring in saying that broken watches had started, mirrors had cracked, cats gone haywire, fridges stopped, and a piggy bank split asunder ... thus proving that the law of averages is a wonderful thing.

While Geller's reputation was certainly affected for some time with the taint of conjuring, his status as the genuine article is still surprisingly intact. Much of this is actually due to some of the scientific backing that he received in the early days of his fame.

Some of the most convincing and controversial scientific studies of Geller and other psychokineticists were carried out by Professor John Hasted of London University in the mid- to late-1970s. Hasted was a kindly, avuncular physicist with a laboratory at Birkbeck College. In response to the growing interest in psychokinetic metal bending he set up complex and sensitive test rigs which measured the strain on keys and other metal objects when submitted to the supposed energies of metal benders.

In one particular experiment Geller managed to bend a key which was held in the rig, merely by stroking one end. Hasted was sure there was no trickery. He became one of a rare breed: a convinced scientist. 'The Geller method of breaking steel,' Hasted claimed, 'is unlike anything described in the [metallurgical] literature.' With the publicity surrounding Geller, Hasted found it increasingly difficult to carry on his work – especially when he started to suffer calls of 'heretic' from his colleagues. Nevertheless he continued with his research – not just on Geller, but on a series of people who came forward in the wake of Geller's fame.

Another metal bender who impressed Hasted was a teen-ager named Nicholas Williams who was able to cause bending in keys that were hung up on a wall a good few yards away. During this well-attested process Williams busied himself with the work of making model aeroplanes. At times the strain-gauges built into the keys demonstrated that a number of keys were bending at once. In another test with Williams, some thin aluminium strips were left in a room by Professor Hasted. When he and Williams returned to the room some minutes later, they found the metal strips had become folded, concertina-style.

While Hasted felt he had good reason to support Geller and his followers, most scientists were afraid, or unwilling, to enter the dangerous business of actual experiments. Nevertheless Geller achieved some notable successes in a few laboratories around the world. Eldon Byrd of the US Navy's Maryland Research Laboratory stated quite categorically that Geller had bent metal 'in a way that cannot be duplicated'. In controlled conditions Geller has caused changes in weight in a one gram mass, affected a Geiger counter so that it registered 500 times its normal count, deflected the needle in a large, marine-quality compass and stopped and erased an image on a computer graphics system.

Geller no longer submits himself to experiments in scientific laboratories, preferring instead the 'megalab' of public television and the exposure it brings. He has confessed to using conjuring tricks at times, but says that whenever he did use fakery he was always caught out. To which the sceptical might reply: 'he would say that wouldn't he!' It may be too early to say whether his work has done the serious study of psychokinetics lasting good. He has built a career on bringing the paranormal to the masses, and has without doubt given the world a great deal of food for thought. The famous writer on the occult Colin Wilson has stated: 'Many scientists who have tested him have concluded that his powers are genuine – or to put this controversial topic at its lowest: no sceptical opponent has been able to prove he is not genuine.'

There are naturally others who would steal his crown:

Miroslaw Magola was born in Communist Poland in the 1960s and now calls himself 'The Magnetic Man'. In a number of television appearances and scientific experiments he has demonstrated the ability to levitate and attract objects to his body. Though 'Magnetic' by name, his power is not limited to metals: pots and pans, china dishes, wooden chopping boards and other household objects will all 'stick' to his naked torso or to his forehead. Once the objects are stuck, Magola can even move and jump around without their falling from him.

Even large, heavy objects – metal sculptures are a favourite – do not appear to present a problem. 'I load myself with energy (I connect myself to it) and at the same time I wish for the object to raise,' he says of his power.

While he feels he has had 'an abundance of kinetic energy' for many years, his talent to attract objects only appeared when he left Communist Poland for Germany in 1987. Through research into psychic energies he claims to have trained his powers, and to have increased his control of the psychokinetic phenomenon – to the point where he claims to be able to make objects levitate, spin around and vibrate in mid-air. Those who have seen him have been impressed – his appearance on the UK television programme *Beyond Belief* with Sir David Frost in February 1996 created strong public interest. Viewers and the studio audience both saw Magola attract objects to his body, but in the live television environment he was unable to perform any levitation effects. The producer of the programme, Trevor Potts, reported that Magola had been more impressive in his magnetic ability when they had originally invited him to their office. Potts felt that when the actual live transmission came, and despite 30 minutes of quiet preparation, Magola was not able to summon his full force for the short period of time during which the spotlight was on him.

Current reports say that Magola has declared himself determined to develop his powers to help mankind, and is offering himself forward for research into the spheres of psychokinesis, telepathy and healing. He has been investigated by Dr Friedbert Karger of the Max Planck Institute in Germany. In January 1997 Magola demonstrated his ability to pick up a cup from the floor without touching it, and to control its suspension in mid-air. Dr Karger video-taped the session, and was entirely convinced that no form of trickery was involved. Further tests in more rigorous conditions are scheduled, during which Magola's physical functions will be monitored along with his claimed PK effects. Magola sees his own work as part of the research into mankind's own development:

> For me every paranormal occurrence, however absurd it may be, is part of something new, a part of something one should get to know in order to understand existence, because it may be a new law of existence. Every paranormal occurrence should be carefully studied. Not ignored because it is not part of our current laws of existence or part of our knowledge database.

Without the weight of comprehensive scientific study, though, it is hard to see how the claims and exploits of people like Magola might change our scientific model of mind and matter.

The formation of the Princeton Engineering Anomolies Research Laboratory (PEARL) at Princeton University in 1979 has gone a long way in continuing the tradition of J.B. Rhine and his colleagues in carrying out detailed scientific studies of the effects of mind on matter. In PEARL's experiments subjects are asked to use their minds to influence the function of one of a number of simple machines. These machines include pendulums with constant frequencies, computers displaying a randomized selection of images, and something called a Random Mechanical Cascade, a device with a working principle similar to a child's pin-ball machine, in which 9,000 small balls fall through a series of pegs to end up in one of 19 columns. All the machines have the potential to be affected in distinct ways, according to the supposed PK powers of the subjects. More than 100 subjects have taken part in some 50 million trials. The current president of PEARL, Professor Bob Jahn, describes the purpose of the laboratory's work:

> The effects we are seeing in a controlled, laboratory-experimental environment are very similar to those which have been presumed over the ages. We are looking at the influence of the wishes and desires of the human operator on the performance of a physical process. Isn't that what we do when we hope for something? Isn't that what prayer is sometimes about? There are many common examples of a human tendency to try to impose desires on the way physical experience unfolds: what we do is look at this in the laboratory.

Dean Radin of the University of Nevada has carried out some fascinating experiments into mass psychokinetic effects, attempting to establish whether group consciousness can affect matter, in the same way that individual consciousness has already been studied by J.B. Rhine and Jahn. Radin's recent experiments have focused on the way large groups of people may affect apparently stable pieces of machinery: in this case an electronic random number generator:

> We know from many years of experiments that if you have one person looking at a random system and you give them the instruction to affect that random system that they can do so to a small degree. So the question then is, what happens when you get lots of people all trying to put their attention on a random system?

In Radin's experiments he focused on the effects that large news events have on the numbers being generated by random number generators. He hypothesized that when large numbers of the population are focused on a particular event, the mental energy of the group consciousness creates increased levels of order in normally random systems. In other words he believed that the news events would cause identifiable patterns to occur in the numbers that his machines spewed out. To test this theory Radin attempted to match the timing of major events to peaks of increased order in five random number generators located in laboratories across America. Radin's big 'hit' occurred around the trial verdict of O.J. Simpson. The televised verdict of the 'trial that gripped the nation' was due to start at 9am. At this very moment, when millions of viewers simultaneously turned on their televisions, there was an increased patterning in all five of Radin's number generators – a patterning which only had a 300-to-1 probability of occurring in each machine. In fact the verdict was delayed for an hour – to be finally delivered to an eagerly waiting public at 10am. As the announcement was made, Radin's machines had another 'spike' of orderly outpourings – this time with a probability of only 500 to 1 in each machine. Probabilities of 300 and 500 to 1 do not sound as incredible as they might, but the fact that all five generators responded with the same orderliness at precisely the key moments of the trial verdict made the event much more significant: the odds against five machines behaving with a probability of 500 to 1 turns out to be some 30 trillion to 1.

While such mass consciousness events are extremely difficult to monitor and, indeed, predict, Radin has suggested that if the focusing of such group mental energy can cause order in a system such as a random generator, then perhaps a similar focus might be harnessed to decrease air pollution or lower crime rates in city areas. This is an identical idea to that put forward by the Transcendental Meditation movement, who claim responsibility for falls in crime statistics in areas where their members have practised meditation with the intention of increasing order and, thus, lowering crime. If Radin's work continues to impress we may start to see armies of meditators and mental 'focusers' travelling to trouble spots around the globe.

THOUGHTOGRAPHY

Ted Serios hit the headlines in the 1960s when his ability to impress thoughts and mental images onto Polaroid photographic film was given a thorough scientific investigation by a professor of psychiatry in Denver named Jule Eisenbud.

When the two men met, Serios was an unemployed hotel porter, with a strong liking for alcohol. Three years later, Serios was one of the most famous cases in psychokinetic literature. He had apparently produced hundreds of 'thought-ographs' – Polaroid photographic images created by the power of the mind. These images were claimed to appear spontaneously, or in response to requests by the experimenter, when Serios looked into the lens and focused the power of his thoughts. Images of buildings, cars, rockets, people and landscapes were all created under Eisenbud's scientifically controlled conditions.

To get these results, Serios would wind himself into a ranting frenzy – fuelled by beer and the attention that surrounded him. Eisenbud described him:

> Ted, in various stages of besottedness . . . became the impresario, the field commander, giving everybody orders sharply and authoritatively, as to what they were going to do, where to stand, what to hold and so forth. As far gone in drink as he sometimes was, he improvised distance experiments with two or more cameras, experiments with cameras out of the room and at queer angles. Sometimes he works himself into a frenzy, ordering cameras to be handed to him one after the other – he almost never reached for one himself or handled cameras between trials.

Serios' talent seemed erratic: as well as recognizable images he would produce 'blackies' and 'whities' – black only, or white only images. These would appear despite the experimenter pointing the camera at Serios' face in normal lighting conditions. His hit rate was unreliable, and he would go for sustained periods without any results. Nevertheless he scored notable successes which initiated further investigation. In May 1965 a series of photos of a shop-front appeared. Its name could be made out in some of the pictures: 'The Old Gold Store'. It was discovered that the photos were of a store in Central City, Colorado, which had once been called 'The Old Gold Store', but was now called 'The Old Wells Fargo Express Office'. Eisenbud searched for photos of the shop from when it had been called by its old name, but was never able to find one. The fact remained though that it had indeed been called 'The Old Gold Store'.

Eisenbud tested Serios inside a steel-walled chamber, checked for X-rays and other magnetic forces, and even had doctors assess whether he possessed any particular physical attribute that made him more able to do this than the average human. But of all the most popular explanations, there was one that would never quite go away: that Ted Serios was a fraud.

When Charles Reynolds of the American journal *Popular Photography* and his friend David Eisendrath Jnr, a photographer and conjurer, visited one of Serios' weekend events they came away with an uneasy and suspicious feeling. At the event Serios made use of a device, or 'gismo', a tube of paper or card. He carried the device continually in one hand and, when questioned about its purpose, pocketed it and refused to allow anyone to view it. When Reynolds and Eisendrath later viewed a television film of Serios in action, they believed they saw an optical device which would be capable of holding a transparency and creating an image in the camera. In their assessment of Serios the two were careful to say that deception was not definite, but that, in their opinion, it was a possibility.

Following the launch of Eisenbud's book *The World of Ted Serios* a number of sceptics put forward theories to explain how the images were made. Professor W.A.H. Rushton – who later became the president of the Society for Psychical Research – actually made up a miniature 'rice grain' optical device which he was able to demonstrate making quite acceptable 'thoughtographs'. Others pointed out that Polaroid film was not immune from pre-tampering. Eisenbud resisted the claims of the critics, accepting that he had held these same objections when he started his research. But Serios was never once caught cheating in all the years of research, and the majority of the thoughtographs happened when Serios had no contact with the camera or even with his 'gismo'.

Gradually Serios' ability to produce the images declined to nothing. His last offering showed, with a neat irony, a pair of drawn curtains.

While Serios' showmanlike approach to thoughtography caught the public's imagination there have been other, less well publicized cases which may deserve equal attention. Stella Lansing from Michigan found a number of strange images on her still and cine-film and was investigated for this and other PK and poltergeist phenomena by psychiatrist Dr Berthold Schwarz. In Russia Dr Gennady Krokhalev tested a number of psychiatric patients, all suffering from hallucinations. Krokhalev placed cameras – both movie and still – over their eyes. In over a third of trials he claims to have captured anomalous images, which in many cases were connected with the nature of the patients' hallucinations. If true, it represents more persuasive evidence that the mind has tremendous power to create ordered and 'patterned' effects on matter.

In an interesting parallel with Serios' work, Krokhalev believed that alcoholics made the best thoughtographers. This could indicate that alcohol in some way liberates the power of thought to create 'at a distance' effects. Certainly the physics of quantum mechanics – while not yet fully integrated into our scientific models – does allow for action at a distance to function. But if this is so, then one might expect PK phenomena such as thoughtography to be more frequent than is reported. Perhaps they are. An alternative explanation that some more spiritually inclined experts might prefer is that alcohol addiction actually permits access to the individual by 'possessive' spiritual entities. These entities may, as in the case of poltergeists, have greater powers than mere humans to affect matter in a deliberate, playful or disturbing manner. Until more reliable practitioners of thoughtography appear and submit to scientific study, though, it is unlikely that a cohesive scientific theory to explain the phenomenon will emerge.

PSYCHOMETRY

Psychometry means 'measuring the soul' or 'measuring the mind'. Many psychics claim to use psychometry to provide evidence of their gifts, and to demonstrate the ability of matter to retain 'residual' patterns of energy. A locket, a coin, a theatre ticket: whatever is provided, the psychic claims to 'read' the energy imprinted in the object, and attempts to identify information about its owner, its background, or its history. Most will hold an object in their hands during this process, while others will simply need to be close to it. To the sceptic this is either a silly parlour game, or a con-trick invented by cunning Victorians to separate the gullible from their money. If genuine, psychometry offers concrete valida-tion of a psychic's ability to detect and tune into powerful emotional and intellectual energies invested in an object, as well as facts about its history. Indeed there is some strong evidence that psychometry has been used in many police cases where psychics have attempted to identify a culprit, or locate a missing person from a fragment of clothing, a piece of hair or even a murder weapon.

Of the psychics and mediums who have been tested as psychometrists, one of the most successful of the modern age was Eileen Garrett who was born in 1893 and died in 1970. She is reported to have identified the location of a missing man from the impressions received by holding one of his

21

shirts. In the 1950s she was thoroughly tested by a New York psychologist Lawrence LeShan. In one particular experiment a small clay tablet of Babylonian origin was wrapped in paper, placed in a box, and sealed inside a further envelope. It was then despatched to Mrs Garrett 1,500 miles away, who, without breaking the seal, identified the object as a clay tablet. She went on to describe a woman connected to the object in such vivid detail that LeShan was positive the woman described was his secretary. LeShan was so impressed by the case that he said the information would have been enough to identify her from 'a line of 10,000 women'. The secretary confessed that she had handled the tablet just before it was packaged up to go to Mrs Garrett.

The Victorian author Robert Browning was a hardened sceptic, convinced that clairvoyants and mediums were nothing but con-artists and charlatans. This remained true in spite (or perhaps because) of his wife Elizabeth's interest in the subject. She had met and 'sat' with the renowed Victorian medium D.D. Home on a number of occasions. When Browning was visiting Italy, however, he was introduced to a clairvoyant named Count Ganniasi of Ravenna. Ganniasi's eyes alighted on Browning's cuff-links: it was the first time Browning had worn them, even though they had been in his family for many years. As soon as Ganniasi held them, the clairvoyant heard the words 'Murder, murder!' Browning somewhat reluctantly revealed that the cuff-links had been worn by his great-uncle on the day he had been murdered by his slaves on the island of St Kitts, some eight years earlier. He had to admit that there was no way that anyone in Florence could have known about this.

Much more recently 'dream detective' Chris Robinson has been tested many times by the British police for the accuracy of his precognitive dreams about impending IRA terrorist bombing incidents. When given an object to investigate, Robinson does not claim to be using psychometry by 'reading energy' as a traditional medium might. He says that any ability to detect the history of an object relies on information gleaned from dream impressions. Because of this he appears to require a number of nights' sleep to focus on an object and uncover information about it.

In one high-profile experiment carried out with the scientific laboratory of Dr Richard Wiseman at the University of Hertfordshire in Hatfield, Robinson was tested for psychometric ability along with a number of other psychics. Two weeks prior to the tests he was asked to focus mentally on three objects which had been chosen by the research team. When the time of the tests arrived, Robinson was 'thrown' by the fact that things were not as he had requested – originally he had asked that the three objects be placed in boxes, and had said that he would provide as much information as he could. In fact Dr Wiseman's team showed the four psychics the objects and asked them to fill in a questionnaire – choosing 6 out of 18 statements to relate to each object. This did not really fit with Robinson's methods: he had brought notes of his dreams about the three objects which he had recorded over the past two weeks, and hoped to have a chance to express these. He felt confident that he had a good fix on two of them at least.

On video he was invited to say what he had gleaned. The first object was a lady's shoe, which he thought belonged to a woman who had been shot. He admitted that instead of a shoe he had expected to see a gun.

The second object was a small part of a bullet. In his dream relating to this he had seen PC Keith Blakelock (who had been killed in a riot on a housing estate in London some years before). He had surmised from this that the object was related to the killing of a member of the police force.

The third object was a red woollen scarf. Unusually for Robinson, as he picked the object up, he had a strong psychometric impression of a woman being strangled. When he put it around his neck he immediately had a clear mental picture of milk bottles. He said 'to camera' that the murder was in some way connected to the milk. Robinson was then asked to fill in Dr Wiseman's questionnaire which formed the scientific part of the process. There was, though, a problem for Robinson here: he couldn't really see how the information he had dreamed about fitted with the statements and, in frustration, was only able to tick some of the boxes.

At the end of the study Dr Wiseman published his results which showed that the psychics were less accurate than chance would predict. This was seized on by a number of sceptical scientists who saw it as evidence that psychometry was still just a phoney parlour game.

Robinson was very disappointed: particularly when the real origins of the objects were revealed. All the objects were in fact from the Essex Police Museum. The shoe had belonged to a woman shot dead by her common-law husband. The bullet fragment was part of that used to kill a PC Gutteridge, in the first English case to convict a murderer on ballistics evidence. The red scarf had been used in the recent murder of a woman. The killer had eventually confessed, saying that he had strangled the woman accidentally with the scarf when she had tried to escape. He was her milkman and they had been arguing over her milk bill! Nevertheless, from Dr Wiseman's perspective Robinson had failed this respectable scientific test.

Another impressive psychometrist is Boris Tulchinski, a Russian now living in Tel Aviv, who, in a series of television appearances has shown remarkable accuracy. In one show he was required to fall in with television showmanship and 'save Uri Geller's life'. Geller was immersed in a tank of water while Tulchinski was given a scrumpled piece of paper on which was written the name of an object to be found somewhere in the studio building. Geller would only be released from the water once Tulchinski had returned to the studio with the object named on the paper.

In this challenge it is worth observing three important facts: Tulchinski does not read English; the paper was fully scrumpled, and never unscrumpled in front of the live audience; the object named on the paper was known to only one man – the producer of the programme – and decided on only minutes before the actual event. In the rehearsal Tulchinski found and returned 'a crushed coke can in the canteen', while in the actual transmission he was able to liberate Geller from his potential watery grave with 'a bunch of red roses from the make-up room'.

Tulchinski also demonstrates a similar, though different, ability to sense remotely: if taken into a room blindfolded and asked to identify objects pointed to by people in the room he appears to be able to give a full description, despite rigorous testing of his blindfold. His gift – if we are to accept it as such – is that his vision does not depend on his eyes, or at least not on his 'physical' sight.

Just as we can recognize the atmosphere or energy in a house after its previous owners have left, it seems reasonable to assume that smaller objects may hold a similar memory of energetic experiences that have occurred to their possessors. But any object may have passed through the hands of many owners during its lifetime. It is easy to imagine that any 'imprint' that may be left on, in or around an object may be prone to confusion with the multitude of other emotional and energetic impressions.

If we are to believe in the reality of psychometry as a psychic gift, then we may also have to accept that a lot of the accuracy is down to the psychic's ability to differentiate between the impressions received from an object – whether short term, long term, owner, handler or even maker. As in many aspects of psychic work, it seems that the quality of the answer depends on the quality of the question.

MEMORIES OF PAST LIVES

In any exploration of past-life memories it is important to register that two of the world's major religions accept or actively promote the idea of reincarnation in some form. For

Buddhism – in both its Asian and Tibetan forms – it is an essential tenet; the same is true for Hindus, who talk of a wheel of life or a wheel of karma, underpinned by the cycles of birth, death and rebirth. In some esoteric circles it is believed that the Bible once contained teachings on reincarnation, but that they were removed at the Fifth Ecumenical Council in AD 553 for political reasons. Some observers have suggested that it is easier for a state to control a population that believes in hell than one that sees the potential for individual spiritual progress through a series of earthly incarnations. In surveys, belief in reincarnation proves remarkably popular: a US survey found that four in ten people believe in reincarnation, and in Britain a survey conducted by *The Times* found that one in six respondents had had an experience which convinced them that they had lived in at least one other lifetime.

Despite its popularity though, hard evidence for reincarnation – proof beyond doubt – is harder to find. If we are not simply to believe or disbelieve first person recollections of those who claim 'far memory', we must dig deeper. To 'prove' reincarnation we need to find cases where people provide information about lives which they should not, indeed could not, know about otherwise. Knowledge of this kind seems to come in two types: conscious and subconscious. Our modern lives are saturated with television and books which tell us a great deal about other cultures, other times. It is not surprising that we know so much about 'other lives'. But did we really live them? Or were they simply *other people's* lives?

The powerful phenomenon of 'cryptomnesia' tells us that, while we may not seem to remember things, our minds have stored virtually every detail of every experience we have ever had. The human mind is a sponge for information, soaking up everything and anything that may prove useful to us. Whether we are able to access it is a wholly different matter: it may only re-emerge when it becomes vital to our well-being or survival. Indeed it may only re-emerge when we are hypnotized, or when we are asked to recall our past lives!

Cases have been recorded of people who, when hypnotically regressed, are able to speak other languages perfectly. This is not necessarily evidence for reincarnation. When asked, they may well reveal that they lived for some years in the relevant country as a child. They did not consciously learn or speak the language. Nevertheless their subconscious mind had absorbed all that is required for them to speak fluently, even after a time gap of many years. It is not just elephants, it seems, who never forget.

With these difficulties snapping at our heels, the serious reincarnation researcher faces a difficult task. Nevertheless there seem to be two main ways in which positive evidence for reincarnation can appear: via spontaneous memories, which often appear most persuasively in children; and via hypnosis which, while it can be monitored more scientifically, is fraught with the problems of the hypnotist's 'suggestion', and the subject's suggestibility.

Hypnosis as a way of revealing past-life memories first came to mass attention in 1952 with the case of Bridey Murphy. Bridey was a young Irish woman, born in 1798, who – it was claimed – manifested herself in the memories of a 29-year-old woman from Madison, Wisconsin, named Virginia Tighe. Morey Bernstein was the hypnotist, although – strictly speaking – he was a businessman with an interest in hypnotism. Over a series of six audio-taped sessions Bernstein took Ms Tighe back to her life in County Cork: to her Protestant father; her marriage to a Catholic barrister and the two wedding services – one for each denomination; their move to Belfast and their life in a cottage in Dooley Road. It all sounds pretty mundane: indeed it is the level of day-to-day detail that marked the case out as both convincing and testable. As Bridey Murphy, Tighe was able to name the family grocers – 'Farr and Carrigan' – who had owned the shop in town. Other similarly verifiable evidence came through: names of places that only appeared on maps from the early 1800s were mentioned, and found to be absolutely correct. A two-pence coin Tighe talked about was only in circulation for 12 years, at exactly the time that she was claiming her memory.

Virginia Tighe had never visited Ireland. Nor indeed had her husband who turned out to be the most sceptical of all observers. Perhaps he had the most to lose: the identity of his wife. Theories to explain the case multiplied quickly: the first was that Tighe had watched a film in which Ireland had been featured. An appropriate film was never discovered. Second, there were relatives of Tighe's who had Irish connections – perhaps they had told her about the Ireland of the early 1800s. A rival newspaper to the one that serialized the Bridey Murphy story attempted an exposé: they claimed that Virginia Tighe had an Irish aunt named Mary Burns who was 'as Irish as the lakes of Killarney', and that she had told her niece tales of her Irish childhood; they also claimed that Virginia Tighe had lived opposite a woman whose maiden name was Bridey Murphy.

None of it turned out to be true, but that was not the point: the Bridey Murphy bubble burst, the 'Come As You Were' parties stopped, and most people forgot that Virginia Tighe had ever existed. The evidence for Bridey Murphy, though, remained intact. One final possibility remained: it was still, of course, possible that Morey Bernstein's entire 'experiment' had been a fraud. In 45 years, though, it has never been proved that Tighe received this remarkably detailed information from anywhere but her own memory of living as Bridey Murphy.

Nowadays such a case would fall under the long shadow of 'false-memory syndrome'. The furore over the regression of 'alien abduction' claimants has left the world of hypnosis and regression in a state of chaos, with no one really knowing who or what to believe. A consensus position seems to have developed that anyone involved in hypnotism or therapy is probably guilty of 'suggestion', of filling their patients' heads with ideas that they would like them to believe. The fact that an entire discipline can appear to have been discredited – at least in the public's imagination – is quite remarkable in itself.

The majority of research into the 'recovery' of past-life memory, following the Virginia Tighe/Bridey Murphy case was carried out by hypnotic regression by a series of university-based psychologists. Perhaps the most influential of these was Dr Allan Cannon who regressed a total of 1,382 volunteers. Originally a sceptic to the idea of reincarnation, he discovered that his subjects could not only remember lifetimes from recent history, but also as far back as several thousand years before the time of Jesus Christ. In 1950 he wrote a book called the *The Power Within*:

> For years the theory of reincarnation was a nightmare to me and I did my best to disprove it and even argued with my trance subjects to the effect that they were talking nonsense. Yet as the years went by one subject after another told me the same story in spite of different and various beliefs. Now well over a thousand cases have been so investigated and I have to admit that there is such a thing as reincarnation.

The work of Cannon and others specializing in hypnotic regression has created a mass of impressive data. All the same, the false-memory syndrome crisis has made the existence of other forms of past-life memory evidence all the more important. This evidence comes in the form of young children's personal testimony. The spontaneity of children's expression, and the absence of what one might call 'learned adult lying', is a feature that makes the testimony of young children so potentially valuable in the search for proof of reincarnation. Probably the greatest champion of children's spontaneous past-life memories is Dr Ian Stevenson, who has, for more than 30 years, provided some compelling evidence. In his original work *Twenty Cases Suggestive of Reincarnation* he documented the apparent memories of children mainly from India, Nigeria, Alaska and the Far East. One of the most interesting of these cases is the story of Bishen Chand who was the son of a railway clerk in Bareilly, northern India. Chand's pronouncements as a four year old had been recorded for some time by a local lawyer named K.K.N. Sahay before any attempt was made to verify the information.

The story, according to Sahay, goes that Bishen Chand had started talking about a place called Pilibhit before he could even say other basic words. Pilibhit was a town some 30 miles away. Chand next said that he was the nephew of a man named Har Narain, of Pilibhit. He also claimed that he had lived next door to Sunder Lal, a gentleman who had a green gate, a sword and a gun. He also told Sahay that Sunder Lal had parties in his courtyard where dancing girls were present.

Sahay determined to take four-year-old Chand to Pilibhit to verify the facts of the case. It should be noted that this was not a scientifically controlled expedition. Nevertheless its findings were remarkable: Chand first 'spotted' Sunder Lal, his green gate, and his past-life uncle Har Narain. A relative from Chand's past life then appeared with a photograph: could he recognize himself and his previous-life uncle in the photograph? 'Here is Har Narain,' said Chand confidently, 'and here I.' He had established his past-life identity as a man named Laxmi Narain. Chand was quizzed about Laxmi, who had not led a completely blameless life: 'What was the name of Laxmi's favourite prostitute?' 'Padma!' said Chand immediately. The crowd nodded their heads; indeed Padma was his favourite. He had clearly not forgotten her.

The final test of Chand's past-life pilgrimage was a meeting with his past-life mother. In response to a series of questions Chand admitted to throwing away some of her pickles – but only because the jar had worms in it. Such is the mundane detail that these stories turn on. Additionally he was able to say that he had worked on the Oudh railway and that he had a servant named Maikua who was a black, short-statured member of the Kahar. On the basis of his answers Chand was accepted back into his past-life family as the reincarnation of Laxmi Narain.

Stevenson also documented a case of twin reincarnations which had occurred in Sri Lanka. Two three-year-old twin sisters – Shiromi and Shivanthi Hettierachchi – described their deaths as two young men who had both died in a Marxist uprising in 1971. It was 1982 when Shiromi claimed that she remembered leaping to her death from a rock. At the same time Shivanthi remembered being shot dead. They both appeared to know their names in these other lives and were able to provide details which were sufficient to satisfy both sets of past-life parents that they had indeed been their sons.

Another set of twins who have provided remarkable evidence are the Pollock twins – Jennifer and Gillian – born in Northumberland in October 1958. Their story, which is both tragic and inspiring, begins some years before they were born, when their elder sisters – Joanna aged 11 and Jacqueline, 6 – were hit by a car while walking home from church. They were both killed instantly. Their father, John Pollock, blamed himself for the accident, as parents of dead children often do. In his own mind John – a devout Catholic who also believed in reincarnation – believed the accident to be some kind of judgement on him. He also believed that the girls would return to him in their future incarnations. Within a year his wife Florence was pregnant, and John's immediate prediction that she would bear twins came true. When Jennifer and Gillian were born John immediately noticed that one of them appeared to carry identical distinguishing features to the departed Jacqueline: a 'thumb-print' birthmark on her left hip, and a thin scar-like line on her forehead: Jacqueline had received this scar as a result of a bicycling accident. As a more conventional Catholic, Florence made her husband promise that he would not talk to them about reincarnation, and that when the topic of their dead sisters eventually arose, that the children would be told they had had sisters who were now in heaven.

The family moved to a new home some miles away when the twins were three months old. When, some three years later, they revisted the area where the tragedy had occurred the girls reacted strongly. Without prompting, they identified their previous home. They knew they were approaching swings and slides – before the playground had come into sight. They also knew they were close to their old school.

When shown the dead girls' dolls one day, Jennifer immediately identified them: 'That's your Mary. This is my Suzanne.' These were the same names their elder sisters had given them. On a number of occasions they were found screaming 'irrationally' at the approach of cars – cars that were at a safe distance, but nevertheless pointing at them. On one occasion, their mother found Gillian cradling Jennifer's head, and saying to her: 'The blood's coming out of your eyes. That's where the car hit you.' Florence Pollock found the incidents increasingly distressing, even though the children's father felt vindicated. By about the age of 6, though, new memories had ceased, and by 13 they couldn't even remember the experiences when told about them by their father. While some investigators have felt that the father's interest in reincarnation weakens the evidence, it is still virtually impossible to see how he might have faked such experiences in the children. It also makes the point that the number of cases of 'suspected' reincarnation may be limited by the sceptical or antagonistic viewpoint of parents in a predominantly Christian country.

A 13-year-old girl who wrote songs in medieval French and who recalled names of people and historical events now known to be real, may have provided some of this century's most compelling evidence for reincarnation. In the literature of reincarnation few writers have researched their subject's 'far memories' as thoroughly as consultant psychiatrist Dr Arthur Guirdham. Guirdham had a successful and highly respected career in orthodox medicine before he wrote two books which changed many people's view of reincarnation forever. Such was the power of what Guirdham discovered from his patient that he felt compelled to spend the rest of his life writing and communicating about the experiences of a woman who was always known simply as Mrs Smith.

In fact Guirdham had the meticulous records of the Holy Roman Inquisition to thank for the verification of Mrs Smith's past life as a member of a little-known religious sect in 13th-century France. This sect, known as Cathars or Albigensians, fell victim to the wrath of the Roman Catholic Church at a time when the Inquisition contained the master persecutors, torturers and executors of heretics of their age. Mrs Smith – it was to emerge – had been one of its victims at a mass burning on the slopes of a mountain stronghold in the Pyrenees known as Montsegur.

Mrs Smith came to Guirdham as a woman in her early thirties – suffering from a nightmare in which she was being attacked by an unknown man. It was some time before she revealed her traumatic yet extraordinary experiences as a teenager. From the age of 13 she had been troubled by bouts of unconsciousness which had remained untouched by conventional medicine. On meeting Dr Guirdham she had little faith that he could offer any help. She was in deep despair about the lack of control that she seemed to exert over her experiences. In January 1965 she wrote of: 'this terrible affliction of "going out of time". I am sometimes so confused that I cannot honestly be sure if a person has just said something, or whether they will say it one day, or did so in the past.'

In her memories Mrs Smith remembered a love affair she had conducted with a troubadour musician called Roger. Such was the clarity of her memory that, at the age of 13, she wrote out the lyrics to medieval songs in an obscure French dialect, despite having very poor knowledge of any modern French. In her dreams she replayed her original meeting with Roger:

I could write a book about Roger and it would not take any effort at all. I have dreamt all of it at some time or other and it is all very easy to set down on paper. It would never be published. I couldn't bear that. It is a comfort to know that other girls dream of lovers. I wish I didn't have the uneasy feeling that this is different . . .

I fell in love with him that very night he came to our house in the snowstorm. I tried not to stare at him but I was terribly aware of his nearness. I was filled with joy because the weather was bad and it was necessary for him to stay the night. That night I kissed him when he was asleep . . .

The day my father beat me and sent me away from home was one of the happiest days of my life. I went to Roger with nothing but the clothes I wore, and I didn't even have any shoes . . . His house was on the top of a hill and the road leading to it was rough and stony. He lived in a large place, not a castle, but something like a fortified house . . . we were sublimely happy.

Their happiness was not to last. They were both persecuted in the crusade against the Cathars, and in February 1966 Mrs Smith was to re-experience her death by fire, some seven hundred years before, at the hands of the Catholic Inquisition.

We all walked barefoot through the streets towards a square where they had prepared a pile of sticks all ready to set alight. There were several monks around singing hymns and praying. I didn't feel grateful. I thought they had a cheek to pray for me. I must be rather a wicked person. I don't think wicked things when I am awake, but I dream awful things. I hated those monks being there to see me die. A girl at school once said she dreamt of Christ's crucifixion. I would rather be crucified than burnt. The pain was maddening. You should pray to God when you're dying, if you can pray when you're in agony. In my dream I didn't pray to God. I thought of Roger and how dearly I loved him. The pain of those wicked flames was not half so bad as the pain I felt when I knew he was dead. I felt suddenly glad to be dying. I didn't know when you were burnt to death you'd bleed. I thought the blood would all dry up in the terrible heat. But I was bleeding heavily. The blood was dripping and hissing in the flames. I wished I had enough blood to put the flames out. The worst part was my eyes . . . I tried to close my eyelids but I couldn't. They must have been

burnt off, and now those flames were going to pluck my eyes
out with their evil fingers.

These stories contain a number of elements which appear in
many other cases where reincarnation is claimed. Birthmarks
and other distinguishing features are often cited as evidence
of past-life injuries, as perhaps some kind of cosmic reminder
of the previous life. In certain cases subjects relate marks to
actual previous death experiences – bullet wounds, scars and
even physical weaknesses can be traced back to previous
violence. So, for instance, some people believe that Soviet ex-
President Gorbachev's birthmark on his head indicates that
he previously died from a blow to the head. The other
consistently claimed indicator of past-life experience is
'irrational' fear, which believers in reincarnation say can be
explained by traumatic death from a previous time. Thus fear
of water may indicate a drowning. Fear of fire may have
arisen from an accidental blaze, but may also be the result of
a fiery death on an execution pyre. The positive aspects of
'attainments' – or past-life skills – are also believed by some
to carry over from one life to another. Not only was Rome
built in significantly longer than a day, but composers like
Mozart and Beethoven may have had a number of lifetimes in
which to develop their musical abilities. All prodigious talent
could be explained in this way, as could all patterns of
limitation and weakness.

For those who claim that DNA is involved in the reincarnation process, these ideas raise some interesting questions.
While fear and other emotional patterns may be carried
genetically – in the same way that instinctive responses in
animals are transmitted across generations – it is harder to
see a gene-based explanation for individual attainments. For
those whose model of life is based around souls as individual
'packets' of complex energies, which can inhabit body after
body, the explanations for such phenomena may appear more
accessible, even if not complete. The great American psychic
and past-life 'reader' Edgar Cayce was once asked 'From

which side of the family do I inherit most?' In keeping with his conviction in reincarnation he replied, 'You have inherited most from yourself, not from your family! The family is only a river through which your soul flows.' The subject of reincarnation is understandably controversial – at its heart is our most fundamental belief about the process of life and death. With so much at stake, the quality of evidence may not be the issue. In the words of American psychologist William James, 'The evidence for life after death shall always be strong enough to reassure the converted, but never conclusive enough to have the slightest influence on the unbelievers.'

TELEPATHY

The Concise Oxford Dictionary defines telepathy as 'the action of one mind on another at a distance through emotional influence without communication through senses.' Perhaps it should say 'without communication through the *known* senses': those five that we take as real before questioning the existence of any further senses. Stories of telepathy and communication by thought are so numerous that they could fill many books on their own. Whether telepathy can stand up reliably to the tests of a scientific laboratory seems to be another, much harder, question.

John Donne, the great metaphysical poet of the 17th century, had a telepathic experience with his wife, which was described by his biographer Izaac Walton.

In 1610 Donne was part of a diplomatic mission that travelled to Paris. Unfortunately, though, Donne had to leave his wife shortly before she was to give birth to their child. Two days after he arrived in Paris he was found by Ambassador Sir Robert Drury 'in such an ecstacy and so altered as to his looks, as amazed Sir Robert to behold him.' Donne's 'ecstacy' was not of the positive kind, 'I have seen a dreadful vision since I saw you: I have seen my dear wife pass twice by me through this room, with her hair hanging about her shoulders, and a dead child in her arms.' Sir Robert tried to reassure him that his vision was simply 'the result of some melancholy dream', but Donne insisted on the importance of what he had experienced. A messenger was despatched from Paris to England to discover 'whether Mrs Donne were alive; and if alive, in what condition she was as to her health.'

Via 17th-century transport, it took the messenger 12 days before he returned – 12 very anxious days for Donne. The news was not good. According to biographer Walton, the messenger reported:

> that he found and left Mrs Donne very sad, and sick in her bed; and that after a long and dangerous labour, she had been delivered of a dead child. And, upon examination, the abortion proved to be the same day, and about the very hour, that Mr Donne affirmed he saw her pass by him in his chamber.

If Donne had been alive in the 20th century he would have sympathized with a well-known modern occurrence. Most people with access to a telephone have experienced the phenomenon of calling a friend, only to be told the recipient was just about to ring them. Perhaps, though, the experience is more credible when we are receiving rather than making the call. Only 'we' know whether we really were thinking of that person at, or just before, the time that they rang. Because of this class of experience, many people believe in telepathy on a day-to-day level – without having tested it scientifically, nor having established its credibility. 'It's an intuitive thing,' we tend to say. Yet in the scientific laboratory telepathy has proved remarkably elusive.

J.B. Rhine, the founder of the parapsychology laboratory at Duke University, was the modern father of scientific research into telepathy – or 'extra-sensory perception' (ESP) as he named it. Rhine had been impressed by the writings of Sir Oliver Lodge the physicist and experimenter in psychic phenomena and by the American psychologist William

McDougall. Rhine had researched psychic, mental and spiritual phenomena with a great keenness, travelling to meet those who claimed to have had extraordinary experiences. He had also met with Carl Jung to quiz him about an incident in which a knife had broken into pieces while stored in a locked drawer in Jung's home. Rhine was desperate to find conclusive, scientifically validated proof of the effects he saw people make claims for.

To test for telepathic abilities, Rhine created a set of cards, called Zener cards. Each pack of 25 cards contained 5 cards, each one showing one of five different, yet simple, designs: square, cross, star, circle and wavy lines. For each experimental run, the experimenter would go through the pack, looking at each card in turn, mentally registering the symbol on the card; at the same time, out of sight of the cards, the subject would attempt to 'guess' which card the experimenter had just turned. By random chance alone the subject would be expected to score 5 correct cards in each run of 25 cards.

In 1931, just prior to the establishment of the Duke University parapsychology laboratory, Rhine tested a Duke economics student named Adam Linzmayer. Linzmayer turned out to be everything Rhine dreamed of in a subject. For Linzmayer's first test Rhine asked him to identify telepathically 9 Zener cards placed face down, out of sight. Taking his time, Linzmayer identified all 9 correctly. Rhine was amazed: the odds against 9 correct 'guesses' were, and indeed still are, about two million to one. The next day Linzmayer was called back for more tests. Again the results were spectacular: in 12 runs of 25 cards (300 in total) Linzmayer identified 119 cards correctly. The laws of probability say that he should have got only 60 correct, and yet he got nearly double. Rhine was inspired by these results, but found that Linzmayer was unable to repeat them 'to order'. While he did have further successes, Linzmayer's abilities, whatever they were, seemed to tail off quite quickly. There is, though, an apocryphal story that he won thousands of dollars in the casinos of Las Vegas.

After Linzmayer, Hubert Pearce, a divinity student, emerged as the laboratory's next star. Over an extended number of trials he would, on average, identify about 9 cards out of 25 correctly – about twice what would be expected, and statistically significant. In one experiment with Rhine, Pearce identified a straight run of 25 cards. The odds against this happening randomly are some many thousands of billions to one. Rhine and his colleagues seemed to be on the brink of a breakthrough: 'Our plan has been to try to catch what looks like ESP and, gradually improving the safeguards as we go, bring the phenomenon, if possible up to the point where there can be no question about the interpretation of the results.' Rhine's techniques, though, came under attack. Many sceptics, keen to debunk any 'real effects' that Rhine was claiming with his subjects, were eager to prove that the methods were not safe, and that they could have been abused by the trickery of subjects. Had Rhine and his colleagues been a naïve audience to the work of tricksters? After all their millions of trials the prospect that they had been duped in some way seemed appalling. And yet it was the charge they were to face.

Mark Hansel was a professor of psychology at the University of Wales in the 1950s when he started actively to analyse claims of ESP. As a conventional scientist he felt it was important to look the claims of unexplained phenomena squarely in the eye and see if they blinked.

If their claims are justified, a complete revision in contemporary scientific thought is required at least comparable to that made necessary in biology by Darwin and in physics by Einstein. On the other hand, if ESP is merely an artefact, it is then important to understand how conventional experimental methods can yield results leading to erroneous conclusions.

Hansel felt he was playing for high stakes when he travelled to Duke University at the invitation of Rhine. Hansel homed in on the experiments that Rhine's colleague J. Gaither Pratt had carried out with Hubert Pearce, the divinity student. His aim was to see if there were flaws in the experimental method, and he had the experiments set up again so that he could see what had happened. In the original experiments Hubert Pearce had been placed in a room on his own in the university library, while Gaither Pratt was in another building some 300 feet away. For each run of tests Gaither Pratt shuffled and cut the cards, and placed them face down on the table in front of him. At an agreed time he would start to turn the cards over one at a time, mentally focusing on each. Back in his room in the library Hubert Pearce would simultaneously write down the order of cards that he believed he was telepathically receiving. After five minutes, Gaither Pratt would repeat the process with another set of 25 cards. After each set of 25, Gaither Pratt would write down the order that the cards had appeared in – his list was given to Rhine, who would compare them with Pearce's. No problems there. As far as Rhine and Gaither Pratt were concerned the method was immune to tampering. Hansel, though, had other ideas. He re-ran a trial, using a member of the Duke laboratory staff – Wadhi Saleh – in Gaither Pratt's role of card turner. Professor Hansel himself played the part of the subject. And he was remarkably successful – 22 out of the 25 cards were identified correctly. Was Hansel a talented psychic? Unfortunately for Rhine he was not: he had found a fault in the method. When Wadhi Saleh was in one building turning the cards, he believed Hansel was in another building. In fact Hansel was right outside the door. 'I slipped back to Saleh's room and saw the cards by standing on a chair and looking through a crack at the top of the door. I had a clear view of them . . . Saleh's desk was about sixteen feet from the door, and he had no suspicion of what I had done until I told them.' When Hansel published his report on Rhine's methods the effect was shattering, nearly blowing Rhine, Gaither Pratt and the whole laboratory out of the academic water. Rhine attempted to defend himself and the laboratory's methods, but the damage was already done. Hubert Pearce, Rhine's most successful subject, was effectively being accused of fraud. He was in no position to defend himself: he had died some years earlier after a lifelong career as a religious minister. Pearce, though, had always denied that he ever cheated in any of the experiments.

Rhine's work was badly damaged by Hansel's exposé, though his work at Duke University continued until his death in 1980. Even though his methods have been questioned Rhine sowed enough seeds of doubt and hope to promote the serious and scientific study of parapsychology.

A less formal scientific test, although a potentially more convincing case, occurred around the same time that Rhine's early tests were being conducted. It was 1937 when Sir Hubert Wilkins, explorer and adventurer, set off by Lockheed plane in search of a group of Russian flyers, led by Sigismund Levanevsky, who were lost somewhere in the Arctic. The rescue mission was to last five months.

Before he left, however, Wilkins had been approached by his friend, the sports journalist and author Harold Sherman. Sherman's interest in the possibility of telepathic communication had led him to an idea:

> Wouldn't it be great, Sir Hubert, if the mind of some humans could be developed to such a point that all you'd have to do, if you were forced down and your radio went out of commission, would be to sit and think of your latitude and longitude, transmit that information to a human receiver, and he would send a rescue plane to pick you up at that point.

Wilkins' reply was encouraging: 'You're jesting, of course, Sherman, but I wouldn't say that, in perhaps fifty to a hundred years, the minds of some humans will not be developed to the point where that could be done.' He agreed to the suggestion of a telepathic experiment with Sherman while he attempted the rescue of the Russian flyers. Sherman was to try to 'make contact' with Wilkins telepathically on three nights of the week, and to keep a log of what he believed to be happening to Wilkins some 3,000 miles away in the frozen North. To ensure scientific rigour, the experiment was to be monitored by Dr Gardner Murphy, head of Columbia University's psychology department. Very soon after Wilkins left, Sherman believed that something extraordinary was happening:

> The very first night I was electrified at getting the sensation that a circuit had been closed between Sir Hubert Wilkins' mind and my own! ... I had never felt this way before and, with the sensation, came a rush of impressions which I commenced to record in a notepad on my desk. It did all seem incredible, as I wrote, since one impression followed another, almost without a break ... as though I were a Western Union operator, taking down a series of messages being telegraphed to me by some distant sender.

Day after day Sherman filled his notebooks with all the impressions that came to him during the sessions when he focused on Wilkins' activities. These he passed on to Dr Gardner Murphy. After some time in the North, Wilkins' log of his journey started to be radioed back to New York, where a radio operator recorded it. When Sherman was shown Wilkins' activities for the preceding weeks he was astonished: though not necessarily accurate all the time, some of the results were remarkably successful. One night Sherman had an impression of an apparently unlikely event:

> I had a feeling you were taking off on a flight this morning for some place that seemed like Saskatchewan. I had the feeling you've been caught in a blinding snow-storm and can probably make a forced landing at some place that sounds like Regina. I see you, Wilkins, roped in on an officer's ball that appears to have been held this evening. I see many men and women in military attire and evening dress. You, Wilkins, are in evening dress yourself.

Even Sherman knew that his impressions sounded a little ridiculous. As he told his wife: 'I know he didn't fly North equipped with an evening dress suit; and yet I saw him in my mind's eye in an evening dress suit.' Nevertheless, when Wilkins' report of that day arrived some weeks later it read:

This morning took off on flight. Hoping to reach Saskatchewan. Was caught in a heavy blizzard. Propose to turn back and make a landing in Regina. Was met at the airport by the Governor of the province who invited me to attend an officer's ball being held there this evening. My attendance at this ball was made possible by the loan to me of an evening dress suit.

Some days Sherman's accuracy was uncanny, as Wilkins himself confirmed for the entries of 7 December 1937. Wilkins added his own feedback on Sherman's recorded impressions:

Sherman: 'Don't know why, but I seem to see crackling fire shining out in darkness of Aklavik – get a definite fire impression as though house burning – you can see it from your location on ice – I first thought fire on ice near your tent, but impression persists it is white house burning, and quite a crowd gathered around it – people running or hurrying towards flames – bitter cold – stiff breeze blowing . . .'

Wilkins: (later) 'While I was in radio office at Point Barrow, the fire alarm rang. A long ring on the telephone. (There were only four telephones at Barrow.) It was an Eskimo's shack on fire. The chimney blazed up, and the roof took fire, but it was soon put out. Some damage resulted, mostly from the efforts of the zealous firemen. Was pretty cold that night with a light wind.'

Sherman: 'Your plane looks like a silvery ghost in moonlight – I seem to be under nose of it – standing in snow, looking up – it towers over me – I've never seen plane, of course, but it seems to have high bow, with two huge propellers either side of cabin or cockpits – motor concealed in great silver metal tub-like cylinders or encasements – don't know technical name

43

for purposes of description – a rounded metal door seems to lift up to admit entrance to cockpits from top of plane – big instrument broad front cockpit – seats for two – pilot and co-pilot or navigator – rear cockpit and space beyond for another passenger and storage – separate rounded metal door with glassed-window covering each cockpit – plane rests on giant skis – dark in colour . . .'

Wilkins: 'Description of plane *practically exact.*'

Sherman was not always accurate in his information, but the detail of the times when he was correct is impressive. The case also remains important because the security of the case was maintained by a highly reputable group of people.

This kind of telepathy is now known as 'remote viewing' and has gained considerable attention in the last half of the 20th century. Most of this interest has focused on remote viewing's use by military and security services to try to gain access to information that would, otherwise, be completely secret or unobtainable.

Most telepathic research is carried out behind the closed doors of scientific, military or educational institutions. It is not often that the general public are asked to participate in large-scale telepathic experiments. Yet with the media's growing interest in parapsychology, television has become a useful medium for study. One television experiment carried out by Uri Geller in 1995 represented one of the first large-scale experiments in mass telepathy. For the experiment Geller used a set of five Zener cards, as used by J.B. Rhine. Prior to the programme, he chose one card and sealed it in an envelope. During the programme he showed the audience the five symbol cards of the Zener pack, and explained that he had already selected one. He proceeded to concentrate on the chosen card and 'beamed' this to the watching public. Of the members of the public who responded via a phone-in, an amazing 48 per cent chose the correct card. Given that the expected, random choice would have given 20 per cent correct responses, 48 per cent represents a statistically very 'real' effect. However, there were some questions raised over the method employed by Geller – particularly in the way he had looked over the five cards prior to the mental experiment. Critics claimed that, even if subconsciously via his body or eye language, he could have given a message to the audience as to which card he had favoured.

If nothing else, the experiment shows those looking for positive evidence that the search for reliable telepathic effects has not disappeared. Nor, with the huge interest in the area still growing, is it likely to. What telepathy has on its side, of course, is that while scientists may find it difficult to prove that telepathy is a real and repeatable phenomenon, it is, and will always remain, impossible to *disprove* its existence.

DREAMS

Everyone dreams. Even those who do not remember their dreams dream. Since the earliest cultures the sleep state has been a mysterious underworld: we all go there but few of us can remember what it is like. The messages we bring back often seem strange, random, surprising and incomprehensible. Yet the work of Sigmund Freud and Carl Jung in the first half of the 20th century, and other dream pioneers who have followed, has offered powerful evidence that dreams offer a cogent and intelligent system of communication between the subconscious and conscious minds. Taken seriously dreams can offer warnings, advice, comfort, initiation, wisdom and intelligence in a symbolic language that can be learnt and understood – just like any foreign language. In some cases they may help to save our health, our sanity, even our lives. On the other hand, if the sceptics are to be believed, they may just be the aimless outpourings of a tired and addled brain, unable to process any more stimuli.

*

45

Many ancient cultures have strong connections with the dreams of their people, dreams that link individuals to the collective unconscious of their tribe or race. For the Aboriginal peoples of Australia, the Dreamtime is a concept that they rely on for their sense of identity. The Dreamtime, or Dreaming, is the story of the creation and of the mythical beings that attended the world's birth. To be in touch with the Dreamtime is to be in touch with past, present and future. Though the beings who created Earth are no longer with us, their spirits have stayed on, living in the creations of Nature – the trees, the rivers, mountains and animals. Through dreams their spirits can be recontacted. Through dreams the Aboriginals can be reconnected with their origins, their Dreamtime. It is this sense of interconnectedness that brings them peace and a sense of wholeness. It is the absence of the Dreaming which leads to the breakdown of the culture.

Medicine men, or healers, still play a forceful role in the lives of many traditional tribal peoples. Their fitness for the role of healer is often determined by their dreams. In Aboriginal cultures a man may see himself put to death and taken up to the 'Rainbow Serpent' in the sky where he is brought back to life and given supernatural powers. In the process the dreamer will often see himself broken into pieces. This dismemberment symbolizes the breakdown of the old psychological self. The self undergoes a spiritual crisis before being made whole again. The crisis forces the man to face himself and to bring about his own healing. Only by healing himself does he become fit to heal others.

The early Greeks conveyed the same idea when they laid the foundations for modern Western medicine. Their advice to doctors was clear: 'physician, heal thyself.' It is sad to note that the professions with the highest suicide rate in the UK are doctors and nurses. Some might deduce that the failure to undergo appropriate 'initiations', such as those in original cultures, puts 'unhealed healers' at great risk from the psychological stresses of their work. Modern medics might benefit from listening more closely to the messages of their own

46

dreams. They have some pioneering examplars to follow. The work of Freud, Jung and other psychiatrists and psychologists can be seen to represent modern Western civilization re-discovering its ethnic dreaming roots – albeit in a scientific context.

Soozi Holbeche, the therapist and writer, has studied the healing potential of dreams. She describes the guidance she gave to the mother of a South African eight year old who suffered from recurrent nightmares:

> I suggested that the next time he had the nightmare she should encourage him to face the monster, point his finger at it, and, while imagining light or colour directed at it, shrink it until it was small enough to pick up. He could then ask the monster its name and make friends with it. To the family's amazement, the child remembered to do this and ran into breakfast talking excitedly about his new friend and what they were planning to do together that night. He never had the nightmare again.

Sleep can be the time when the subconscious mind releases our greatest creativity. Many great works of literature, many inventions and ideas have owed their inspiration to the mysterious workings of the sleeping mind. Leonardo Da Vinci attributed the birth of many of his greatest inventions to his dream images. Robert Louis Stevenson, the author of classic works of fiction such as *Treasure Island* and *The Strange Case of Dr Jekyll and Mr Hyde*, trained himself to recall his dreams. When he started writing novels, he wrote them as serializations for newspapers. Each night he would dream a further segment, and in the morning write down the story. He claimed that he had no clear idea what direction the story was travelling in or where it would end. In later life he was able to dream the stories for entire novels in one single night. Many other poets and authors received help from the creative muse of their dreams, Wordsworth, Coleridge and Edgar Allen Poe among them. Coleridge dreamt the entirety of his epic poem *Kubla Khan*, and on waking started to write it down. When he was disturbed in the middle of the process he lost his thread, and the poem remained forever unfinished.

Science is not immune from such sources of inspiration. The French chemist Friedrich Kekulé struggled for weeks to understand the structure of the benzene molecule before receiving a dream image of snakes devouring their own tails. When he awoke Kekulé immediately understood the symbolic significance of the coiled snakes, which expressed in pictorial form the geometry he had been seeking: what we now call the 'benzene ring'.

Another scientific dreamer was Alan Turing, the great mathematician, who invented the world's first modern computer after being shown how it worked in a dream. From this raw material he developed the Enigma code-breaking computer which successfully deciphered many of Hitler's secret messages during the Second World War. Some experts believe it was crucial to the Allies' victory.

Strangely, though, there is a paradoxical parallel to this story, which shows that dreams do not always favour those that history dubs the heroes. It centres on a warning dream that came to Adolf Hitler while he was fighting in the trenches of the First World War. While asleep inside a defensive bunker, alongside other exhausted, war-weary soldiers of the German army, he dreamt that he was being buried under molten earth: buried alive and suffocated. He woke suddenly, in a terrified state. He rushed out into the cold night air to calm himself. While he stood there, recovering from his fright, an Allied artillery shell scored a direct hit on the bunker, killing every man inside. Hitler attributed his escape to divine intervention: God had saved him through his dream, that he might save the Fatherland. When Germany suffered the humiliation of losing the First World War, Hitler's dream inspired him to strengthen and expand the Fatherland so that it might never be conquered and subdued again.

The pattern of history owes much to dreams and the inspiration that the dream-state has provided. When Bismark was a young child he discovered that many of his dreams came true. These dreams continued throughout his military career, and he took them very seriously – seriously enough to relate them to his Emperor William:

> Your majesty's communication encouraged me to relate a dream I had in the Spring of 1863, during the worst of the days of struggle. I dreamed that I was riding on a narrow Alpine path, a precipice on my right and rocks on my left. The path grew narrower and narrower so that my horse refused to proceed and it was impossible to turn round to dismount. Then, with my whip in my hand I struck the smooth rock and called on God. The whip grew to an enormous length, the rocky wall dropped like a piece of stage scenery and opened out into a broad path with a view over the hills and forest like a landscape in Bohemia: there were Prussian troops with banners and even in my dream the thought came to me that I must report it to your majesty.

This dream inspired Bismark to pursue his aim. His Prussian homeland took over the leadership of the German Federation of States, which was to lead, eventually, to Hitler's establishment of the Third Reich.

All dreams can bring us important messages, vital information – information from a level of knowledge that we are not normally in touch with. The information that we receive may not be welcome either. Before he was assassinated Abraham Lincoln dreamt of his death: he saw a coffin being guarded by soldiers, and people standing around the coffin weeping. In the dream Lincoln asked: 'Who is dead?' 'The President, killed by an assassin,' came the reply. In 1963 a number of people claimed to have had dreams predicting President Kennedy's death. One woman phoned the White House the day before his assassination to say she had dreamt he was going to be killed in Dallas.

The author Mark Twain was only a boy when he had a dream of death which was to affect him all his life. He and his brother Henry worked on the riverboats that ran up and down the Mississippi between New Orleans and St Louis. One night, while Twain was staying at his sister's house in St Louis, he had a particularly vivid dream that his brother's body was lying in a metal coffin in the room downstairs from where he was sleeping. The coffin was supported by two chairs, and on top rested a bouquet of white flowers with another red flower at its centre.

The dream was so vivid that Twain awoke, believing his brother had actually died, and that his body was in the sitting room below. He could not face going in to see his brother's coffin, however, and decided to take a walk outside. Within a few minutes he realized that the dream had been just that. He rushed back, opened the sitting room door, and, with what he described as a 'trembling revulsion of joy', found the room empty. Twain immediately confided the dream to his sister, but then tried to put it out of his mind.

A few weeks later Twain and his brother Henry were in New Orleans, ready to return again to St Louis. As it happened, Henry was to take the first boat, the *Pennsylvania*, while Twain followed on two days later in the *Lacey*. When his boat passed through a small town called Greenville, Twain heard people shouting from the bank: 'The *Pennsylvania*'s blown up, just below Memphis, at Ship Island! One hundred and fifty people lost!' When Twain arrived at Memphis he learned the full horror of what had happened. One of the worst disasters in Mississippi shipping history had killed 150, and left a further 40 seriously injured, including Twain's brother Henry. Twain stayed with him for six days and nights, watching his life slip away. Biographer Albert Bigelow Paine described the last days:

> And then, the long strain of grief, the days and nights without sleep, the ghastly realization of the end overcame him ... A citizen of Memphis took Sam [Twain's real name was Samuel Clemens] away in a kind of daze and gave him a bed in his home, where he fell into a stupor of fatigue and surrender.

Many hours passed before he awoke. When he did, at last, he dressed and went to where Henry lay.

All of the victims' coffins were of unpainted wood – except for Henry's. His youth and good looks had attracted special attention. The women of Memphis had raised 60 dollars for a special coffin – a metal coffin. When Twain entered the room where his brother's body lay, he saw the coffin just as he had in his dream – only lacking the flowers that had adorned it. As he sat looking at the coffin in grief, an elderly woman entered the room and placed a bouquet on top, a bouquet of white flowers with a single red rose at its centre.

In this century the scientific study of dreams has progressed a long way from the original work of Freud and Jung. In the 1960s scientific research was carried out at the Moses Maimonides Medical Center in New York into the precognitive and telepathic aspects of dreams. The research focused on the question of whether the subjects of the experiments could dream about the content of pictures which had been chosen, secretly, by the research staff. At the end of the project the subjects had scored a remarkable hit rate of 233 out of 379 tests. Perhaps, though, the most remarkable results of the research came from a British healer and psychic named Malcolm Beasant. In one of a number of successful trials he dreamed about a concrete building, from which he saw a medical patient dressed in a doctor's white coat, trying to escape. He felt an antagonistic atmosphere in the scene of the dream, where a group of doctors and nurses were also present.

When he woke up, and before he was allowed any contact with the staff of the dream research, the 'target' picture was chosen by a random process. It turned out to be Van Gogh's painting entitled *Hospital Corridor at St Remy*. The painting depicts exactly the content that Beasant had described, only Beasant had managed to dream about the image *before* it had even been chosen.

*

One area of dreaming that has attracted a lot of recent research interest is *lucid* dreaming. A lucid dream is one in which you become aware that you are dreaming and yet, instead of waking up, you continue on your dream journey. In the cases of some 'advanced' dreamers, they are able to control and guide their lucid dreams, and some even claim to have high levels of precognition and even communication with spiritual entities through their dreams.

While the majority of the population do experience a lucid dream during their lifetime, it remains a rare event. Dr Peter Fenwick, a neuropsychologist at London's St Thomas's Hospital, and Dr Keith Hearne, a British parapsychologist, have carried out extensive research with people who claim to have regular lucid dreams. As well as a greater understanding of the lucid dream state, their motive has been to make lucid dreaming more possible for more people. By 1994 Dr Hearne had released an electronic device called a 'dream machine' which may help to stimulate dream recall and lucid dreaming by sensing when users are in the deepest regions of sleep and then stimulating the dreamer to wakefulness.

Many people now record their dreams in a dream diary. There seems little doubt that with practice, and a conscious intention to remember and record, dreams can become more lucid, easier to remember and more accessible to interpretation. Some experts liken it to a two-way conversation between the subconscious and conscious minds, with the subconscious often acting as a form of wise guide. As the conscious mind becomes a more studious pupil the subconscious mind opens up and reveals more wisdom and helpful information for the conscious mind to chew on, wrestle with and, ultimately, to benefit from. As anyone who has worked in this way knows, however, dreams do not often speak in a direct or simple language.

The language of symbols is often a more memorable and more subtle system than the mere language of words. Symbols – such as animals, natural forces, the elements, specific events

– may be the universal language of the collective unconscious, as 'dream dictionaries' seem to imply. In the 1930s before the Second World War eventually started, many of Carl Jung's patients shared dreams of storm clouds, destruction, bloodshed and mayhem rolling across the lands of Europe. Jung's theory of the collective unconscious seems very helpful in explaining the way that we 'tap into' the *Zeitgeist*, the psychic projections of a particular time-frame. It is as if some people can read the collective thoughts of the group consciousness. Nevertheless dreams inevitably contain images, people and events that are unique to us, and that speak, in a sense, our own unique language. Perhaps no one can tell us what they mean, but others may help lead us to understand a dream's meaning more fully. Until someone has attempted the process of dream recording and interpretation with some diligence and application it might be churlish to say, with any confidence, that last night's apparent ramblings were, really, 'only a dream'.

PRECOGNITION

One morning in 1933 an 80-year-old Quaker awoke from a curious dream. John Williams had been a clean-living man all his life. Some would have called him a puritan, for he avoided alcohol, smoking and betting. But this morning, the morning of the 1933 Derby, he awoke with a dream clearly in his mind: in the dream he heard a radio commentary of the big race, with the names of the first four horses past the post clearly mentioned. Unfortunately he could now only remember the first two: Hyperion and King Salmon. Surprised by the content of the dream, he told two friends what had happened. Later in the day – out of curiosity alone – he decided to listen to the radio commentary. To Williams' amazement, Hyperion was the winner, with King Salmon the runner-up. True to his beliefs, Mr Williams had not staked his savings on the horses' winning. He told the story to a few people, and eventually the case was investigated by H.F. Saltmarsch of the Society for Psychical Research, who concluded – unsurprisingly – that Mr Williams had indeed had a precognitive dream.

Stuart Wilde, one of the prosperity gurus of the 1980s and 1990s tells a similar story of a participant in one of his 'abundance workshops'. The American lady awoke one morning with a set of numbers, which, as a regular player of the state lottery, she felt to be the numbers for the coming draw. On her way to the shop where she chose her numbers she had a feeling that some of the numbers were not quite correct, so she changed them – in her own mind improving her chances. When the numbers were drawn, guess what? The original numbers came up – exactly as she had dreamt them. Just a few million dollars down the drain . . .

There are many similar stories of people who dream winners, which of course must be balanced with the less often heard stories of people who dream losers: they tend to keep quiet about their feats. Betting and gambling are only one obvious example of precognition – the abilitity to 'know before' something has happened. In fact the most common examples of precognition are in cases where people have had dreams, mental pictures, or strong intuitions about danger and disaster – particularly, though not exclusively, where they themselves are likely to be at risk. In these cases the precognition can be seen to act as a kind of warning. It is also common for recipients of the message to attribute it to a benevolent deity, an angelic or spiritual being. Unfortunately it can also happen that those who experience precognitive visions are unable to act upon them, or even to influence events in order to avert disaster.

It was October 1966 when the Welsh village of Aberfan was hit by a tragedy which still haunts the small coal mining community over 30 years later. The village's junior school was engulfed by the collapse of a massive slag heap. In all there were 144 victims. Dr John Barker, a psychiatrist, was later able to collect evidence of around 60 cases of people who had experienced some premonition of the tragic events in the preceeding days and weeks. Twenty-two of the cases involved reports that had been told to others, and were considered to be corroborated. A few stuck out as being particularly uncanny: Mrs Monica McBean was working in an aircraft factory some 200 miles from Aberfan when she had a waking vision of 'a black mountain moving and children buried under it'. Mrs McBean was so distressed by the images that came to her mind that she had to go to the ladies' room to recover. This happened half an hour before the actual disaster.

Eryl Mai Jones was nine years old when the disaster struck, and killed her, along with many of her classmates. Two weeks earlier she had told her parents that she had no fear of dying because she knew she would be going to heaven with two of her best friends. On the morning of the tragedy she had dreamt that there was no longer any school, that it had been covered by something black. When her body was recovered from the debris, she was found to be seated between the two other children she had named.

It could be said that in this case those around the young girl chose not to act to at least remove her from the potential disaster. Yet her own sense of the future included her tragic death and, indeed, her acceptance of it. Some would conclude that she simply had a clear understanding of her own 'plan'. Indeed many (though by no means all) bereaved parents of young children report that, in retrospect, they felt their child instinctively knew that they would die 'early'. Could they be fulfilling their 'life-plan' as much as those who live to a ripe age. This is not necessarily a popular view in our culture, but it may fit with other cultural models – such as that of India and many Hindu and Buddhist countries – which incorporate the teachings of reincarnation and karma. While we may fear death, and use modern medicine and other techniques to try to prevent it from ever impinging on our reality, we might take note of Carl Jung's message about death and our attitude to it: 'our myth of death determines the way we live our lives.'

There are many people who claim to have avoided death following an experience of precognition: the American actress

Lindsay Wagner was checking onto an American Airlines DC10 at Chicago's O'Hare airport in May 1979 when she had an overwhelming feeling not to take the plane. Within moments of take-off the plane she would have taken rolled over and crashed, causing the death of all its 273 passengers. She was not the only person to have had a sense that something terrible would happen. David Booth of Cincinatti, Ohio, had been seeing the details of a crash for nearly two weeks before the Chicago disaster actually occurred. In his dreams he saw a large, three-engined American Airlines jet, apparently trying to land. The engines were not working properly: he could tell from the sounds they made. Next he saw the plane turn over and crash into the ground, engulfed in flames. 'It was like I was standing there watching the whole thing, like watching television.' It was as if Booth was seeing the reports of the crash after it had happened. The dream repeated with the same terror for the next eight nights until he decided to do something about it. He contacted American Airlines. He wasn't taken seriously. He rang the Federal Aviation Administration. He still wasn't taken seriously. He rang his nearest airport – Cincinatti – and was asked to come in. On Thursday 25 May he described his distressing dreams to an airport official, Paul Williams. From the description, Williams could only deduce that Booth was 'seeing' an American Airlines DC10 or a Boeing 727. Both have three engines, one on the tail. The description of the crash, though, was not enough to locate the image. The next day the crash happened, just as Booth had dreamt. Despite his attempts he had not been able to prevent it.

The evidence for precognition being possible is very strong, but as yet there has been no scientific study that has shown conclusively that it is a repeatable and reliable phenomenon. It appears to occur relatively randomly, and while some people may use their precognition to avoid a personal disaster, or even death, not everyone gets to avoid the fatal danger. One unusual study by the paranormal researcher William Cox appears to show that on aeroplane flights that have crashed there are significantly lower numbers of passengers than one would normally expect. Even if those who had 'avoided' the crash had not been consciously aware of any danger by precognitive means, it is possible that their precognition may have been at a subconscious level. It still leaves a question over those who do die in crashes – is it possible that some have, tragically, ignored subconscious promptings? Or is it the case, as many religious or spiritual people may feel, that when our time is up, it is time to leave?

Perhaps an even more important question about precognition is exactly how it might work. If we accept the evidence that people really are 'seeing the future' before it has happened, there are a number of ways that this may be possible. Some psychics say that when they see future events for their clients, they are often reading the desires and projections that the person has started to express through their mental and imaginative powers. These pictures, they say, register in the person's aura, or in the astral world to which we are all connected. These pictures could also be of a person's fears as well as their desires – for both can start to create and manifest reality equally powerfully. In a case of precognition, is it possible that people are subconsciouly 'reading' the projections – of both hopes and fears – that the 'players' of an event are already projecting? In cases of large events involving many people we may be reading the picturings of a group, or the results of its 'collective unconscious', as Carl Jung called it.

This explanation may have been at work when an author named Morgan Robertson published a novel in 1898 called *The Wreck of the Titan* about the tragic loss of a ship called the SS *Titan*. In the story, the new passenger liner – with an unthinkably large displacement of 75,000 tons – was believed to be unsinkable. Yet when the *Titan* made her maiden voyage across the Atlantic Ocean, she hit an iceberg. Most of the 3,000 passengers drowned because there were only 24 lifeboats – such was the confidence in *Titan's* invincibility.

If this story sounds more than a little familiar, it's hardly surprising: the story appeared 14 years before the SS *Titanic* made her maiden voyage in April 1912 – only to strike an iceberg with the loss of most of her 2,200 passengers. Other features of the real ship were remarkably similar to her fictional counterpart: the *Titanic*'s displacement was 66,000 tons; she carried only 20 lifeboats; and while the *Titan* was travelling at 25 knots at the time of her fictitious crash, the *Titanic* was actually travelling at 23 knots.

Morgan Robertson had not been the only person to have foreseen disaster for the *Titanic*. W.T. Stead, the writer and social campaigner, wrote an article for the *London Review of Reviews* in 1894 detailing the failings in safety precautions for ocean-going liners. In the article he described the terrible loss of life when a fictitious liner hit an iceberg in the north Atlantic. In a terrible irony, Stead ignored his own inner promptings: he died on the *Titanic*'s tragic maiden voyage.

While we might expect some people to fear for the safety of a new venture such as the *Titanic*, there were many other unexplained precognitive experiences that occurred close to the time of the disaster. Dr Ian Stevenson, professor of psychiatry at the University of Virginia, has collected 19 cases of precognition connected to the sinking of the *Titanic*. In one account a 14-year-old girl (later to become a Mrs Charles Hughes) had a strange dream on the very night that the *Titanic* was sinking. She dreamt that she was walking in a local park, but, 'Suddenly I saw a very large ship a short distance away, as if in Trentham Park. I saw figures walking about on it. Then suddenly it lowered at one end and I heard a terrific scream.' She woke up immediately, terrified by what she had seen. She was comforted by her grandmother, before going back to sleep. Again the dream came to her. Again her grandmother comforted her. The grandmother's own son – the young girl's uncle – was a man called Leonard Hodgkin, and at that very moment he was about to die as a member of the crew on the *Titanic*.

It almost seems that the key moments in history have all been foreseen ahead of time: prior to President Kennedy's assassination, the security forces received a higher than usual number of phone calls from people claiming to have dreamed or foreseen his death. On 28 June 1914, the First World War was triggered by the assassination of Archduke Ferdinand of Austria at Sarajevo. It appears, though, that the news arrived with one person before it happened. Bishop Joseph Lanyi had, some years before, been the Archduke's tutor. On the early morning of the 28th, though, Bishop Lanyi awoke from a terrible nightmare:

I dreamed I had gone to my desk early in the morning to look through the post that had come in. On top of all the other letters there lay one with a black border, a black seal and the arms of the Archduke. I immediately recognised the latter's writing, and saw at the head of the notepaper in blue colouring a picture like those on picture postcards which showed me a street and a narrow side-street. Their Highnesses sat in a car, opposite them sat a general, and an officer next to the chauffeur. On both sides of the street, there was a large crowd. Two young lads sprang forward and shot at their Highnesses. The text of the letter was as follows: 'Dear Dr Lanyi, Your Excellency, I wish to inform you that my wife and I were the victims of a political assassination. We recommend ourselves to your prayers. Cordial greetings from your Archduke Franz, Sarajevo, June 28th/3.15am' Trembling and in tears, I sprang out of bed and looked at the clock which showed 3.15. I immediately hurried to my desk and wrote down what I had read and seen in my dream. In doing so, I even retained the form of certain letters as the Archduke had written them. My servant entered my study as a quarter to six that morning and saw me sitting there pale and saying my rosary. He asked whether I was ill. I said: 'Call my mother and the guest at once. I will say Mass immediately for their Highnesses, for I have had a terrible dream.' My mother and the guest came at a quarter to seven. I told my mother the dream in the presence of the guest and of my servant. Then I went into the house chapel. The day passed in fear and apprehension. At half past three, a telegram brought us news of the murder.

The fact that many precognitive experiences seem to occur in the dreaming state is significant in itself. Many psychologists and seers believe that the sleep state actually allows us to 'slip out of time', and to access the astral world where time does not operate in the way that we normally understand it. We access a state where time is not linear, where the future does not follow the past, and where all time periods are equally 'available'. What we find most frightening in the idea that we may be able to see the future is the notion that the future already exists: that it has already been decided, and that, whatever we do, however hard we try, we cannot help but fulfil what time expects of us. In the novel *The Strange Life of Ivan Osokin* by the Russian metaphysician P.D. Ouspensky, Ivan Osokin is given the chance to live his life again, to right the wrongs of his past. Yet even with this gift he still makes exactly the same mistakes again and again. Despite every attempt to exercise his free will, the course of his life is immutable – a kind of living hell. Perhaps this kind of primal fear is at the heart of our objections to a known future. If the future can be known, then are we not truly passive observers? And then where is our encouragement to act responsibly? Many people who have experienced precognition have wondered why they were able to see a terrible future event when they were unable to act to stop it. Is this just some terrible cosmic joke?

There are, however, some people who have acted on their impressions and do appear to have averted disasters. It seems likely that 'dream detective' Chris Robinson's description to the police of an IRA terrorist cell in Cheltenham, England – gleaned from his dream – may well have led to their arrest. Robinson, though, has put forward an explanation for the way that time works: he claims that this explanation comes from 'Robert', one of the spirit guides who provide him with his dream information:

Time: what is time? . . . Time is the interval between two events or a series of events. If there were not an action or event, time, it could be argued, would not exist. It must follow from this that the gap is also an action or event as it does and must exist.

Try to imagine a gap between two events that is small enough that no other action or event, however apparently unrelated, could have occurred. This gap or unit of time is time itself. It can be argued that this gap could not exist, and if that is correct, time cannot exist either. As time is something that we could not deny must at least exist in our minds, it could then be argued that everything that has existed, or will ever exist, must have existed at the same time.

It is worth at this point trying to consider this: everything that has existed, or will ever exist, must exist now and have always existed, and will always exist.

If all things exist always, then travel between one event and another could be a possibility. Try to imagine it as a sideways, rather than a forwards or backwards step.

This compares interestingly with the material on time from the channellings of Jane Roberts' spirit guide named Seth. The Seth material, which is strongly premised on the concept of reincarnation, says that all lifetimes are occurring simultaneously. In other words all the events of all lifetimes, of all times, have all been 'compressed' into one moment called 'NOW'. It is only our minds that are structured to experience time in a linear fashion. This, Seth and other spiritual sources say, is a vast illusion, and we will only wake up to 'reality' when we realize that the events of our lives have, in a sense, already happened. While this directly contradicts our normal experience of reality, it may help to explain how precognition is possible.

PSYCHIC DETECTIVES

At 6am on 3 December 1967, Dorothy Allison, a New Jersey housewife, awoke from a disturbing dream. She had seen the body of a young boy, trapped in some kind of pipe. In her mental picture, the boy was wearing a green snow suit and had his shoes on the wrong feet. She thought he was Polish. A few days later, after much worrying about her vision, she rang the Nutley police in New Jersey. The police were initially sceptical of a woman claiming to have information from a dream about a missing boy, yet when she described the details of what she had seen and felt, they revised their opinion. The reason was a Polish boy called Michael who had been walking by a canal in a green snow suit. He had slipped and fallen into the freezing cold waters, and, despite extensive searches, his body had not yet been recovered. It was also established that Dorothy Allison's dream had occurred two hours *before* the boy had disappeared.

As in all such cases of tragedy, the police were keen to find the body as quickly as possible so that the boy's parents could know the truth and start the painful grieving process. Dorothy Allison wanted to help. She had also been brought up by a clairvoyante mother. Although Dorothy had not practised as a psychic, she had a respect for information that came from dreams and mental images. With the help of a police-approved psychiatrist, Dr Richard Ribner, Dorothy was put into a semi-hypnotized state: she repeatedly saw the numbers 8 and 120; the child's body, with its shoes on the wrong feet, was trapped in a bend in the pipe. She also saw a car-parking area behind a factory that belonged to ITT. The police did not think the information could be of much help. The ITT factory was a good distance away from where the child had fallen. A connection was highly unlikely. Dorothy now thought that the body would come to light on 7 February.

When the 7th came, the freezing weather was beginning to thaw. Near the ITT factory on the other side of the town, a pipe started to drip with melting ice. By the end of the morning the drip had become a regular trickle, until finally at 1.20pm, the body of the little Polish boy in a green snow suit, Michael Kurcsics, was released from its icy grave. His shoes were still on the wrong feet. The site was close to the local school – Public School Number 8.

Since this case, Dorothy Allison has assisted police with their enquiries around 4,000 times. In all cases she has responded to direct calls from the police for help. She only works on cases where the police are willing to be open about using her psychic skills. In a more recent case in February 1989 she was contacted by a missing persons bureau about a girl called Heather Church. Dorothy told them that Heather had been kidnapped by a man called Charles Browne. 'Browne with an "e",' she insisted. In fact the police were already suspicious of a man named Robert Charles Browne, but there was insufficient evidence to bring a case against him. The police dug deeper, discovering that Browne had been in jail in New Orleans. Armed with a set of fingerprints from Browne, the police were able to find a match at the scene of the crime. Yet they still needed more evidence if they were to secure a conviction. Dorothy's psychic information told her that a tan-coloured car would be likely to contain the most incriminating evidence. After an extensive search, the tan car linked to Browne was found. Even though Heather Church's disappearance had occurred some five years before, traces of her blood were found in the car. Browne was arrested and sent for trial.

Chris Robinson's dreams have got him into some serious trouble. Since 1989 he has been successfully predicting the location and type of terrorist attacks mounted by the IRA well in advance of their actual happening.

In the very first dream that he felt to have some significance, he was 'taken' to a town in England's West Country, he was 'shown' a small hotel where he saw an IRA cell of five people plotting a terrorist attack. When he woke up he knew the place to be Cheltenham, identifying it from his dream images of large, information-gathering satellite dishes. These dishes belonged to the Government's defence communication centre GCHQ. He knew immediately that it was the IRA's target, and that many people working there could be killed.

Robinson immediately contacted Paul Aylott, a detective inspector he had known for some years. Aylott had contacts at Scotland Yard, the London Metropolitan Police Headquarters, who had further contacts with special branch. He agreed to do what he could. What they both knew was that if something did happen to confirm Robinson's information, not everyone would believe them when it came to revealing his sources.

Only eight days later news broke that police had arrested a group of IRA terrorists in a hotel in Cheltenham. In the raid, guns and explosives had been found. Suddenly Robinson knew what he had only previously suspected: that he was on to something very important. With Aylott, another policeman, a priest and a newspaper reporter, Robinson agreed that he would keep a 'dream diary' recording all his dreams, and that he would forward material to the group. When he started the diary he discovered something almost as shocking as the dreams themselves. He had expected that he would wake up and write his dreams down, but when he woke up after the first night he found that the first page of the dream diary was already covered in writing: his own writing. Whether he had woken up without remembering, or whether this was some form of automatic writing, Robinson was not yet sure.

On the night of 8 January 1990 Robinson dreamt of the kidnapping of a very young baby from a hospital adjacent to a river – which he believed to be the Thames. Only three days later Alexandra Griffiths was snatched from her mother at St Thomas's Hospital, Westminster, overlooking the Thames. Within hours there was a knock on the door. Two policemen wanted to know where he had hidden the baby. The officers were convinced that Robinson had wanted and needed his dreams to come true: so he had driven to the hospital and snatched the child – truly a self-fulfilling prophecy.

It was not to be the last time that the shadow of suspicion

would fall on Robinson himself. After all, how could he know things before they happen? It just did not make sense to rational minds. As Robinson's dream diary developed he found a symbolic code emerging that, from dream to dream, he seemed to be learning more and more about. He was not always accurate – but often because he was not able to interpret the symbols or words. It was almost like a crossword puzzle, and some of the clues were surprisingly cryptic.

The next big breakthrough came on 16 February 1990. His dreams gave him three potential locations for IRA bombs, received in the form of postcodes: two in 'BT' and one in 'LE1'. LE1 is the postcode for the centre of Leicester, BT the code for Belfast, where Robinson believed the bombs were being sent from. About four days later Robinson was invited to a police station to make a statement detailing his thoughts on this. Within two hours of the visit a bomb went off in the centre of Leicester. The postcode? A very small part of the city centre, called LE1.

Robinson started to dream about bombs near Stanmore, Middlesex, and Wembley High Road, where he, himself had worked in an electrical store which had subsequently become a branch of Dixons – the electrical retailer. As the dreams progressed he gathered more information on both cases: finally, as the pieces of puzzle fell into place, he passed his conclusions to Paul Aylott, his police colleague. A bomb would be placed under a van or small lorry in Wembley High Road. He hoped that Aylott could do something. About six hours later, Robinson switched the television on: Sergeant Charles Chapman of the Army Recruiting Office had been killed by a bomb as he started the engine of his vehicle. The vehicle was a Sherpa van, parked outside Dixons in Wembley High Road.

When he dreamt of dogs with guns outside the RAF base at Stanmore in Middlesex, Robinson knew what it meant: dogs were IRA terrorists who intended to attack. But Robinson did not know when. Frustrated by his inability to prevent the terrible actions of the terrorists and feeling that the police were not acting fast enough, he decided to take things into his own hands. He drove to RAF Stanmore and walked up to the gate. He told the guards that he was psychic and that their base would be bombed – just as their colleague had been the previous day in Wembley.

Robinson was put under arrest, searched and interrogated. At last he was being taken seriously! After a good many hours of questioning by officers who firmly believed him to be a hoaxer or a madman, a fax arrived from the head of the anti-terrorist squad saying that he should be released. A month later a terrorist bomb was found on the RAF base. Fortunately it was detonated safely and no one was killed. Yet there were still members of the police force who believed that Robinson was actually working for the IRA – trying to infiltrate the police's intelligence network by posing as a clever psychic.

After one terrorist bomb attack, Robinson decided that he was going to try to locate the perpetrators of the attacks via his dream information. Within a few days, and with the help of a London A-Z street guide, he felt he had narrowed down his search to about 500 yards square in the Kilburn area. He decided to call Chris Watt, his contact at London Metropolitan Police Headquarters. Watt was pretty sceptical, but Robinson explained how his dream had helped him arrive at the conclusion. There were lots of flats to be checked out, but he knew that the names Sidmouth and Chamberlayne were connected.

About a month later Robinson bought a copy of the *Daily Express* with the headline: 'IRA Bomb Factory Smashed'. One hundred pounds of explosives recovered, six people arrested and two cars full of guns and explosives seized. The flat was in Kilburn, in a block called Sidmouth Court in Chamberlayne Road. Robinson was elated. He rang Chris Watt to celebrate. But Watt was in no mood to celebrate. He wanted nothing more to do with Robinson. There has been no contact between them since. Did Watt believe that Robinson actually knew where the IRA cell was? That he shopped them? Was it all just too much for the rational policeman?

It has not stopped other prominent people from taking him seriously. Towards the end of 1990 Robinson started to write to his local MP Graham Bright. John Major had just become Prime Minister, and the dreams had started to contain information about an attack on Major. It was fortuitous when Bright became the new Prime Minister's private parliamentary secretary. Robinson's letter was responded to with more seriousness than previously:

> Thank you for your letter of 4 December listing all the various incidents that you have forseen. As you know, I have been in touch with the police and have spoken personally to the Chief Superintendent at Luton. The Cambridgeshire police are aware of you and of the fact that you have information to give them.
>
> If you would like to let me have any additional detail, particularly of what you are predicting for the future, I will ensure that the appropriate authorities are fully aware.

Robinson had dreamt about the postcode SW1, and the Prime Minister's home – 10 Downing Street – is in SW1. By 1 January 1991 Robinson knew the attack would be by rocket and be carried out by two men. On 10 January he dreamt of IRA terrorists re-spraying a white transit van. On 3 February he dreamt that the van would be written-off in the attack. On 6 February dreams showed three rockets firing into space. Additionally there were more indications of SW1 postcodes, and a strong feeling that the attack would come the same day or the next day. Later that morning the phone rang. It was Graham Bright: there had been a mortar attack on Downing Street; three rockets had been fired from a white transit van that had then exploded. Two men had been seen making a getaway. Bright was now a believer.

When Robinson put the phone down he realized what had just happened: the Prime Minister's own private secretary had rung him – within an hour of a major assassination attempt on the country's leader. If that was not confirmation of being taken seriously, it would be harder to think of a better one.

Ever since Robinson started to dream of events that had not yet happened he has questioned why this was possible. Why, in his own terms, was he being allowed to see this information? Particularly as he was often unable to do anything about the events that were being revealed? How could he respond in the best way possible to the information that he was being given?

In some cases it seemed that it was possible to change the future, but other events showed him that the future was seemingly immutable. His early revelation of the IRA cell in Cheltenham may indeed have led to the arrest of the terrorists before they were able to cause any harm. The Stanmore incident may also have made people more aware of a potential threat. But then there were other times when he was helpless to do anything, and when he only managed to piece the clues together hours, or even minutes before tragedy actually struck. On these occasions he often blamed himself for his failure to interpret the messages. If only he could have understood better. If only the dreams could have been clearer.

Even now, Robinson has no fixed theory of time: what he knows from his own evidence, and what many are prepared to believe, is that he can indeed see what has not yet happened.

In the autumn of 1979 the county of Yorkshire was in shock: 12 women had been killed and another 4 had only just escaped the murderous intentions of the man dubbed the 'Yorkshire Ripper'. The police were under siege from a public eager to catch the murderer before he struck again. In addition to people who were offering ordinary information about the circumstances surrounding the previous deaths, they were also receiving calls from people claiming to offer psychic information which might identify the 'Ripper'.

One of these psychics was Nella Jones, a London woman who worked as a clairvoyante for private clients. It was October 1979 when, as well as contacting the police, Mrs Jones had rung the *Yorkshire Post*, the local newspaper for the terror-stricken area. From their London office they despatched a reporter named Shirley Davenport to visit Mrs Jones and interview her. Davenport knew that the story would never be printed: first there was a fear that it might lead to a copy-cat killing; second, the paper would not necessarily want to muddy the waters for the already overwhelmed police. Nevertheless Davenport went to Mrs Jones' address and dutifully recorded what she was told. Afterwards she wrote the interview up, before the story was 'spiked' as she had expected.

Three months later in January 1980 Mrs Jones contacted Shirley Davenport again. Davenport listened to what she had to say, but never wrote it up. Nella Jones called again in November 1980 to say there would be a further killing on 17 or 27 November.

On the night of 17 November the Yorkshire Ripper killed his thirteenth victim. Davenport talked to her editor about publishing an article, but the paper decided against it. Within weeks Peter Sutcliffe was caught and charged with the 13 murders. Details emerged about the man, his life, his home. When Davenport reviewed her notes of her meetings with Nella Jones she began to realize the significance of what she had been told. Sutcliffe had worked as a lorry driver for a company called Clark Transport. In their first meeting Nella Jones had told her that the 'Ripper' was a lorry driver called Peter and that she could see a name beginning with 'C' on the side of the cab.

On television Davenport watched with some amazement a report showing Peter Sutcliffe's home in Bradford. Jones had told her in January 1980 that the 'Ripper' lived in a large house in Bradford, number six in its street, with iron railings and steps leading up to the door. Here, on television, was 6 Garden Lane, Bradford: a large house with iron railings and steps leading to the door. Not all Jones' information was completely reliable, but of her meetings and contacts with her, Davenport says:

It was still the most weird experience. It went far beyond anything coincidence or guesswork could possibly have provided. And you have to remember that for the previous two years all the public signs had been that the police were looking for a man who came from the north-east of England, a hundred miles away and who worked in an engineering plant.

It is very hard to know just how much the police and military forces around the world work with psychics. Where they do, there is little willingness to admit to the fact: where would the logical and deductive powers of the detective be if psychics were able to pinpoint the perpetrators of crime? Psychics like Chris Robinson also face a dangerous truth: the more reliable their information turns out to be the more vulnerable they become to forces such as terrorists who might prefer their actions not to be predicted. Secrecy may be valuable in such cases. In truth, also, for every psychic offering accurate information there may well be many who are not, and the police will inevitably only work with those whom they have established to be reliable over a period of time. We may never know the extent to which security forces work with psychics – and that may indeed be the most effective way for it to be.

SPIRITUAL HEALING

From the loud and miraculous claims of the evangelical Church healing services to the calm and peaceful sanctuaries of spiritual healers around the world, the mystery of healing can take many forms. To add to the confusion healing also takes many names: spiritual healing, faith healing, psychic healing, therapeutic touch, natural healing, absent healing. There are so many forms of healing that it is not always easy to understand what is being claimed.

There has been a recent upsurge in the biblical style of evangelical healing – typified by the emotional outpourings and miraculous happenings that accompany the healing missions of evangelical preachers like Morris Cerullo who travel the globe giving healing services to audiences of thousands. Many have claimed miraculous healings, which they have attributed to Jesus Christ, the Holy Spirit or the preacher taking the service. The images of people throwing away their crutches, or getting out of their wheelchairs to walk for the first time in years have made these meetings famous, but they have also attracted sceptics and detractors who have questioned the authenticity of these events. There is no doubt that some of these evangelical healers have stooped to the tricks of the charlatan's trade: evangelism is big business, particularly where television and mass fund-raising is involved. There are, though, just as many devout people willing to testify to the power of prayer and the healing of the spiritual forces. What differentiates practising spiritual healers from these 'miraculous healers' is that the spiritual healers do not make overblown claims for what they do: they generally say that they assist the body's normal healing process to work, or that they channel healing energy to a person. To generalize somewhat: the miraculous healers look for *cures*; the spiritual healers help to catalyse self-healing. Harry Edwards, perhaps the most famous spiritual healer of this century, described the requirements for a spiritual healer:

> People who have a deep inner yearning to give of themselves in healing the sick, to take away pain and stress, who possess compassion and sympathy for those who are afflicted, and are willing to sacrifice their time without any pecuniary reward; people who are generous in their nature, and who render willing service for good causes, are those who possess the spiritual qualities which mark the healing gift. This healing potential, then, only needs the development of the faculty of attunement with the spirit source of healing and the opportunity to give it practical expression.

Spiritual healing is now acquiring an acceptability in the UK alongside conventional therapies: this is borne out by the fact that the treatment is now available to patients courtesy of the National Health Service. There are currently 7,000 members of the National Federation of Spiritual Healers who are all qualified to give this service to patients. The fact that many doctors are still extremely sceptical of the ability of healers to have any positive effect, may simply be the result of prejudice: there are now many scientific studies that have shown the efficacy of 'healing energy' in a range of experimental, laboratory-based situations.

The first experiment to attract attention in this field was carried out in the early 1960s by Professor Bernard Grad of McGill University in Canada. The experiment involved a faith healer named Oskar Estabany applying his 'laying on of hands' to a group of 150 mice who had all been inflicted with small, yet identical, wounds: the removal of a small patch of skin from their backs. Another group of 150 mice, who had been given the same wounds, were left to heal normally. To address the experimental objection that any animal that is handled will recover faster than one which is not, the animals in the control group – those not receiving the healer's touch – were handled for an identical 15 minutes a day by people who were not healers. It was found that the mice that had received the laying on of hands from the healer recovered significantly faster.

In an ingenious experiment to try to isolate the healing effect even further, Grad went on to apply a similar technique to plant life – in this case to barley seeds. In order to 'injure' the barley seeds they were treated with salt water and then mildly baked in an oven. Some 480 seeds were planted in 24 pots and the pots split into two groups. The first group was watered with ordinary tap water, while the second group was watered with tap water that had been held and influenced each day for 30 minutes by the healer, Oskar Estabany. The 'blind' aspect of the experiment was that none of those applying the water knew which plants were receiving the healer's treated water. After two weeks it was found that the plants which had been watered with the treated water had not only germinated more successfully, but that they had grown taller, and produced a larger yield.

The advantage of these 'non-human' experiments is that they manage to exclude the suggestibility of human patients and our susceptibility to the 'placebo effect'. The placebo effect emerged in medical studies earlier this century, when it was discovered that subjects given sugar pills containing no active medicine will experience an improvement in their state – in some cases an improvement as large, if not larger, than the positive effects of a real drug or treatment. Some scientists have described the placebo effect as the 20th century's greatest medical discovery, revealing the enormous power of the mind in the healing process. For those who want to study the effects of drugs and other treatments, though, it can make the measurement of 'real', treatment-induced, effects surprisingly difficult to isolate.

In an attempt to study the effects of healing on human patients Californian psychologist Dr Daniel Wirth developed an experimental method that seems to rule out the role of the placebo effect in the healing process. Very much like Professor Grad's mice, 44 volunteers were given identical half-inch deep wounds on their arms. They had been told that they were participating in an experiment to test a new kind of medical photography. Following the 'wounding', they visited daily, and were asked to put their arm through a screened off 'hole in the wall' beyond which, they believed, was the photographic equipment they had been told about. In fact, for half of the subjects, there was nothing on the other side of the wall. For the other half, though, a healer was present, who, without touching the patients, channelled healing energy to their wounds. To make the experiment secure from any stray influences – or 'double blind' as it it known – even the staff involved in escorting the subjects in and out of the experiment room believed that the experiment was concerned with medical photography.

The healing of the wounds was measured after 8 and 16 days. By the end of the experiment, 13 of the healer-treated group were 'completely healed', while 10 showed marked improvement. For the untreated control group, the wounds showed little healing at all. The experiment had demonstrated a statistically very significant result in favour of the power of healing.

Carol Everett is a British healer who has worked closely with orthodox medicine. In 1994 she was invited to Tokyo to take part in a challenging experiment with Professor Yoshio Machi at Denki University. Machi had set up a test for Everett which would place her psychic healing abilities in direct competition with the powers of high technology. She was taken to a laboratory and connected to a complex set of sensors to monitor her heart, breathing, blood and brain-wave activity. Everett was then introduced to a young woman and asked to use her psychic sense to diagnose the woman's medical condition. At the same time the professor and his doctors in the laboratory were using an expensive thermal imaging machine to view the patient's body.

Everett sensed a problem in one of the woman's ovaries – a small lump. Professor Machi's equipment confirmed the presence of the lump – just under an inch across. The healer then started to apply her healing power to the tumour. The sensors attached to Everett revealed that her brain activity changed quite dramatically. The left half of the brain – the part normally used for intellectual and rational tasks – became almost completely inactive, while the right half – associated with artistic, creative and intuitive functioning – was highly active. Alpha waves were also being recorded from her brain – waves that normally only appear when someone is asleep.

The thermal image scanner, which records the relative heat of different parts of the body, and displays them in different colours on a computer monitor, was telling an interesting story. The heat being given off by the tumour was reducing, and after some minutes the diseased area seemed to disappear completely. By the end of the session Everett felt that the tumour had been healed. Further scans a month later seemed to show that the diseased lump had indeed disappeared.

The possibility of healers working in conjunction with

modern science in a complementary way may offer great potential for the future. The well-known British healer Matthew Manning is always keen to stress that healing can work very well alongside conventional treatments. Manning came to healing after a childhood filled with psychic adventures: persistent poltergeist activity and automatic drawing were just two of his manifestations. He now runs a successful healing clinic in Bury St Edmunds, England. Many of those who come to him are suffering from serious illnesses such as cancer. He claims that the spiritual healing offers clients an emotional strength which other treatments may not provide: and with emotional and mental strength, the body's own self-healing mechanisms can be encouraged to function more powerfully. He sees that the healer's energy is often only the catalyst that mobilizes a patient's own self-healing powers.

When another spiritual healer Lorraine Ham appeared on British television's popular show *Strange but True?* to demonstrate her gift, she was not prepared for the public's response that followed. Within weeks she had received 20,000 letters detailing health problems ranging from the minor to the very serious, from the youngest child to those nearing the end of their natural life-span. All were desperate for some form of healing. Lorraine could evidently not deal with the huge demand herself — she already had her own practice, and worked regularly at a National Health Service clinic in her native Yorkshire. She decided to set up a network of healers who could cater for the needs of this spontaneous demand — and the National Healing Centre was born. While Lorraine Ham works mostly with patients who visit her, what might surprise many observers is that the great majority of clients of the National Healing Centre never get to meet a healer: they are the subjects of a form of treatment called 'absent' healing.

Three times a day — at 6.30am, 12.30pm and 10.30pm — a group of healers 'focuses' healing energy on those people named on their local list. How or why this should work is most certainly a mystery to science, and yet there is strong evidence that it does.

Of the thousands of patients of the National Healing Centre who have received absent healing, many have written letters testifying to a positive effect: Ruth Dorrington is a runner who competes for her club in the national road-racing season. Preparing for the 1995 season she developed a serious hip injury that threatened to put her out of action. Her physiotherapist was unable to bring any relief, and her ambitions seemed to be under threat. When Ruth saw Lorraine Ham's television broadcast, she felt instinctively that Lorraine could help her:

> When I got the letter back I didn't really know what absent healing was. I didn't really try to find out, either, but I thought it might help. And I did start to feel better. I was not entirely sure why, but it seemed too coincidental that I had started to feel better at that period of time.

To the scientist there are many explanations for this, and not all of them involve the power of 'healing energy'. People do get better of their own accord: our natural healing ability is remarkable. Equally, when a number of people are focused on you, there are good reasons for believing that you are getting better – either by simple peer pressure or by the placebo effect.

In the case of absent healing, there have been relatively few scientific studies. One particular experiment carried out in the USA, though, may have gone a long way to demonstrating the power of 'remote' healing techniques. Dr Randolph Byrd is a cardiologist at San Francisco General Hospital who also happens to be a committed Christian. In the early 1980s he decided to test the effects of prayer on the recovery rates of his heart patients. Four hundred patients undergoing major heart surgery were chosen randomly from a patient database. Dr Byrd then split the group into two: 200 would receive healing prayers for their recovery from prayer groups around the country; the other 200 patients – the 'control group' – would only receive the normal medical treatment. In 1985 Dr Byrd presented his results to a meeting of the American Heart

Association in Miami, Florida. Of the patients who had received the absent prayer healing there was a significantly lower incidence of both post-operative infections and 'pulmonary odema' – water on the lungs. Since this result a number of groups in the UK and the USA have attempted similar experiments, with some significant positive results.

One branch of the healing arts that spiritual healers often steer clear of is diagnosis. It is a tenet of the National Federation of Spiritual Healers' ethical code in the UK that all healers should refrain from making diagnoses. That, they say, is the job of doctors who have been trained to diagnose. These are litigious times, and any error in diagnosis could end up as the subject of a lawsuit. That said, there are people who offer intuitive or psychic diagnosis, and who make a living from doing it. One of the greatest pioneers in this field was Edgar Cayce (1877–1945) who became perhaps the most famous American psychic ever. Admired by many as a highly principled man, Cayce had dedicated himself at an early age to healing people – particularly children. Cayce discovered that he could enter a hypnotic state in which information would 'come through' about people's afflictions and the actions that needed to be taken. Through this gift he is said to have saved his own wife's life, as well as his son's sight.

'The Sleeping Prophet' – as he became known – would lie down on a couch and dictate 'readings' about the patient in question (always known as 'the entity') from a hypnotic trance state. It was quite normal for the person requesting the reading to be many miles away. Distance, it seemed, was no object. Cayce claimed that through his 'super-conscious' mind he was able to access information about the patient from the Akashic Records – the 'records of all life', sometimes also known as the 'Book of God's Rememberance'. His readings would start with the phrase, 'we have the body' meaning that a link had been established with the person seeking treatment. The readings described the nature of the person's condition and its causes, and would go on to suggest practical and often complex suggestions for treatments or medicines that were required by the patient. Dietary advice, exercises, tonics, poultices, medicines, massages, tinctures, salt-packs – the variety of advice was incredibly broad, and in nearly all cases successful when followed. Occasionally the readings would even identify the actual shop or supplier where the particular ingredients or medications could be found. All this from a man who was not a doctor, was not trained in any form of medicine, and who had not studied medical text books.

Needless to say there were those who did not agree with Cayce's approach. Some of them set out deliberately to damage his reputation. Fake cases were brought to him to see if he would provide a reading. Cayce's response to every false patient was that 'no body' could be found. In 1931 his work had reached its nadir when undercover policewomen from the New York force arrested Cayce on the charge of fortune-telling. The policewomen had posed as interested students of Cayce's work and requested readings, for which they had not been asked to pay. In the event the judge threw the case out for lack of merit, but the circumstances caused Cayce to question his own work. If God had wanted him to do this kind of work, he railed at his ever-supportive wife, why hadn't He just made him a doctor. With her typical acuity she replied that then he would have been just another doctor. And no one could ever accuse Cayce of that.

Patients came with ailments as diverse as acne, cancer, heart problems, arthritis and Alzheimer's disease. He gave a total of about 10,000 medical readings in his lifelong career. In a number of cases the solutions he proposed were viewed as strange at the time, but many years later have been shown to agree with modern discoveries. The only recommendation Cayce's readings made for Alzheimer's was to avoid the use of aluminium pans in cooking. The first scientific papers to make the connection between aluminium and Alzheimer's disease were not published until 1980.

It might be expected that this level of success made Cayce a rich man. The reverse is true. He charged very little for his readings, and lived with his wife and children in relative poverty – despite many offers to commercialize his work. The 14,000 readings he left behind him on topics as diverse as healing, reincarnation, astrology, sex, parenting and prophecy are still the subject of intense study today. A hospital, a research centre and over 1,500 study groups worldwide continue to examine his legacy. Cayce himself died in 1945. Many people say this was as a result of overwork. His readings for himself had told him to produce only two readings a day, yet right up until his death he would routinely go into trance between four and six times each day. He is one healer of whom many would say his healing work truly does live on after his death.

A more recent arrival to the world of psychic diagnosis is Caroline Myss, who describes herself as a 'medical intuitive'. Before her talent to diagnose emerged, Caroline Myss had formed a publishing company which produced books on alternative health strategies. Nevertheless she had no personal interest in the healing field, preferring to smoke, drink coffee and overwork in the true style of the journalist she had once been. However, she began to find that when people talked about their ailments, very clear images of their bodily and 'energetic' conditions would appear in her mind. When these images turned out later to be correct, she realized that something was happening to her that was, in her own words, beyond her control.

In her practice today, Myss works closely with doctors (she has so far worked closely with 15) and provides them with valuable information about their patients' conditions – information which a doctor can then use to assist in providing a treatment. Some of Caroline Myss's work has been with patients who have AIDS, or who have been HIV positive. In one of her first cases, a man asked Myss to talk to his grown-up son, Peter, as he suspected that something was seriously wrong with him. As she was talking with the son on the phone she suddenly had a very strong impression that he was HIV positive. Rather than dump this terrible news on him without warning, she explained how his father had asked her to make contact, told him what she did as a medical intuitive, and how she 'read' a person's energy field. She went on to say that, having evaluated his energy field, she felt that he had AIDS. His response was immediate: he had already had two tests which had shown he was HIV positive. He was scared for his life. Together with a doctor – Norman Shealy – Myss created a programme of healing therapies for Peter. These included dietary recommendations, exercise, castor oil packs and psychotherapy to address the underlying problem that Peter had not yet revealed to his family that he was gay. Peter pursued the therapies with a strong commitment, and today Peter is HIV negative. A miracle, some might say?

> Some people referred to Peter's case as a 'miracle', implying that he had received a special grace from God that assisted his healing and that without that grace he would never have gotten well. While that might be the case, one must still ask, 'What does it take to make a miracle happen?' I believe that our cell tissues hold the vibrational patterns of our attitudes, our belief systems, and the presence or absence of an exquisite energy frequency or 'grace' that we can activate by calling back our spirits from negative attachments.

The modern resurgence of interest in spiritual healing has roots in older forms of medicine practised in many indigenous cultures. Medicine men and women, as well as shamans and witch doctors have always played a vital role in the physical and psychological health of tribal and native peoples. After many hundreds of years in which these traditions have been destroyed and repressed by the invasions of Western civilization, peoples in Africa, Australia and the Americas are once more gaining respect for their healing wisdoms. Many Western healers now go to learn ancient healing techniques from what remains of these native peoples. Soozi Holbeche is a healer and writer who has studied with Aboriginal healers in Australia and now uses their techniques:

I put my right hand on his chest and my left hand on his back. I closed my eyes, and after five minutes sensed a terrible turmoil in his chest with something like a snake coming into my right hand. It took all my strength to keep pulling it out, and as I did so it coiled itself further and further up my arm. It was not a physical snake, but the energy of deep repressed rage against his father since childhood. Eventually I felt his chest grow empty and clean, and he began to cry.

I opened my eyes to find us surrounded by a circle of absolutely still and silent birds. They continued to watch us with bright, beady eyes until I threw the snake-like energy off my arm and into the air. The birds lifted as one; they appeared to take it in their beaks – as if I had thrown a live snake – and then carried it away. It was one of the most profound experiences I have ever had.

It seems that with the reintegration of other cultures' healing traditions, the superstition and fear that has surrounded the activities of healers, may be coming to an end. To many in the field it seems very likely that the ancient and simple skills of spiritual, psychic and natural healing will become a normal part of 21st-century medicine, working alongside surgery, drug therapy and other complementary therapies in a new alliance of the healing arts – even though it's still far from clear just how, exactly, healing works.

PSYCHIC SURGERY

One of the most strange and inexplicable forms of healing medicine is psychic surgery. Though dismissed by conventional medicine as dangerous charlatanism, there is strong evidence that psychic surgeons may have helped many people, and that their popularity is growing. What so many sceptics find impossible to accept is the claim of psychic surgeons that they are able to enter the patient's body without an anaesthetic, and without causing severe bleeding. Using bare hands or an instrument of some kind they appear to remove diseased or malignant tissue without physical harm, and without the need for any stitches. Are they all charlatans, and if not what exactly are they doing? How can the hands of psychic surgeons move through solid flesh? And how can they know what they are doing when none of them are trained surgeons?

Under the nickname of 'Arigo' – meaning 'country bumpkin' – a Brazilian named José Pedro de Freitas became the world's most famous psychic surgeon of the 20th century. If Arigo's story is to be believed, he first discovered his talent for psychic surgery in 1950 when a colleague in a political campaign fell ill. Unknown to Arigo, his friend Lucio Bittencourt actually had lung cancer, and was about to fly to America for treatment. As his colleague slept, Arigo appeared in a trance-like state, holding a razor, and telling Bittencourt in a strange voice that he required an operation. Bittencourt then became unconscious. When he came round he found his pyjamas bloodstained, and an incision in his chest. Arigo was as surprised about the event as anyone – he had no memory of going to Bittencourt's bedroom. He worried that he had done serious harm to his colleague. Bittencourt went to a doctor whose X-rays told him that the tumour had been removed – by a technique 'unknown in Brazil'.

Looking back to his childhood Arigo remembered being troubled by hallucinations of bright lights and a voice that spoke to him in an unknown language. In early adulthood he worked in a local iron mine where he was active in union politics, becoming president of the mineworkers union at the tender age of 25. Arigo was fired from his job at the mine after a labour dispute, and became the owner of a local bar. It was during this time that he started to have strange, haunting dreams that left him debilitated with severe headaches. In the dreams he was witness to an operating theatre: a large, bald surgeon was addressing an assembled group of doctors and nurses in the voice that Arigo remembered from his earlier childhood hallucinations. In desperation, Arigo, who had been brought up as a devout Catholic, would go to pray in the church of Bom Jesus do Matosinho. Within a short time the source of the voice would reveal its identity. It was Dr Adolphous Fritz, a surgeon who had died some 30 years before. According to Arigo it was Fritz, and not he, who had controlled the healing event with his friend Bittencourt.

Adolphous Fritz had been a young doctor when his medical career was cut short by an early death. Wishing to continue his healing work, he had chosen Arigo to 'work through'. Arigo – through an original desire and willingness to heal others – had accepted Fritz's influence. He claimed to hear Fritz's voice in his left ear – telling him what to do – while he was performing the surgery.

Following the healing of Bittencourt, and the media coverage that the event created, Arigo started to use his talent. Soon the world was knocking on his door, requesting the seemingly miraculous benefits of his unorthodox and inexplicable techniques. In most operations he used an ordinary pocket knife, observed no conventional hygiene codes, and never used any form of anaesthetic. His patients did not complain of pain from the operations – indeed there seemed to be no sensation at all. At times he would perform surgery on as many as 300 people a day. As far as we know Arigo never accepted money for his healing work, and supported his family by working in an ordinary office job during the daytime.

Yet in 1956, 'The Surgeon of the Rusty Knife', as Arigo was now known worldwide, came under pressure from the medical authorities and the Catholic Church, and was charged with practising illegal medicine. In the court case that followed Arigo was frank about his unorthodox methods:

'How do you go about your practice?' Judge Soares asked him.

'I start to say the Lord's Prayer. From that moment I don't see or know about anything else. The others tell me I write out prescriptions, but I have no memory of this.'

'What about the operations?' asked the judge.

'It is the same with them. I am in a state I do not understand. I just want to help the poor people,' Arigo asserted.

'But you are doing what you are charged with, are you not?'

'I am not the one who is doing this. I am just an intermediary between the people and Dr Fritz.'

Judge Soares requested Arigo to make Fritz appear and account for himself. He would not, it seemed. Despite the massive support of the local people and his patients, Arigo was sentenced to 15 months in prison and a fine equivalent to $300.

The sentence, which was later reduced, was not enough to stop Arigo. With the return of his headaches, he started to practise again, albeit without the knowledge of the authorities. He was later imprisoned again for practising medicine without a formal licence, but never lost his devout following.

His techniques were filmed and investigated many times, and he was never caught performing any fraud or illusion. The American researcher Dr Andrija Puharich investigated Arigo's work thoroughly in the 1960s, even allowing Arigo to remove a small benign tumour on his elbow. He went back home convinced of Arigo's genuine talent and sincere approach. His reputation as a genuine psychic surgeon has remained intact well after his death in a car crash on 11 January 1971.

The same cannot be said for all practitioners of this unusual healing art. A number of studies of psychic surgery were carried out in the 1970s, particularly in the Philippines where it has been popular since it emerged there in the 1920s. The studies revealed that as many as 80 per cent of practitioners were practising conjuring tricks. In many cases the bloody and diseased tissue removed by the surgeons was in fact chicken or other meat offal. When challenged over this sleight of hand some of the surgeons made the case that in order for the patients to treat the surgery seriously it was necessary for them to see some real blood – albeit that it wasn't their own. There are, though, psychic surgeons who practise for no money and seem genuinely dedicated to their profession. One Filipino named Jun Toting accepts no payment for his healing work, and practises almost exclusively in the poor districts of Cebu City. Many witnesses claim to have seen him open bodies for surgery, and – once the operation is complete – to close the wound again instantaneously with his hands.

In Chelmsford, England, a psychic surgeon named Stephen Turoff has a continuous stream of patients from all over the world. Turoff sees 50 patients a day, 5 days a week, 52 weeks a year and has a waiting list of many months. On the walls of his waiting room are letters from those who believe his psychic surgery has helped them. Like Arigo he claims to be working with a spirit guide. In Turoff's case the guide is a doctor named Dr Joseph Kahn. Dr Kahn is supposed to have died in the early part of the 20th century after a long and successful surgical career. Turoff says that Dr Kahn worked at the front during the First World War, healing the sick and wounded. His dedication to his healing work, it is claimed, lives on beyond the grave. Dr Kahn had apparently been looking for a 'body' to work through after some rehabilitation and education on the 'other side', and Turoff fitted the bill.

Turoff had been an 'orthodox' spiritual healer for 15 years until 1985 when, in a healing session with a friend of the family, he started to hear a voice telling him what to do. With the patient in agony from a severe back problem, he was 'guided' to give her 'an etheric injection' and to operate immediately. Turoff says he was not sure what to do at first but found that his arms and hands were completely under the control of the spirit doctor. 'I am like a puppet,' he explains. 'I just let him [Kahn] get on with it.' Following this first operation the woman revealed that X-rays had recently found an ovarian cyst. Later X-rays showed no cyst. Since then Turoff claims to have healed literally thousands of people. During this time he has attracted fierce critics. Dr Peter May, a general practitioner from Southampton who has tried to debunk many healers who claim to use spiritual powers, was asked to comment on Turoff's work for a television programme:

> To believe that Turoff is inhabited by a dead doctor is, to my mind, sheer nonsense and for people to believe this is gross gullibility. In my view the medical advice given ... was ignorant. Many of those who see him are desperate – they want to believe. You can't protect people from their own stupidity.

While many people find it acceptable and understandable that spiritual healers may work with energy, the idea of a person's hands entering a body and removing tissue under the influence of some spirit guide seems mind-boggling to say the least. Turoff's patients report, without fail, that his hands and implements are definitely inside them. Not just pushed into their flesh, but actually moving their internal organs. They have seen and felt it. They are adamant about this. If we are to believe them, that they are not the subjects of hallucination, hypnosis or trickery, then we are duty bound to look for a scientific answer that may allow for such a possibility.

It certainly does not appear to fit with our current scientific model: matter is not meant to pass through other matter, except perhaps in the case of neutrinos and other small particles passing through earthly substance. Einstein told us that matter is only energy vibrating at a certain rate. Following his lead there are some scientists who are willing to entertain the idea that under certain circumstances it may be possible to increase the vibration of matter to a point where it is less dense – closer to a 'pure' energy state – and may be able to pass through other dense matter. Could a spiritual influence be sufficient to raise the vibration of a human body? This is a theory and, as yet, not a popular one. But in this area, as in many others, it may be science that has to change to accommodate phenomena. Ultimately, this is, and always will be, the only way that science can progress.

NEAR-DEATH EXPERIENCES

The recording of near-death experiences is not, as many people believe, simply a recent phenomenon. The Swedish scientist and mystic Emanuel Swedenborg (1688–1772) reported many extraordinary experiences in his writings which bear striking similarity to contemporary reports of near-death experiences. He describes what happens at the moment when breathing and circulation stop: 'Still man does not die, but is only separated from the corporeal part which was of use to him in the world . . . Man, when he dies, only passes from one world into another.' Swedenborg describes the moment when he left his body:

> I was brought into a state of insensibility as to the bodily senses, thus almost into the state of the dying; yet the interior life with thought remaining entire, so that I perceived and retained in memory the things which occurred, and which occur to those who are resuscitated from the dead . . . the first state of man after death it similar to his state in the world, because then in like manner he is in externals . . . hence, he knows no otherwise than that he is in the world . . . Therefore, after they have wondered that they are in a body, and in every sense which they had in the world . . . they come into a desire of knowing what heaven is, and what hell is.

He goes on to record the meetings that occur with other spiritual beings, who offer support and instruction. 'The spirit of man recently departed from the world is . . . recognised by his friends, and by those whom he had known in the world . . . wherefore they are instructed by their friends concerning the state of eternal life . . .' The phase of confronting the life just past is also described by Swedenborg:

> The interior memory . . . is such that there are inscribed in it all the particular things . . . which man has at any time

87

thought, spoken, and done ... from his earliest infancy to extreme old age. Man has with him the memory of all these things when he comes into another life, and is successively brought into all recollection of them ... All that he had spoken and done ... are made manifest before the angels, in a light as clear as day ... and ... there is nothing so concealed in the world that it is not manifested after death ... as if seen in effigy, when the spirit is viewed in the light of heaven.

From a totally different time period and cultural background comes 'The Tibetan Book of the Dead' – a vital document to all Tibetan Buddhists. Originally compiled from the oral accounts of Tibetan mystics in the 8th century AD, this influential work was finally translated into English in 1927 by the American academic and Tibetan cultural historian W.Y. Evans-Wentz. The book, also known as the 'Bardo Thodol', was originally used as a religious text and was read or recited at a person's death. In later times it became a guide for the living as much as for the dead. Tibetan Buddhists would read the book's description of the soul's passage through progressive levels of consciousness in the realms of 'Bardo'. This knowledge would prepare the soul for its journey on the 'other side', and help it to retain its consciousness through the challenges and tests that would face it. This manual goes as far as describing the process whereby souls choose rebirth in a human womb for a further life in a human body. *The Tibetan Book of the Dead* also had a function for those who might mourn the dead: it acted as an encouragement to the grieving to let go of their link to the dead person in the knowledge that 'clinging on' would only serve to tie their deceased to the earth-plane and so hinder the departed soul's progress through the spiritual planes.

In the modern, scientific era, one important pioneer in near-death research was Albert Heim, a professor of geology from Zurich. In 1871 Heim had been leading a climbing party in

88

the Alps, when his hat was blown off by the wind. When he made a grab for the hat he lost his footing. As he fell from the mountain he experienced an expansion of time: a fall of just a few seconds took on a sense of the eternal

> Mental activity became enormous, rising to a hundredfold velocity . . . I saw my whole life take place in many images, as though on a stage at some distance from me . . . Everything was transfigured, as though by a heavenly light, without anxiety and without pain. The memory of very tragic experiences I had had was clear but not saddening. I felt no conflict or strife; conflict had been transmuted into love. Elevated and harmonious thought dominated and united individual images, and like magnificent music a divine calm swept through my soul. I became ever more surrounded by a splendid blue heaven with delicate and rosy and violet cloudlets. I swept into it painlessly and softly and I saw that now I was falling freely through the air and that under me a snow field lay waiting.

The fall had taken him 70 feet down the mountain to a snow-covered ledge where he was later revived from unconsciousness. The experience led Heim to start collecting other climbers' experiences of their accidents. Over a period of 20 years he was to discover that around 95 per cent of the victims reported similar experiences to his own. From this he concluded that for those who did not survive such falls, their experience of death was one of peace, rather than of violent suffering as, perhaps, we might conventionally suppose.

> A man is dying and, as he reaches the point of greatest physical distress, he hears himself pronounced dead by his doctor. He begins to hear an uncomfortable noise, a loud ringing or buzzing, and at the same time feels himself moving very rapidly through a long dark tunnel. After this, he suddenly finds himself outside of his own physical body, but still in the immediate physical environment, and he sees his own body from a distance, as though he is a spectator. He watches the

resuscitation attempt from his usual vantage point and is in a state of emotional upheaval.

After a while, he collects himself and becomes more accustomed to his odd condition. He notices that he still has a 'body', but one of a very different nature and with very different powers from the physical body he has left behind. Soon other things begin to happen. Others come to meet and to help him. He glimpses the spirits of relatives and friends who have already died, and a loving, warm spirit of a kind he has never encountered before – a being of light – appears before him. This being asks him a question, non-verbally, to make him evaluate his life and helps him along by showing him a panoramic instantaneous playback of the major events of his life. At some point he finds himself approaching some sort of barrier or border, apparently representing the limit between earthly life and the next life. Yet, he finds that he must go back to the earth, that the time for his death has not yet come. At this point he resists, for by now he is taken up with his experiences in the afterlife and does not want to return. He is overwhelmed by intense feelings of joy, love and peace. Despite his attitude, though, he somehow reunites with his physical body and lives.

Later he tries to tell others . . . he finds that others scoff, so he stops telling other people. Still, the experience affects his life profoundly, especially his views about death and its relationship to life.

This is not anyone's near-death experience. It is, rather, the 'model' near-death experience described by Dr Raymond Moody in his 1975 book *Life After Life*. Moody had been inspired to research the subject by Dr George Ritchie of Virginia, who, as a young soldier in 1943, had physically 'died' and been brought back to life. Ritchie had been in hospital with a respiratory problem: he had started to spit blood, and then lost consciousness. He woke up to see his own body lying, apparently dead, on the hospital bed. He started to move around the building, a hospital assistant walked straight through him in the corridor. He tried to attract someone else's attention by tapping him on the shoulder: he took no notice. When he tried to return to his body on the bed, he found it was simply impossible. What Ritchie described next could be called a religious, or mystical, experience. The room lit up, shining 'brighter than a thousand arc lights'. A figure appeared, whom Ritchie identified as Jesus. He was shown around a huge city by the figure, where the consequences of 'sin' were made vividly clear to him. When Ritche woke up he was sure he had died. He had not: he was simply 'back in his body'.

Dr Raymond Moody took this starting point, and over a period of some 11 years conducted interviews with 150 people who had reported near-death experiences in a variety of circumstances – such as the aftermath of car crashes and hospital operations. Moody collected and examined the evidence for the reality and validity of these experiences, and explored the ways they had affected people's lives. One of Dr Moody's subjects recalls how he felt on returning from what he believed to be the 'other side':

I suppose this experience molded something in my life. I was only a child when it happened, only ten, but now, my entire life through, I am thoroughly convinced that there is life after death, without a shadow of a doubt, and I am not afraid to die. I am not. Some people I have known are so afraid, so scared. I always smile to myself when I hear people doubt that there is an afterlife, or say, 'When you're dead, you're gone.' I think to myself, 'They really don't know.'

I've had many things happen to me in my life. In business I've had a gun pulled on me and put to my temple. And it didn't frighten me very much, because I thought, 'Well, if I really die, if they really kill me, I know I'm still alive somewhere.'

In his later book, *Reflections on Life after Life*, Moody reported a particular experience he called 'the vision of knowledge', a mystical experience that characterized the near-death experience for some fortunate individuals:

> For a second I knew all the secrets of all the ages, all the meaning of the universe, the stars, the moon – of everything ... This all-powerful knowledge opened before me. It seemed that I was being told that I was going to remain sick for quite a while and that I would have several close calls. And I did have several close calls after that. They said some of it would be to erase this all-knowing knowledge that I had picked up ... that I had been granted the universal secrets and that I would have to undergo time to forget that knowledge. But I do have the memory of once knowing everything.

Dr Moody's books caught the imagination of the public and could be said to have popularized the idea of near-death experiences, or NDEs as they became known. Moody's work also spawned a new area of academic enquiry. This was led by Dr Kenneth Ring, a professor of psychology at the University of Connecticut, who took a more systematic and rigorously statistical approach to the subject. His findings confirmed Moody's conclusions. In 1980 Ring categorized near-death experiences into five levels of depth. He discovered that the least common were the most 'deep' where people felt they were faced with the question as to whether they wished to return to life or not. His research suggested that about one in five people believed that they had experienced some form of 'out of body' experience, but only about one in twenty testified to the deeper levels of the near-death experience. Those who felt deeply affected by the experience often 'came back' with a new sense of purpose, a reduced or non-existent fear of death, and a wish to communicate about the experience.

In the 1980s, television programmes about the phenomenon multiplied, and soon led to increasing research into the nature of death and a 'scientific proof' for the continuation of life after death. These scientific studies of near-death experiences have not all concluded that the perceptions should be taken as 'reality'. Dr Susan Blackmore of Bristol University's psychology department – who admitted to having had an out of body experience herself – was adamant that these experiences are hallucinatory, and that they generally represent the images put out by the oxygen-starved brain's dying consciousness.

This conclusion has been challenged, though, by further research focusing on experiences in hospital operation theatres. Dr Michael Sabom, a cardiologist working in Georgia, USA, has been a leading pioneer in this area. A five-year-old boy, on waking up from major surgery, was able to describe a plastic valve that had been inserted into his heart. Many were able to report the content of conversations between members of hospital staff, or even between relatives in other rooms. One saw a shoe lying on a window ledge, not visible from the operating theatre.

Later studies have formalized some of these experiences into an experimental methodology. These later experiments generally involve the planting of 'strange', or out of context, objects in parts of the operating theatre, or in the roof-space, where they would not normally be visible to patients. Following surgery patients have been asked whether they had experienced any sensations of 'hovering' over their body on the operation table. If so, they were asked further questions to see whether they had seen any of the planted objects. Continuing researches in this field, both in the UK and the USA, have yielded very positive results that indicate that the consciousness of patients exists independently of their physical bodies. Some experts now believe that research into near-death experiences is potentially the most fruitful area in bringing together science and the paranormal.

POWERS OVER HEAT AND COLD

Much of civilization's effort has revolved around our common need and desire to remove pain from our lives. In earlier times, before the advent of central heating systems, the ability to control the temperature functions of the body had a very real role to play in our survival as a species. If we could not survive extremes of heat or cold, then we would, simply, die. In some cultures who live in extreme climates it is still a current practice to test the viability of young babies in extreme temperatures. There have been reports that in some Himalayan cultures babies are routinely dunked in the freezing water of mountainous streams. Only the strong survive, or to put it another way: only those who could survive as adults are given the chance to become adults.

Alexandra David-Neel, the French scholar, writer and traveller of the early 20th century, spent 14 years in Tibet studying the ways of the Buddhist monks and lay-people. She gave an account of one particular skill entitled 'The Art of Warming Oneself without Fire up in the Snows.'

To spend the winter in a cave amidst the snows, at an altitude that varies between 11,000 and 18,000 feet, clad in a thin garment or even naked, and escape freezing, is a somewhat difficult achievement. And yet, numbers of Tibetan hermits go safely each year through this ordeal.

The endurance of these monks is ascribed to the power which they have acquired to generate *tumo* . . . The word *tumo* signifies heat, warmth, but is not used in Tibetan language to express ordinary heat or warmth. It is a technical term of mystic terminology . . .

It is kept by the lamas who teach it, and they do not fail to declare that information gathered by hearsay or reading is without any practical result if one has not been personally taught and trained by a master who is himself an adept . . .

Sometimes, a kind of examination concludes the training of the *tumo* students.

Upon a frosty winter night, those who think themselves capable of victoriously enduring the test are led to the shore of a river or lake. If all the streams are frozen . . . a hole is made in the ice. A moonlight night, with a hard wind blowing, is chosen . . .

The neophytes sit on the ground, cross-legged and naked. Sheets are dipped in the icy water, each man wraps himself in one of them and must dry it on his body. As soon as the sheet has become dry, it is again dipped in the water and placed on the novice's body to be dried as before. The operation goes on that way until daybreak . . .

It is said that some dry as many as forty sheets in one night. One should perhaps make large allowances for exaggeration, or perhaps for the size of the sheets which in some cases may become so small as to be almost symbolical. Yet I have seen some 'respas' (monks who have mastered *tumo*) dry a number of pieces of cloth the size of a large shawl . . . (Respas wear but a single cotton garment in all seasons at any altitude.)

It is difficult for us to get a perfectly correct idea about the extent of the results obtained through *tumo* training, but some of these feats are genuine. Hermits really do live naked, or wearing one single thin garment during the whole winter in the high regions I have mentioned. I am not the only one who has seen some of them. It has been said that some members of the Mount Everest expedition had an occasional glimpse of one of these naked anchorites.

In 1981 His Holiness the Dalai Lama – the spiritual leader of the Tibetan people – invited a group of scientists from the Harvard Medical School to witness and investigate the ability of three Tibetan monks to control their body temperature. The team, led by Dr Herbert Benson, carried out a number of experiments using temperature sensors attached to different parts of the monks' bodies. Using meditational techniques the three monks were all able to raise the temperatures of fingers and toes substantially – at times by as much as 15 degrees Fahrenheit. They were able to increase the temperature of other skin areas, but not by such extreme amounts. During the exercise, temperatures inside the body appeared to remain constant.

Dr Benson believes the monks are able to dilate the blood vessels under the skin: this increases the flow of blood and raises the surface temperature. The normal bodily response is to constrict the blood vessels, and so to lower the temperature of the limbs and extremities. The research seems to show that it is this physical mechanism that the monks have learned to control.

The control of the body's pain response to extreme heat, though, may be quite a different physical challenge. Claims of fire-walking and, particularly, the handling of hot coals and live fire, seem to introduce an investigation of supernatural powers, rather than simply the mental control of the body's functions.

Daniel Dunglas Home, the world renowned Victorian medium and pretender to the crown of all-time greatest levitator, was reported many times to have demonstrated immunity to fire and heat. Many who sat in his seances and meetings testified not only to Home's ability to handle fire, but to the apparent 'infectiousness' of the ability. If we are to believe the reports, it seems that in some sympathetic, sha-manistic way, Home may have been able to share his gifts with some of those who were present at seances. Lord Adare wrote down his experiences of a seance given by Home at Norwood, England, in 1868. He describes how Home went into his customary trance, and was attracted to the fire:

... and with his hand stirred the embers into a flame; then kneeling down, he placed his face right among the burning coals, moving it about as though bathing in water. Then, getting up, he held his finger for some time in the flame of the candle. Presently, he took the same lump of coal he had previously handled and came over to us, blowing upon it to make it brighter. He then walked slowly round the table, and said, 'I want to see which of you will be the best subject. Ah! Adare will be the easiest, because he has been most with Dan' (Home's spirit guide is referring to Home himself). Mr Jencken held out his hand, saying, 'Put it in mine.' Home said, 'No, no, touch it and see.' He (Jencken) touched it with the top of his finger and burnt himself. Home then held it within four or five inches of Mr Saal's and Mr Hurt's hands, and they could not endure the heat. He came to me and said, 'Now if you are not afraid, hold our your hand'; I did so, and having made two rapid passes over my hand, he placed the coal on it. I must have held it for half a minute, long enough to have burned my hand fearfully; the coal felt scarcely warm. Home then took it away, laughed, and seemed much pleased. As he was going back to the fire-place, he suddenly turned round and said, 'Why, just fancy, some of them think that only one side of the ember was hot.' He told me to make a hollow of both my hands; I did so, and he placed the coal in them, and then put both his on the top of the coal, so that it was completely covered by our four hands, and we held it there for some time. Upon this occasion scarcely any heat at all could be perceived.

In a witness statement to the Dialectical Society in 1869, Lord Lindsay – later to become the Earl of Crawford and Balcarres – testified to the remarkable happenings at one of Home's seances:

I have frequently seen Home . . ., when in a trance, go to the fire and take out large red-hot coals, and carry them about in his hands, put them inside his shirt, etc. Eight times I have myself held a red-hot coal in my hands without injury when it scorched my face on raising my hand. Once, I wished to see if they really would burn, and I said so, and touched a coal with the middle finger of my right hand, and I got a blister as large as a sixpence; I instantly asked him to give me the coal, and I held the part that burnt me, in the middle of my hand, for three or four minutes, without the least inconvenience. A few weeks ago, I was at a seance with eight others. Of these, seven held a red-hot coal without pain, and the two others could not bear the approach of it; of the seven, four were ladies.

It appears from these reports that not only Home's mediumistic abilities, but also the state of mind of the sitters, affected whether they were able to handle the coals without burning. Home himself claimed it was his link with spirit entities that made fire-handling possible for both himself and his sitters. William Crookes, one of the greatest physicists and chemists of his day, was present at one of Home's seances on 28 April 1873, when he was asked to become involved in an unorthodox experiment. For a scientist he showed himself surprisingly willing to participate in something he knew to be potentially very dangerous:

> ... Mr Home told me to leave my seat and come with him to the fire. He asked me if I should be afraid to take a live coal from his hand. I said, No, I would take it if he would give it to me. He then put his hand among the hot coals, and deliberately picked out the brightest bit and held it in his hand for a few seconds. He appeared to deliberate for a time, and then returned it to the grate, saying the power was too weak, and he was afraid I might be hurt. During this time I was kneeling on the hearth-rug, and am unable to explain how it was he was not severely burnt ... After Home had recovered from the trance I examined his hand with care to see if there were any signs of burning or of previous preparation. I could detect no trace of injury to the skin, which was soft and delicate like a woman's.

Not all 'fire-handlers' have attributed their ability to any spiritual or supernatural source. Nathan Coker was born into slavery in Hillsborough, Maryland, in around 1814, and, following a life of cruel treatment, eventually became a blacksmith in the town of Denton. On 7 September 1871, a report appeared in the *New York Herald* describing a demonstration given by Coker, in the office of a Dr Stack, to a group of eminent witnesses, including two newspaper editors and four doctors:

A brisk fire of anthracite coal was burning in a common coal stove, and an iron shovel was placed in the stove and heated to a white heat. When all was ready the negro pulled off his boots and placed the shovel upon the soles of his feet, and kept it there until the shovel became black. His feet were then examined by the physician, but no burns could be found, and all declared that no evidence of a heated substance having come in contact with them was visible.

The shovel was again heated red hot, taken from the stove and handed to him. He ran out his tongue as far as he could, and laid the heated shovel upon it, licking the iron until it became cooled. The physician examined the tongue, but found nothing to indicate that he had suffered in the least from the heated iron.

A large handful of common squirrel shot ... was next placed in an iron receptacle and heated until it melted. The negro then took the disk, poured the heated lead into the palm of his hand, and then put it into his mouth, allowing it to run all around his teeth and gums. He repeated the operation several times, each time keeping the melted lead in his mouth until solidified. After each operation the physicians examined him carefully, but could find nothing upon his flesh to indicate that he had been in the least affected ... [Then] he deliberately put his hand into the stove, in which was a very hot fire, took therefrom a handful of hot coals and passed them about the room to the gentlemen present, keeping them in his hand some time. Not the slightest evidence of a burn was visible upon his hand after he threw the coals back into the stove.

Coker had discovered his remarkable gift while he was still a teenage slave. His master of the time had kept him virtually starved, and Coker had to resort to desperate measures to keep constant hunger at bay:

> I shied around the kitchen one day ... and when the cook left I shot in, dipped my hand into the dinner pot, and pulled out a red hot dumpling. The boiling water did not burn and I could eat the hot dumpling without winking; so after [that] I got my dinner [that] way. I has often got the hot fat off the boiling water and drank it. I drink my coffee when it is boiling, and it does not give me half so much pain as it does to drink a glass of cold water. I always likes it just as hot as I can get it.

In recent times one form of fire-immunity has emerged as a kind of new-age initiation rite. Fire-walking workshops – often open to the public – are now regular events all around the world. Until this century, however, the knowledge behind fire-walking remained part of the secret traditions of a number of native cultures – particularly those of the south and central Pacific Ocean. One of the first Westerners to perform a fire-walk with a native culture was the anthropologist Dr William T Brigham. Brigham was the director of the Bishop Museum of Ethnology in Honolulu in the 1880s, when he agreed to take part in a walk on red-hot lava under the guidance of three 'kahunas' or Hawaiian shamans:

> When the rocks we threw on the lava surface showed that it had hardened enough to bear our weight, the kahunas arose and clambered down the side of the wall. It was far worse than a bake oven when we got to the bottom. The lava was blackening on the surface, but all across it ran heat discolorations that came and went as they do on a cooling iron before a blacksmith plunges it into his tub for tempering. I heartily wished that I had not been so curious. The very thought of running over that flat inferno to the other side made me tremble ...
>
> The kahunas took off their sandals and tied *ti* leaves around their feet, about three leaves to the foot. I sat down and began

tying my *ti* leaves on outside my big hob-nailed boots. I wasn't taking any chances. But that wouldn't do at all – I must take off my boots and my two pairs of socks. The goddess Pele hadn't agreed to keep my boots from burning and it might be an insult to her if I wore them.

I almost roasted alive before the kahunas had finished their chanting although it could not have taken more than a few minutes ... One of the kahunas beat at the shimmering surface of the lava with a bunch of *ti* leaves and then offered me the honour of crossing first. Instantly I remembered my manners; I was all for age before beauty.

The matter was settled at once by deciding that the oldest kahuna should go first, I second and the others side by side. Without a moment of hesitation the oldest man trotted out on that terrifically hot surface. I was watching him with my mouth open and he was nearly across – a distance of about a hundred and fifty feet – when someone gave me a shove that resulted in my having a choice of falling on my face on the lava or catching a running stride.

I still do not know what madness seized me, but I ran. The heat was unbelievable. I held my breath and my mind seemed to stop functioning. I was young then and could do my hundred yard dash with the best. Did I run! I flew! I would have broken all records, but with my first few steps the soles of my boots began to burn. They curled and shrank, clamping down on my feet like a vise. The seams gave way and I found myself with one sole gone and the other flapping behind me from the leather strap at the heel.

That flapping sole was almost the death of me. It tripped me repeatedly and slowed me down. Finally after what seemed minutes, but could not have been more than a few seconds, I leapt off for safety.

There is little more I can tell of this experience. I had a sensation of intense heat on my face and body, almost no sensation in my feet. When I touched them with my hands they were hot on the bottoms, they did not feel so except to my hands. None of the kahunas had a blister, although the *ti* leaves which they had tied on their feet had burned away long since.

While religious fire-walking appears in a number of different cultures, the reasons for the emergence of the practice can be equally diverse. A religious fire-walk that is still performed every year in Greece started as the result of an accident over 700 years ago. It was AD 1250 when the church of Saint Constantine in the village of Kosti in Thrace was consumed by fire. The villagers, hearing the groaning of the icons, rushed into the church to rescue them. Just as it seemed that they had been lost along with the pictures, the villagers appeared from the intense flames, completely unharmed. Since that time, on 21 May each year, the descendants of the original villagers – who have since moved to the Greek village of Lankadas – have remembered their ancestors with a ritual fire-walking dance. Early on the morning of the dance, the 12 foot square fire pit is lit. Those who will dance prepare themselves for many hours through meditation and contemplation on the very icons that were rescued so many years before. When the fire glows red-hot, the first of the dancers enters the fire pit carrying a copy of one of the sacred images. He is soon followed by others who tread the fire until it is finally put out, perhaps half an hour later.

In the 1970s a doctor from Athens General Hospital – Christo Xenakis – measured the temperature of the coals at somewhere between 500 and 850 degrees Fahrenheit. On witnessing the fire-walk, the doctor expressed his amazement: 'I would have expected third-degree burns in all cases.' And yet only a few of the entranced dancers even suffered blistering on their feet. The phenomenon was explained by one of the village's fire-walkers, Constantine Kitsinos:

It is almost exclusively a question of faith ... [one must] first overcome the feeling that it is impossible ... Once guided by faith and concentration, the actual dancing on the burning coals is painless. You feel something but it is no more than like walking in a prickly field. Despite the heat the strange thing is that your feet sometimes even feel cool.

Unfortunately for George Mills, a young American man who enthusiastically joined the local people in their fire-dance, he had to receive hospital treatment for third-degree burns to both feet.

2

MYSTERIOUS BEINGS

Our universe is a sorry little affair unless it has in it something
for every age to investigate ... Nature does not reveal her
mysteries once and for all.

Seneca

Psychotherapists, anthropologists, sociologists and other
people-watchers often claim that the *mysterious beings* that
form the basis of these unexplained encounters are merely
psychological 'projections', the results of either wishful thinking or fearful dreaming. Like our childhood dreams and
nightmares, we conjure up beasts and angels to give vent to
the often incomprehensible workings of our inner worlds.

So is that it? Does this explain every strange meeting, every
genuinely new experience? Is everything in the world simply
the triumph of hope and fear over reality? Are all the witnesses
of the strange and extraordinary described below simply
deluded, or, perhaps worse, liars? I trust not.

The 19th and 20th centuries' explorations have revealed
much. Every year, as many as a hundred new species of land
creature are discovered, and probably more from the other
world under the sea. There are still many, many new life-
forms yet to be discovered. Whether monstrous, mysterious
or ethereal, the full range of living beings that inhabits our
extraordinary world is far from familiar to us yet.

SEA MONSTERS

In July 1724 Hans Egede, a Norwegian missionary of impeccable integrity, was travelling to Greenland via the Danish colony of Good Hope when he saw something he was never to forget.

On the 6th, appeared a very terrible sea-animal, which raised itself so high above the water, that its head reached above our maintop [sail]. It had a long, sharp snout, and blew like a whale, had broad, large flappers, and the body was, as it were, covered with a hard skin, and it was very wrinkled and uneven on its skin; moreover on the lower part it was formed like a snake, and when it went under water again, it cast itself backwards, and in doing so it raised its tail above the water, a whole ship-length from its body. That evening we had very bad weather.

In his book *In the Wake of the Sea Serpents* the famous cryptozoologist Bernard Heuvelmans brought together 587 reports of mysterious sea creatures which had been documented up to 1966. Heuvelmans categorized the evidence into nine identifiable categories including the many finned, the super-eel, the many humped, the super-otter and the merhorse. While reports of all these creatures go back throughout history, the advent of reliable motorized sea transport has increased sightings, and provided more opportunities to confront inexplicable beasts of monstrous proportions.

Perhaps the most famous and terrifying of all recorded sea monsters is the beast known to Norwegian sailors as the Kraken. Its first reported appearance seems to have been recorded by Eric L. Pontoppidan, the Bishop of Bergen, in the 18th century. The bishop's sea voyage was interrupted by the beast, as it decided to surface close to his boat. The bishop starts his commentary with the fact that it was so large that the entirety of its body was never fully visible. He goes on to describe what he did see:

> ... its back or upper part, which seems to be in appearance about an English mile and a half in circumference, (some say more, but I chuse [sic] the least for greater certainty) looks at first like a number of small islands, surrounded with something that floats and fluctuates like sea weeds ... at last several bright points or horns appear, which grow thicker and thicker the higher they rise above the surface of the water, and sometimes they stand up as high and large as the masts of middle-siz'd vessels.
>
> It seems these are the creature's arms, and, it is said, if they were to lay hold of the largest man-of-war, they would pull it down to the bottom.

On 30 November 1861, the French gunboat *Alecton* struck a huge sea monster in the Atlantic Ocean. Lieutenant Bouyer, commander of the ship, tried to capture the beast. The crew managed to harpoon and rope the creature but it snapped the harpoon and slipped away, leaving just a small piece of its tail, weighing around 40 pounds. Bouyer wrote a report for the then minister of the navy:

> It was in fact the giant calamary, but the shape of the tail suggested it belonged to a species not yet described. The body seemed to measure about 15 to 18 feet in length. The head had a parrot-like beak surrounded by eight arms between 5 and 6 feet long. In aspect it was quite appalling; brick red in colour, shapeless and slimy, its form repulsive and terrible.

Bouyer had recognized the creature as a giant calamary or giant squid: 'the Poulpe Geant whose existence has been so much disputed and now seems to be relegated to the realms of myth.' For Bouyer, though, it was far from myth and now its existence is no longer disputed. Its proper name is *Architeuthis*. This example was by no means the largest possible size for these creatures. Examples have been caught that are 60 feet long, with a reach of 90 feet from the tip of one arm to the opposite tip of another. The tales of 19th- and 20th-century whalers have often provided evidence of these massive beasts. Whales in their death-throes have often vomited pieces of squid of huge proportions: tentacles the thickness of a man's chest, with suckers the size of saucers. Modern divers and scientists are now discovering that the giant squid is not the monster that once spelt fear. It has an intelligence and learning ability that makes its place in the animal kingdom special for very much more positive reasons than its monstrosity.

Sightings of the sea serpents occur with an intriguing regularity, yet for scientists and oceanographers they remain the stuff of legends. After Hans Egede's encounter in 1724, the next reliable sighting of a sea serpent seems to have been in August 1817, when an impressively large beast appeared in Gloucester Harbor, Massachusetts, and was seen by a number of people simultaneously. The testimony of Matthew Gaffney, a ship's carpenter, was backed by many others, and stated:

> That on the 14th day of August, AD 1817, between the hours of four and five o'clock in the afternoon, I saw a strange marine animal, resembling a serpent in the harbor in said Gloucester. I was in a boat, and was within 30 feet of him. His head appeared full as large as a four-gallon keg, his body as large as a barrel, and his length that I saw I should judge 40 feet at least. The top of his head was of a dark colour, and the underpart of his head appeared nearly white, as did also several feet of his belly that I saw ... I fired at him when he was nearest to me.

Gaffney went on to tell how the beast turned, as if to charge his boat, but then sank like a stone and resurfaced about 100 yards away. He estimated its swimming speed at between 20 and 30 miles an hour.

One of the most famous sightings of a sea serpent occurred when Captain Peter M'Quhae and the crew of the HMS *Daedalus* were travelling back from the East Indies to Plymouth, England, in 1848, and were 300 miles off the west coast of Africa. At 5pm on 6 August, 'something very unusual was seen by Mr Sartoris, midshipman, rapidly approaching the ship before the beam.' When Sartoris told his superiors, they gathered with the rest of the crew to look at the strange sight – a huge, snakelike beast 'with head and shoulders kept about four feet above the surface of the sea.' Captain M'Quhae judged the serpent to be at least 60 feet long, with a thick neck of some 16 inches in diameter. There seemed to be some kind of mane along its back.

Different geographical areas may, of course, contain their own particular species of unidentified swimming object. In 1885 Gunnar Hylten-Cavallius published a collection of 48 reports of a Scandanavian sea serpent which had become known as the Lindorm:

Usually the Lindorm is about ten feet long, but specimens of 18 or 20 feet have been observed. His body is as thick as a man's thigh. His colour is black with a yellow-flamed belly. Old specimens wear on their necks an integument of long hair or scales, frequently likened to a horse's mane. He has a flat, round or squared, head, a divided tongue and a mouth full of white shining teeth. His eyes are large and saucer shaped with a frightfully wild and sparkling stare. His tail is short and stubby, and the general shape of the creature is heavy and unwieldy.

In modern times the sightings of sea serpents appear to have been quite rare, but the serpent's case was strengthened by a 1966 sighting involving two very reliable witnesses who later went on to become world famous for their exploits at sea. The two were then British paratroopers on leave from the British

Army – Captain John Ridgeway and Sergeant Chay Blyth –
and they were rowing their way across the Atlantic Ocean.
Their 92-day survival test turned out to contain more than its
expected share of extraordinary experiences. It was early on
25 July. Blyth was still asleep. Ridgeway was tired but still
rowing hard in their 20-foot boat. Then, out of the semi-
darkness came . . . something:

> I was shocked to full wakefulness by a swishing noise to
> starboard. I looked out into the water and suddenly saw the
> writhing, twisting shape of a great creature. It was outlined by
> the phosphorescence in the sea as if a string of neon lights
> were hanging from it.
>
> It was an enormous size, some thirty-five or more feet long,
> and it came towards me quite fast. I must have watched it for
> some ten seconds. It headed straight at me and disappeared
> right beneath me. I stopped rowing. I was frozen with terror at
> this apparition. I forced myself to turn my head to look over to
> port side. I saw nothing, but after a brief pause I heard a most
> tremendous splash.
>
> I am not an imaginative man, and I searched for a rational
> explanation. Chay [Blyth] and I had seen whales and sharks,
> dolphins and porpoises, flying fish – all sorts of sea creatures
> but this monster in the night was none of these. I reluctantly
> had to believe that there was only one thing it could have been
> – a sea serpent.

For followers of the sea serpent, recent interest has focused on
appearances of the oarfish. Examples of this extraordinary
fish could account for a number of historical sea-serpent
sightings. With its narrow, silver, ribbon-like body, which
carries a garish red fin the full length of its 50-foot body, it is
the longest bony fish in the seas. Its large head is reminiscent
of a horse, and is adorned with blue gills. Accidental catches
of oarfish speciments, usually in tropical or sub-tropical
waters, has led them to be classified zoologically as *Regalecus
glesne*. What we do not yet know is just how widespread such

a species may be – and whether it has relatives living in colder climates.

The story of the oarfish is similar in important ways to that of the coelacanth, and both give a great deal of credibility to those who believe there are still many mysteries to be solved. The coelacanth is a genuinely prehistoric fish which was only known about through the fossil record, and which was thought to have become extinct about 70 million years ago. Yet in 1938 the first modern coelacanth was discovered swimming in the seas around the Comoro Islands. These islands lie off the coast of south-east Africa, amongst waters as deep as 1,300 feet. Adult coelacanths are known to grow up to a length of about six feet, but there is currently concern that their rarity is attracting hunters to kill them – either for sport, or simply for their curiosity or rarity value. While the coelacanth can justly claim to be the dinosaur of the deep, it seems a sad prospect that it might become genuinely extinct within a mere century of being rediscovered. Its appearance, though, has given a boost to cryptozoologists who study the seas: after all, if one animal can survive undetected for so long, why shouldn't many others?

Another prehistoric animal was at the centre of one of this century's most controversial sea-monster encounters. On 25 April 1977, the crew of the Japanese fishing vessel *Zuiyo-maru* were deeply shocked by the contents of their nets. A huge decomposing carcass was hauled out of the seas off Christchurch, New Zealand. About 33 feet long and weighing in at around 4,000 pounds, the beast was neither fish nor whale, nor, apparently, anything else from the natural history books. The smell from the rotting corpse was so bad that the crew, also fearing that their catch might become contaminated, decided to throw it back. Fortunately, though, Michihiko Yano – assistant production manager of Taiyo Fisheries – had taken samples and photos and made measured drawings of the beast. From these sketches, which clearly show the animal's skeleton, the most likely candidate appeared to be some kind of plesiosaur. The only problem with the plesiosaur explanation is that this dinosaur is thought to have died out some 60 million years ago. But if the coelacanth can survive, figured many hopeful observers, then, just perhaps . . .

Japan went plesiosaur crazy: there was even a stamp depicting the un-extinct beast. Unfortunately, it was revealed the following year, a tissue sample from the carcass pointed not to a dinosaur, but to a very large basking shark – a known, and thus 'not interesting', monster. So ended a cautionary tale for all cryptozoologists.

BIGFOOT

In our modern world filled with tales of alien abduction, Albert Ostman's story of his encounter with a Bigfoot has a strangely reassuring tone. It was 1957 when Albert Ostman, a British Columbian, announced to the world that he had been abducted, over 30 years earlier in 1924, by a family of Bigfoot, or Sasquatch, the humanoid apes reputed to live in the backwoods of America and Canada. Ostman's extraordinary claim was, to say the least, met with some scepticism.

His story ran that he had been on a prospecting trip, close to Vancouver Island. One night he and the sleeping bag he was asleep in were picked up and carried for some miles before being put down again. When he emerged from the bag he found himself the prisoner of a family of giant ape-people. It was an archetypal family of mother, father, son and daughter. He was not threatened in any way, but they did not want him to leave. He stayed for some days before he managed to get away, apparently after the adult male choked on Ostman's chewing tobacco.

It may sound like an unlikely, uncorroborated piece of evidence – perhaps the very reason why Ostman kept it to himself for so long – but of the experts who interviewed him, not one found Ostman crazy, deluded or insincere. Even John Napier, the respected scientist and yeti expert, remarked on his 'convincing account ... which does not ring false in any particular'. Ostman's own account makes fascinating reading:

> I was awakened by something picking me up. I was half asleep and at first I did not remember where I was. As I began to get my wits together, I remembered I was on this prospecting trip, and in my sleeping bag.
>
> My first thought was – it must be a snow slide, but there was no snow around my camp. Then it felt like I was tossed on horseback, but I could feel whoever it was, was walking.

Ostman believed that some hours passed, as he was carried along, still encased in his sleeping bag. He could not reach his knife to cut himself free. When they arrived at their destination he was let down on the ground. He heard the creatures talk in a strange, incomprehensible language. When he finally struggled out of his sleeping bag he saw his captors – four human shapes covered with hair, and completely without clothing. Ostman believed himself to be amongst the Sasquatch giants that a native Indian boatman had told him about. The family treated him well, and the adults seemed keen, for whatever reason, to keep him. Ostman described the family:

> The young fellow might have been between 11–18 years old, about seven feet tall and might weigh about 300 lbs. His chest would be 50–55 inches, his waist about 36–38 inches. He had wide jaws, narrow forehead, that slanted upward round at the back about four or five inches higher than the forehead. The hair on their heads was about six inches long. The hair on the rest of their body was short and thick in places. The women's hair was a bit longer on their heads and the hair on the forehead had an upward turn like some women have – they call it bangs, among women's hair-dos nowadays. The old lady could have been anything between 40–70 years old. She was over seven feet tall. She would be about 500–600 pounds.
>
> She had very wide hips, and a goose-like walk. She was not

112

built for beauty or speed ... The man's eyeteeth were longer than the rest of the teeth, but not long enough to be called tusks. The old man must have been near eight feet tall. Big barrel chest and big hump on his back – powerful shoulders, his biceps on the upper arm were enormous and tapered down to his elbows. His forearms were longer than common people have, but well proportioned. His hands were wide, the palm was long and broad, and hollow like a scoop. His fingers were short in proportion to the rest of his hand. His fingernails were like chisels. The only place they had no hair was inside their hands and the soles of their feet and upper part of the nose and eyelids. I never did see their ears, they were covered with hair hanging over them.

Albert Ostman claimed to spend six days in the company of the Sasquatch family, before deciding enough was enough and making his escape.

In 1955, a hunter named William Roe took his rifle for an exploratory trip close to the town of Tete Jaune Cache in British Columbia, Canada. Somewhere in the Mica mountains he came across what he first thought was a grizzly bear. As he watched, though, he soon realized that it was something very different. His sworn affidavit continues the story:

This, to the best of my recollection, is what the creature looked like and how it acted as it came across the clearing directly towards me. My first impression was of a huge man, about six feet tall, almost three feet wide, and probably weighing somewhere near three hundred pounds. It was covered from head to foot with dark brown silver-tipped hair. But as it came closer I saw by its breasts that she was female.

And yet its torso was not curved like a female's. Its broad frame was straight from shoulder to hip. Its arms were much thicker than a man's and longer, reaching almost to its knees. Its feet were broader proportionately than a man's, about five inches wide at the front and tapering to much thinner heels.

Roe was hiding himself behind a bush as he watched the creature feed on leaves from a bush. It had a flat nose, beady eyes, a thick neck and a skull that seemed to 'peak' at the back. It was no more than 20 feet away when it seemed to pick up Roe's scent: it looked directly at him, eye to eye. Roe described a look of comic amazement passing across its face, before it stood up tall and started to walk away.

> The thought came to me that if I shot it, I would possibly have a specimen of great interest to scientists the world over. I had heard stories about the Sasquatch ... Maybe this was a Sasquatch ...
>
> I levelled my rifle. The creature was still walking rapidly away, turning its head to look in my direction. I lowered the rifle. Although I have called the creature 'it', I felt now that it was a human being and I knew I would never forgive myself if I killed it.

As it reached the edge of the nearby clearing, Roe heard it make a kind of whinnying sound, 'half laugh and half language', the last that he saw and heard of the creature.

A few years later, in the autumn of 1958, a news story broke in north-western California. Jerry Crew, a logging driver, had found some giant human footprints in the dirt where he had been bulldozing. Crew had tried to authenticate his findings. *The Associated Press* of 6 October tells the story:

> Jerry Crew, a hard-eyed catskinner who bulldozes logging roads for a living, came to town this weekend with a plaster cast of a footprint. The footprint looks human, but it is 16 inches long, seven inches wide, and the great weight of the creature that made it sank the print two inches into the dirt.
>
> Crew says an ordinary foot will penetrate that dirt only half an inch. 'I've seen hundreds of these footprints in the past few weeks,' said Crew.
>
> He added he made the cast of a print in dirt he had bulldozed Friday in a logging operation in the forests above Weitchpeg,

50 miles north and a bit east of here in the Klamath River country of north-western California.

Crew said he and his fellow workmen never have seen the creature, but often have had a sense of being watched as they worked the tall timber . . .

'Every morning we find his footprints in the fresh earth we've moved the day before,' Crew said.

Crew said Robert Titmus, a taxidermist from Redding, studied the tracks and said they were not made by any known animals.

The event that really brought the Bigfoot search to public attention was the film of a large black-haired hominoid shot by Bigfoot buff Roger Patterson in 1967. It was October when Patterson headed off to camp in Bluff Creek Valley, northern California, in an effort to capture Bigfoot tracks with a 16 mm cine camera. A little after 1.15pm on 20 October, Patterson, and his friend Bob Gimlin, were riding their horses when, according to their story, they witnessed something rare and extraordinary. Squatting in the shallows of a partly dried river was a dark, female figure, entirely covered in hair. The horses shied at the sight, throwing Patterson and Gimlin to the ground. Patterson struggled to get the movie camera from his bag as the creature got up and started to walk away. Eventually, with the creature some 80 feet away, Patterson pointed the camera, squeezed the trigger and used up the last 28 feet of film – in the process capturing the only credible footage of 'Bigfoot' filmed anywhere in the world. After the event Patterson also showed casts he had made of the creature's footprints, some 14½ inches long, as well as more still photos of the tracks.

The frames from Patterson's movie film have probably generated more controversy than any other Bigfoot evidence. Is it a bear, is it an ape, is it a prehistoric human? Or is it, as some would suggest – given Patterson's well-known pro-Bigfoot sympathies – just Bob Gimlin, or someone else, in a hairy ape suit? Frames of the film have been subjected to every possible form of manipulation and enhancement in order to reveal any further information. Some researchers claim that these photographic enhancements strengthen the Bigfoot case, by showing the creature's musculature, her breasts, shaggy hair and patchy skin – so dispelling any idea that there is a 'suit' involved. For others, though, the doubts will always linger.

On 19 August 1970 Mrs Louise Baxter was driving close to her home town of Skamania, Washington, when she stopped to check her tyre for a puncture:

I kicked the tire, which was okay, and then bent over to see if possibly something was stuck under the fender to make the noise.

I suddenly felt as if I was being watched and without straightening up I looked toward the wooded area beside the road and looked straight into the face of the biggest creature I have ever seen except the one the time nearly a year before.

The creature was coconut brown and shaggy and dirty looking ... The mouth was partly open and I saw a row of large square white teeth. The head was big and seemed to be set right onto the shoulders. The ears were not visible due to the long hair about the head. It seemed the hair was about two inches long on its head.

It had a jutted chin and receding forehead. The nose and upper lip were less hairy and the nose was wide with big nostrils.

The eyes were the most outstanding as they were amber color and seemed to glow like an animal's eyes at night when car lights catch them.

It seemed contented there and seemed to be eating as the left fist was up toward the mouth as though it had something in it.

I screamed or hollered but whether I made any noise I can't tell I was so terrified. I know it didn't move while I looked. I don't remember how I got back in the car or how I started it.

As I pulled out I could see it still standing there, all 10 or 12 feet of him.

This uncorroborated sighting was typical of many that occurred throughout the 1970s, but the Bigfoot's apparent unwillingness to show itself to more than one or two people at a time helped to maintain its status as an unrecognized species. Perhaps the most convincing and important Bigfoot sighting after Roger Patterson's film was Paul Freeman's alleged encounter in 1982. Freeman worked part-time for the US Forest Service, and was driving through the mountainous country of the Umatilla National Forest one June morning when he saw some elk and decided to follow them on foot. Suddenly a figure stepped out: an enormous creature Freeman described as an eight and a half feet tall Bigfoot. After some seconds of mutual staring, both fled ... Shaken by the experience Freeman called for assistance from his Forest Service colleagues. When they searched together they found 21 footprints measuring 14 inches long by 7 inches wide. They took photos and casts of the prints.

Over the next days and weeks further prints were found in the surrounding area. Freeman came under media scrutiny and pressure which led to his resigning from the service, citing stress from the experience. The footprints came under even more scrutiny than Freeman, particularly for their 'dermal ridges' – lines like those on fingerprints which only feature on primate-type feet and hands. Some researchers were deeply impressed by the prints, but others felt they were too regular, too perfect. Doubts also surfaced about Freeman's credibility – he later claimed further sightings and even took a photo of what he said was a Bigfoot. He also admitted that he had previously faked some footprints. Many experts now believe his sighting to have been a hoax – albeit an impressive one!

In 1987 more Bigfoot tracks seem to have been found by James A. Hewkin, an employee of the Oregon Department of

Fish and Wildlife in a remote region of the Cascade Mountains. From his findings Hewkin came to this conclusion:

> A species of giant, bipedal primate, weighing up to 800 pounds and standing as tall as eight feet, and known as Sasquatch, does, in fact exist. Its diet is probably omnivorous, with feeding habits similar to those of bears (grubbing for roots, larvae etc.). It searches for rodents in stumps, logs, and rock slides. It might cache meat for winter use.

With the absence of great quantities of photographic, film or video evidence, much of the testimony to the existence of Bigfoot relies on tracks and the kind of information they provide. All of the evidence put forward has inevitably been called into question by sceptics eager to deny the existence of Bigfoot and his relatives. Yet scientist and Bigfoot expert John Napier refutes the idea that all the tracks could be fakes:

> For all tracks to be fakes we must be prepared to accept the existence of Mafia-like ramifications with cells in practically every township from San Francisco to Vancouver. Even if we accept the conspiracy angle there is still another hurdle to be jumped. How could footprints of such realism and functional consistency have been made? Rubber latex moulds bonded to a boot or shoe might explain how the footprints are repro-duced, but the mechanical problems would be immense, par-ticularly when it is borne in mind that the hoaxer would have to walk considerable distances over difficult terrain wearing such unwieldy contraptions.
>
> There is also the problem that footprints are found in conditions where an ordinary man is too light to make any impression in the substrate. However, it is not impossible that some of the footprints were made in this way.

One form of evidence that has only recently made an appear-ance is hair. On 4 August 1995 Wes Summerlin, a local resident of Walla Walla in south-east Washington state, headed into the Blue Mountains following a series of strange howling noises and cattle disturbances. Summerlin was accompanied by Paul Freeman, the veteran Bigfoot hunter who had claimed an encounter in 1982, and a former game warden named Bill Laughery.

On the trail of a musky smell the three found a clearing where creatures had been stripping trees. Then, suddenly, they caught sight of a seven-foot-tall animal, which was reported to be eating wood violets. They also heard the screaming sounds of two other creatures. Most significantly of all they found clumps of hair – some black, some brown – on the broken trees. The hair samples were subsequently given to Frank Pourier, the chairman of the anthropology department at Ohio State University. While there have been problems with contamination of the sample, Pourier still hopes to carry out conclusive DNA tests – similar to those used by the FBI for identifying criminals. If the hair is discovered to be from a primate, Pourier intends to carry out comparative tests with samples believed to be from a Chinese Wildman specimen, found in 1989.

It seems hard to believe that in a country like America, with a relatively high population density, that it is impossible to find and capture a Bigfoot or Sasquatch, or even to detect its skeleton. It has, after all, been sighted thousands of times, had its footprints cast as often, and even – if we are to believe Roger Patterson – been filmed for posterity. Yet Bigfoot researchers point to the abundance of dense woodland, particularly in the north-western states of America. The failure of a recent five-year Bigfoot Research Project to unearth conclusive evidence has, for some, been a disappointment. Nevertheless the Bigfoot legend lives on, as fresh and magnetic as ever. It has spawned the successful television series *Bigfoot and the Hendersons* and is even attracting new adherents who claim experiences linking it to UFO phenomena. The story has, if anything, become as much about the hunters who make the claims, as about the Bigfoot itself.

YETI

The very first reconnaissance expedition to Everest in 1921 brought back reports of a mysterious man-beast in the mountainous regions of the Himalayas. The expedition, led by Lt Col C.K. Howard-Bury, was on its way to Lhakpa La in Tibet when members saw dark shapes moving in a snow-field high above their position. When, on 22 September, they reached the point where they believed the 'shapes' to have been, they found groups of large footprints. Howard-Bury reported that at first sight the prints appeared human, but could not have been, since they were three times the size of a normal human foot. He went on to speculate that perhaps they had been made by a grey wolf which had strayed outside its normal habitat.

This did not impress the Lt Col's Sherpa porters who had seen the figures from lower down the mountain. They believed the footprints had been made by half-human creatures which they called *metoh* or *mehteh kangmi*, meaning 'snow creature' or 'wild creature' in Nepalese. When reports reached the West, the inexplicable beast was soon given its most enduring Western name: the Abominable Snowman.

For the Nepalese Sherpas who live in the Himalayan region, the *metoh*, or yeti, has been a normal part of their fauna for well over 200 years. Their descriptions give a picture of a hairy, half-human, half-ape figure with long arms and bowed legs – very much like the mountain gorillas of Africa. The difference between the yeti and apes, though, lies in its face, which is described as white, with humanoid features.

The fact that a yeti has never been captured, alive or dead, and that no body or skeleton has ever been found, leads most Western observers to doubt the creature's reality. Many wonder whether the Sherpas are simply believers in an enduring monster myth, perpetuated by the remote and difficult terrain of the Himalayan region. Reports that Buddhist monasteries may hold the scalps of yetis as religious artefacts have proved inconclusive, as the monasteries have rigidly refused to give up their holy relics for scientific investigation.

As more and more Western mountaineers have attempted to conquer the Himalayan peaks, sightings of yeti-like creatures have certainly increased. From these sightings, together with the Sherpas' descriptions, Edward Cronin of the 1972 Arun Valley Wildlife Expedition put together a generalized description of the man-beast:

> Its body is stocky, apelike in shape, with a distinctly human quality to it, in contrast to that of a bear. It stands five and a half to six feet tall and is covered with short, coarse hair, reddish-brown to black in color, sometimes with white patches on the chest. The hair is longest on the shoulders. The face is robust, the teeth are quite large, though fangs are not present, and the mouth is wide. The shape of the head is conical with a pointed crown. The arms are long, reaching almost to the knees. The shoulders are heavy and hunched. There is no tail.

Most Nepalese and Tibetans believe the creature lives, not in the mountainous regions, but in the dense Himalayan forests just below the snow zone. When the creatures are seen in snowy regions, the local people say it may simply be travelling between wooded areas, or looking for mosses or lichens that grow on the rocky outcrops. One of the first climbers to give an eye-witness account of a yeti was the Italian N.A. Tombazi, a member of a 1925 expedition. The habitat description in his report seems to match the local interpretation:

> The intense glare and brightness of the snow prevented me from seeing anything for the first few seconds; but I soon spotted the 'object' referred to, about two or three hundred

yards away down the valley to the east of our camp. Unquestionably, the figure in outline was exactly like a human being, walking upright and stopping occasionally to uproot or pull at some dwarf rhododendron bushes. It showed up dark against the snow and, as far as I could make out, wore no clothes. Within the next minute or so it had moved into some thick scrub and was lost to view.

With only a few scarce first-hand sightings of the yeti, the most tangible and pictorial evidence to support the yeti's existence has often been provided by footprints. The photographs brought back by pioneering mountaineers during the 20th century have stimulated a now global fascination with the Himalayan yeti. Particularly significant in the search for evidence have been photographs from F.S. Smythe's 1937 expedition, and a now world-famous image taken by Eric Shipton on the Menlung glacier on a 1951 reconnaissance expedition. Shipton's photo shows a crisp snow imprint of a very large, wide foot, alongside an ice axe to provide the impression of the foot's size. Shipton's co-mountaineer Michael Ward described the prints: 'They were really well defined . . . we could see the toes of all the feet . . . There was absolutely no blurring round the edges.' Measurements taken showed the prints to be 13 inches long and 8 inches wide. Some cryptozoologists believe such feet could bear the weight of an eight-foot-tall beast. Shipton's description goes on: 'Where the tracks crossed the crevasse, one could see quite clearly where the creature had jumped and used its toes to secure purchase on the snow on the other side.'

A 1955 RAF expedition also resulted in photos of footprints, as did a 1979 British expedition led by John Edwards. In 1980 a Polish mountaineer photographed a footprint 14 inches long and 7 inches wide. Sceptics tend to explain 'yeti footprints' as those of other animals such as snow leopards or bears, or even as the tracks of Buddhist monks who sometimes walk barefoot in the snow. It is also often claimed that the large size of many tracks that have been found – some up to 18 inches long – is due to melting of the snow since the impression was first made.

In 1970 the world renowned climber Don Whillans gave an eye-witness account of a yeti he had seen on Annapurna, an encounter which also resulted in photographed footprints:

> ... this creature, which looked to me in its movements ape-like, sort of bounded along in a funny gait towards what obviously in a few weeks time, when the snow had gone, would be a clump of trees ... I got the binoculars out and all I could make out was a black ape-like shape. Then, quite suddenly, it was almost as if it realised it was being watched, it shot across the whole slope of the mountain. It must have travelled half a mile before it disappeared into the shadow of some rocks ... And the actual tracks that I saw had very peculiar indentations between the actual footprint, which didn't strike me until about twelve months later when I was looking at a picture of a gorilla in a normal animal book.

In 1987 Rheinhold Messner, the German mountaineer often considered to be the best climber of his generation, claimed to have had a face-to-face encounter with a yeti: 'He was bigger than me, quite hairy and strong, dark brown-black hair falling over his eyes. He stood up on two legs, and seeing him I immediately thought he corresponds to all the descriptions I'd heard from the Sherpas and Tibetans.'

The next year another famous mountaineer and climber, the Briton Chris Bonington, led a British yeti expedition to the Menlung glacier region. Bonington had been inspired to make a conclusive search after an experience in 1987 when he and a party of three other Norwegian and British climbers had come across a set of day-old tracks at 16,000 feet after being forced down the mountains by a fierce storm. Bonington had reported that each print was seven inches by four inches and about the same size as a small human.

On this 1988 expedition a BBC television producer named John Davidson was working on a film of the project when he claimed to see a yeti near base camp. His report described a dark figure hiding behind a rock, watching him as he progressed through a blizzard: 'My first impression was that it was probably a bear. But it didn't act like one.'

One of the facts that has always strengthened the sceptics' case has been the absence of any photographic or filmed evidence of an actual animal. In March 1986, however, this problem seemed to have been solved: Anthony Wooldridge, a British man on a charity run through the Himalayas, observed a yeti-like figure, and managed to photograph it:

> Standing behind a shrub was a large, erect shape, perhaps up to two meters tall. Convinced that whatever it was it would disappear quickly I took several photographs rapidly and then moved up about 50 meters nearer to a rocky outcrop ... It was difficult to restrain my excitement as I came to the realisation that the only animal I could think of which remotely resembled this one in front of me was the yeti ... its head was large and squarish, and the whole body appeared to be covered in dark hair, although the upper arm was a slightly lighter colour. The creature was amazingly good at remaining motionless.

Wooldridge's photos attracted worldwide media and scientific attention. But while there were many ready to accept the figure as real, others had their doubts. Further stereoscopic photos the next year at the same site revealed a very yeti-like outcrop of rock ... Wooldridge had to accept his error: '... this is obviously very disappointing. I appear to have jumped to a false conclusion which has taken nearly two years to sort out.'

The yeti lives on, not just in myth, but in the popular imagination. With an ever-increasing number of expeditions to the Himalayan peaks, there is hope amongst the crypto-zoologists that some conclusive evidence will at last bring this beast the recognition they so wish for it. Whether a yeti might wish for such recognition is another matter . . .

THE LOCH NESS MONSTER

Of the world's 300 lakes that are claimed to harbour 'monsters', none is more famous than Scotland's deep, dark Loch Ness. Once linked to the sea, but now an inland lake, its surface covers 21 square miles. Up to 800 feet deep in places, the loch's murky waters support a strong population of eels and fish, including salmon. Enough, some say, to feed a family of Nessies. For certainly, if Nessie does exist, it does not exist alone. The simple laws of nature demand that at least a pair of Nessies continue to reproduce.

An estimated 3,000 reported sightings have intensified the controversy since the first sighting by Saint Columba in the 6th century AD. More recently photographs, video footage and detailed scientific exploration of the loch have provided more evidence for the existence of a large creature living somewhere in the depths. As yet, though, it seems that the concrete, clinching proof that Nessie-hunters crave has yet to surface.

The modern sighting that brought the Nessie legend into the 20th century occurred on 22 July 1933. Londoners Mr and Mrs George Spicer were driving south from Inverness along the shore of Loch Ness, on their way to the small town of Foyers. Their Scottish holiday had, so far, been uneventful. The peace, though, was not to last. As Mr Spicer looked on, the bracken on the hill some 200 yards away began to move. Very suddenly an enormous animal with a long neck appeared. In jerky movements the animal hauled itself across the road. Mr Spicer sped up to get a better look at the beast, but by the time he arrived at the spot where it had crossed the road it was already into the bushes on the loch side of the road. Later, describing their encounter to the press, the Spicers said that the creature stood about four feet high and was about six feet long (although later reports seem to have stretched it to 25 or even 30 feet). Its neck, they said, undulated 'in the manner of a scenic railway'. All in all the beast was 'a terrible, dark, elephant grey, of a loathsome texture, reminiscent of a snail'. Mr and Mrs Spicer's report was one of five major sightings in 1933, and did a great deal to popularize the idea of Nessie. Circus owner Bertram Mills was inspired to offer £20,000 to anyone who could deliver the monster, alive, to his circus.

At least a further five reports were recorded the following year. The first of these was in January when another land sighting occurred close to the loch. A young medical student Arthur Grant was riding his motorcycle along the loch side when a large dark blob appeared in the shadows of bushes beside the road ahead. As Grant approached, the creature leapt across the road in front of the motorbike. Grant could now see the animal more clearly: on its long neck was a small, eel-like head with oval eyes; its bulky body thickened towards a long tail. It moved with the help of its four, flipper-like legs. Grant estimated its length at between 18 and 20 feet and it had a dark skin like a whale's. Grant managed to see where the creature splashed into the loch, presumably from where it had originally emerged: 'Knowing something of natural history, I can say that I have never seen anything in my life like the animal I saw. It looked like a hybrid – a cross between a plesiosaur and a member of the seal family.'

If the monster from Loch Ness is not a known species that exists elsewhere – a sea cow, a large eel or an elephant seal – then theorists often turn to the prehistoric. The animals that fit most closely with the sightings are dinosaurs of a particular type thought to be extinct for many millions of years: either the plesiosaur (as Grant had mentioned), a flippered creature with a large body, long neck and small head, or the zeugladon, a strange prehistoric cross between snake and whale. Other, less exotic theories revolve around large eels or the giant sturgeon, a large cartilaginous fish with a long snout – more famous for giving the world caviar.

However it might be classified, the wealth of sightings since the 1930s has been enough to convince some researchers that Nessie is real. Others have looked at the quality and standing of the witnesses. Doctors, lawyers, businessmen, even priests have testified to the creature's reality. Father Gregory Brusey claims to have seen Nessie on 14 October 1971. A monk at the Fort Augustus Benedictine Abbey on the shores of the lake, Father Gregory was well aware of the legend, and of the fact that many of his colleagues at the abbey had already seen a creature in the waters. Father Gregory was in the grounds of the abbey with a visitor, when they both saw a creature's head rear out of the water as high as seven feet. The two watched the animal swimming away from them for about 20 seconds before it dived. 'We felt a sort of awe and amazement. In fact, my friend said if I hadn't been with him, he'd probably have run. It gave us a feeling of something from another world.'

In 1972 science stepped in to try to settle the matter once and for all. A team led by Dr Robert H. Rines arrived from the Academy of Applied Sciences, based in Massachusetts. They brought with them sophisticated sonar equipment as well as a 16 mm camera system able to capture time-lapse images with a synchronized flash unit. The team's great hope was to capture a combination of photographic and sonar traces at the same time, but, like all researchers of the deep waters of Loch Ness, they faced two considerable challenges: the sheer size of the loch and the murkiness of its water. Their answer was to set up the equipment in places where there had been sightings previously, and where they felt Nessie was most likely to reappear.

On the night of 8 August members of the team were stationed in their boats in Urquhart Bay, a little way out from the shore. They lowered their equipment into the water and started recording. At around 1am the sonar started to pick up traces of a large object moving in the sonar beam. The American team were beginning to get excited. Forty minutes later a group of salmon showed up, along with two more large objects. As the objects appeared on the sonar, the time-lapse camera took shots of them, illuminated by flash.

When the photographic frames were processed it was not entirely clear what the team had captured. Yet when the images were put through a computer enhancement process at the Jet Propulsion Laboratory, two of the frames revealed what clearly seemed to be the flipper of a sea creature. Each of the two frames showed the unmistakable shape in a slightly different position. By analysing the data an estimate of the flipper's length came out at between four and six feet. A third picture seemed to show that the two large objects were two living creatures, swimming through the water, about 12 feet apart.

The evidence was everything that the team had dreamed of: simultaneous photographic and sonar images of at least one large beast swimming in Loch Ness – flippers and all. What more could the sceptics ask for? The answer was 'quite a lot'. So, in 1975, the team returned with improved imaging equipment. Now two cameras were deployed: the original system from 1972 and a new system with an improved strobe light. Both cameras also carried more sensitive, higher speed film. The new system was put at a depth of 80 feet, in line with the sonar beam, while the older camera system was positioned at 40 feet. Images of large objects regularly appeared on the sonar system, but the camera failed to see anything, its view obstructed by clouds of silt from the lake floor. Nevertheless the original camera continued to take regular frames for 24 hours in the clearer water nearer the surface. In a few of these frames is possibly the most compelling evidence for the monster ever seen. One frame shows a part of a large pink body, another seems to capture the upper body, neck and head of a flippered creature. In later frames the camera seems to have been disturbed by something, as it starts to point in different directions. Then, in a single frame, we can see what many people believe is the first close up of the monster's face: a dragon-like head, with mouth open, nostrils visible, and horn-like protuberances sticking out about six inches.

Time Magazine and the BBC were now talking as if Nessie was a reality. Sir Peter Scott, the famous naturalist, put his full weight behind the campaign to make Nessie real. Together with Robert Rines he gave the creature a 'proper' Latin name, *Nessiteras rhomboteryx*, which means the Ness monster with the diamond shaped fin. Unfortunately for Scott and Rines, the name also forms a number of anagrams. One London newspaper could hardly contain its delight when it published its reworking of the Latin name 'Monster hoax by Sir Peter S.'

There are still many sceptics who can find acceptable explanations for Dr Rines' photographic images which do not involve a monster – a tree stump, or an old car engine, the carcass of a deer, perhaps. But definitely not a monster.

Perhaps predictably, there was a rash of sightings following the Academy of Applied Science's 1975 expedition. Only 18 days later, in fact, came one of the most remarkable records of all: Allen Wilkins had four sightings in one memorable day. On 8 July 1975 at 8.20am Wilkins and his son saw something dark, about 20 feet long, appear on the surface of the lake, only to disappear again after a few moments. At 10.12, Wilkins, now with his wife and some other holidaymakers, photographed three triangular humps, moving along in the water. When a boat appeared the humps submerged. Later that evening, at 9.25pm, Wilkins was with others when another dark shape broke the surface and showed two humps before again disappearing. An hour later the same group saw more humps moving in the water: a group of three this time, each about four feet high, swam along curving in and out of the water, before submerging again.

*

Another busy day in Loch Ness sighting history was 17 June 1993. Edna McInnes, a young mother, and her boyfriend David Mackay, both from Inverness, Scotland, claimed to have watched a 40-foot monster swim around in the loch for ten minutes: 'It was a very light coloured brown. You could see it very clearly.' It seemed to wave its long, giraffe-like neck as it moved swiftly. Ms McInnes ran along the shore, trying to keep up with the beast: 'I was scared when the wash from its wake lapped on the shore, but I just kept running behind it. By the time it plunged below the surface I was running as fast as I could go.' They ran to get a camera from a relative's house, and returned to the shore. Soon after, the creature reappeared only 20 feet from the edge of the loch. David Mackay's attempt to photograph the creature showed a wake, but no monster. It was not the end of the day's activity however. That evening, James MacIntosh, also of Inverness, was driving home along the road beside the loch when his young son, also named James, spotted something strange: 'Dad, that's not a boat.' MacIntosh senior takes up the story: 'I was concentrating on my driving but I looked over at the loch and I suddenly saw this brown thing with a neck like a giraffe break the surface. It was an eerie experience. It was swimming quite swiftly away from the shore at the time.'

The next year, however, despite continued sightings, the Nessie fans took a blow when the photograph known as 'the surgeon's photo' was revealed to be a fake. In 1934, London surgeon R.K. Wilson took four photos of a head and neck sticking out of the water. The image of the long neck with the small head became the archetypal image of the Loch Ness monster. Throughout most of the 20th century it stood, for many, as the incontrovertible proof of Nessie's existence. It was, after all, taken by a surgeon. Sixty years after it was taken, however, and some time after Wilson's death, a friend revealed that the photo was a hoax, taken for a joke. Unfortunately the joke had got somewhat out of hand, and it had never been possible to go back on the story. At the time of the revelation it was a big public relations setback for the Nessie fans, giving fuel to the sceptics' fire.

In late 1996, however, progress again seemed to be made when coastguard and Nessie hunter George Edwards revealed sonar evidence of a network of caves at the bottom of the loch. This caused bookmakers to cut their odds on Nessie's discovery from 150–1 to 100–1. A spokesman from the gaming organization Ladbrokes shared his concerns: 'Every year, thousands of bets are placed on Nessie being discovered. If George Edwards manages to solve this famous mystery, it will cost us a fortune.' Edwards has been offered technical assistance from an oil exploration company to explore the cave with the company's remote-controlled, video-carrying submarines. Dr Robert Rines, the most successful of all the scientific hunters so far, has promised to come out of retirement to help Edwards explore the loch's deep caves. The story goes on . . . Yet, until a creature is brought to the surface – alive or dead – and displayed for all the world to see, the silent majority will continue to think of Nessie as nothing more than a harmless myth.

LAKE MONSTERS WORLDWIDE

Loch Ness is not alone. The presence of lake monsters is recorded in as many as 300 separate lakes around the world – from Tibet to Africa, from Scandinavia to Russia. Reports from many lakes predate encounters at the Scottish loch by many years. What links many of these lakes is that they have, at some time in the past, been connected to the sea. Generally, too, they all play host to a population of migratory fish that have the potential to feed the kind of creature that could lurk in the cold depths of their home waters. It's obvious to us all, however, that the right conditions are nowhere near enough to prove the existence of a monster. If these monsters are to be properly recognized as some new species, their witnesses and supporters will need some first-rate evidence. So does this evidence exist?

On the North American continent perhaps the most famous contender for genuine lake monster is Ogopogo, who reputedly lives in British Columbia's Lake Okanagan. Reports of its presence have been regular for around a hundred years, and many of these sightings have been strengthened by the fact that groups of people have often shared the sighting.

On 2 July 1949 a close-range multiple sighting occurred when the creature was seen by a group of people on a boating trip. Mr Leslie Kerry, whose house overlooked Lake Okanagan, had invited his friends from Montreal, the Watson family, for a journey around the lake in his boat. As they were heading out, they spotted a large, snakelike shape moving in the water. Its body seemed to undulate – sometimes above the water, sometimes below. The trippers described the beast as 30 feet long, about a foot in diameter, with a forked tail that lashed the water as it swam. Interestingly Mr Kerry's wife, watching the incident from the shore, also saw much of what was happening. She was so shocked that she called her neighbours, the Underhills, who rushed down the beach to view the scene through binoculars. Dr Underhill later described the coils of the body standing above the water – each about seven feet long. Indeed its body seemed so long that Dr Underhill later reported that there may have even been two of the strange beasts. Altogether the witnesses were able to view the creature for what seemed a very long 15 minutes before it eventually returned to the depths of the lake.

Ten years later, almost to the day, was an even rarer occurrence: a sighting by a journalist. On the 17 July 1959, Mr R.H. Miller, the editor of the local *Vernon Advertiser*, was out on the lake with his wife, another couple and their son, when the party became aware of a creature following in the wake of their motor cruiser. They turned around to get a better view and saw very clearly a blunt-nosed head, much like that of a snake, sticking out of the water. It was not like any creature Mr Miller, or any of the rest of the crew had ever seen. Needless to say the story provided good copy for the local paper!

In 1974 a woman named Mrs B. Clark described her brush with Ogopogo:

> It was travelling north, away from me. It did not seem to be in much of a rush, and it swam very slowly . . . five to ten feet behind the hump, about five to eight feet below the surface, I could see its tail. The tail was forked and horizontal like a whale's, and it was four to six feet wide. As the hump submerged, the tail came to the surface until its tip poked above the water about a foot.

A composite description based on 200 sightings dating back to 1850 was put together by one Ogopogo expert: 'The animals look most like a log, elongated, serpentine, not thickened in the body centrally, about 12 meters long, although a range of smaller sizes has been reported and a few larger, up to say 20 meters . . .' Some descriptions have described the beast as having a head like a horse or a goat, with a kind of mane running down its neck. Cryptozoologist Roy Mackal has analysed the reports on the creature, and has now rejected the theory that Ogopogo is similar to the Loch Ness monster. Instead he now believes that Ogopogo must be a form of primitive whale named *Basilosaurus cetoides*.

Whatever it is, though, it manages to make fairly regular appearances: in recent times photographic and video evidence has been on the increase. At least seven separate groups of photos have been taken since the 1960s, with about half a dozen videos apparently showing a creature of some kind. As yet, though, there is no conclusive physical evidence – the only kind of evidence that would transport Ogopogo from the uncertain realms of cryptozoology to the text books of zoology.

Stories of a monstrous serpent in America's Lake Champlain also go back over a hundred years, and sightings of 'Champ', as it is fondly known, now number over 240. Many experts believe the creature, or family of creatures, to be a 'plesiosaur' – a prehistoric throwback thought to have become extinct some 60 million years ago. About a third of the sightings describe a creature with a long, sinuous neck, able to stand proud of the water; its body is dark, between 15 and 25 feet long, often with a number of humps.

Lake Champlain, which has often been described as America's Loch Ness, is 109 miles long and shares a number of features with its Scottish counterpart: both are deep, fresh-water lakes that were created about 10,000 years ago. While Lake Champlain, at 400 feet, is only half as deep as Loch Ness, both lakes carry a sufficient population of fish to support, in theory at least, a family of such creatures.

Over the last hundred years or so Champ has caused some extreme reactions, and in an age less interested in 'the natural world', the serpent has become the victim of aggressive hunts. In the 1880s a serpent was claimed to have been killed in Lake Champlain:

> Only about 25 feet was between us and the infuriated serpent. [We] discharged each a shot at it, when the head was seen to turn, the immense body begin to curve .. Streams of blood spurted from its head . . . At last the excited party observed the serpent give one spasmodic twist of its immense length . . . never to rise more by its own exertions . . .

The most convincing evidence for Champ's existence is a photo taken in 1977 by Sandra Mansi while she was holiday-ing with her partner and two children. The huge animal with humped body, long neck and small head appears clearly in the photo, which, despite close scientific analysis, has so far revealed no evidence of tampering or retouching. In 1981 the picture appeared in the *New York Times* and *Time* magazine. Asked to testify at a public hearing about the lake monster Sandra Mansi was strident in her testimony: 'I just want you to know that "Champ" is there. Believe me, "Champ" is there.'

Of Champ's modern champions, perhaps the most dedicated is Joseph W. Zarzynski, the founder of the Lake Champlain Phenomena Investigation. He is a firm believer in Champ's reality, but admits: 'the evidence is scanty when compared to the wealth of eyewitness testimony, photographic and sonar evidence from Loch Ness.' In 1979 Zarzynski and Jim Kennard, an engineering expert colleague, used high-tech sonar to search for Champ. On 3 June they got readings indicating the presence of a 10 to 15 foot long object moving in the waters beneath their boat. Their more recent searches have used remotely controlled underwater camera equipmnent: they do not necessarily hope to film Champ, or rather 'a Champ'. Zarzynski would be happier to find a carcass or a skeleton on the bottom of the lake and to remove it to a laboratory for examination. As in Nessie's case, it makes little sense to suggest that there is, or has been, only one example of Champ. If he or she exists, there will need to be at least one *he* and one *she*!

On 6 October 1980, partly in response to the Mansi photograph, the civic elders of Port Henry, New York, a village at the southern end of Lake Champlain brought into force a measure of protection for Champ (and possibly the local tourist trade). They resolved that: 'all the waters of Lake Champlain which adjoin the Village of Port Henry are hereby declared to be off limits to anyone who would in any way harm or destroy the Lake Champlain Sea Monster.' The following year Champ made a record number of appearances: at least three dozen people claimed to have seen it – including 17 from one Bible class.

Whether or not Champ decides to reveal its full identity, the creature's immortality is virtually guaranteed by local entrepreneurs: its name and image will live on in the marketing and products which bear its name: Champ 101.3 FM radio station, the Champ car wash, and Champ's chips (made from an extinct recipe!)

*

All of America's Great Lakes have generated monster sightings, with 'South Lake Bessie' of Lake Erie attracting the most attention. Sightings of other lake monsters from the inland waters of the world now appear regularly on the news services. In December 1996 a story started to appear of a 'Russian Nessie' in Lake Brosno. The local reports described a serpent-like creature about 16 feet long. A local palaeontologist added flesh to the bone by saying that the shape indicated an extinct type of reptile with mammal-like teeth. Interestingly there have been reports from as far back as the 1850s.

When an expedition set out from Moscow University in 1964 to survey mineral deposits in Siberia, they were not prepared for the encounter they would have at Lake Khaiyr. G. Roskuev, the leader of the team, described how one of the group, N. Gladkikh, ran into the monster: 'Here is how it happened. Gladkikh went out to the lake to draw water and saw a creature that had crawled out onto the shore, apparently to eat the grass – a small head on a long gleaming neck, a huge body covered with a jet-black skin, a vertical fin along the spine.' Gladkikh returned to base with his extraordinary experience still fresh in his mind. The group, armed with rifles and cameras went back to find the strange animal – but it had disappeared, leaving Gladkikh's credibility with his team at an all-time low. Within a short time, though, the creature re-appeared, in full view of the whole team: 'Suddenly a head appeared in the centre of the lake, then a dorsal fin. The creature beat the water with its long tail, producing waves on the lake. You can imagine our astonishment when we saw with our own eyes that the stories were true.' The drawing Gladkikh produced bore a remarkable resemblance to the plesiosaur-like images of Nessie.

China, too, has claimed its own vapour-breathing lake creature. Dubbed 'Chan', meaning toad, the monster is believed to live at the bottom of a deep gorge in a mountainous area of Hubei province. Its existence was first acknowledged when a group of peasants were chased by the beast after they had been trying to catch fish by blowing them out of the lake with explosives.

With the ubiquity of video cameras the quality of visual evidence might be thought to increase, but recording on video is not everyone's first instinctive reaction to a strange experience. In 1996, however, Gun-Britt Widmark, aged 67, recorded images of what he believed was Storsjoodjuret – Lake Storsjon's monster – Sweden's most famous lake creature. Widmark was boating with a group of pensioners when the beast apparently showed itself. It appeared to have humps and was about 35 feet long. Unfortunately for Widmark, however, it disappeared before he could get close enough to produce good-quality images. Lake Storsjon has already generated 500 claimed sightings dating back to 1635 – most of them in the summer season. Avoiding the theory that this is a tourist generation ploy, local experts point to the fact that Storsjoodjuret has obeyed the same seasonal movement patterns since 1899.

Here, as in all lake monster cases, even video will never provide the kind of evidence that would satisfy biologists and zoologists. Only when a living, or dead, specimen has been examined and classified will science take seriously the idea that a lake monster is anything more than a misperception, a mistake, a hoax, or even some strange hallucination.

THE CHINESE WILDMAN

It was 1940 when a biologist named Wang Tselin claimed to be present when a 'yeren', or 'Chinese wildman', was killed. He said that it was a female of the species, about six and a half feet tall; its hair was greyish brown, and its face combined ape features with human. He said that it reminded him of the prehistoric Beijing Man – an early humanoid ancestor of *homo sapiens*. For many centuries the people of southern China have talked about a 'yeren' as more than simply a myth. Its local names, like 'man-bear', 'hill-ghost' and 'monster of the mountains', give a flavour of this elusive beast, and of the seriousness with which it is regarded.

One of the most important encounters in wildman history happened on a May afternoon in 1957. Xu Fudi, a woman from the Chinese province of Zhejiang, heard a scream from her young daughter who was tending cattle. She rushed out to see the girl in the grasp of an ape-like beast, about four feet nine inches tall. Xu Fudi hit the beast with a stick to make it release the terrified youngster. The beast let go and ran off into a paddy field with Xu Fudi in pursuit. A group of women then joined in the chase and managed to beat the animal into submission. It lay in the field, not quite dead, but unconscious. It recovered consciousness, grunted and lay with tears in its eyes. The women, still scared by the creature, now beat it to death. Some days later they cut it into pieces. The following day screams and grunts were heard from the hills.

The local area newspaper, the *Sonyang Daily*, investigated the story and subsequently gave a description of the creature: the young male weighed around 88 pounds; its large-chested body was covered in long, dark-brown hair; its face resembled a human's although its nose was sunken. The skin of the beast was pale and soft under its dark hair. It was also reported that Zhou Shousong, a biology teacher from a village nearby, had removed the feet and hands to preserve them for posterity, an action that was later to prove important for a yeren research team of 1980.

Meanwhile, a 1961 enquiry into the yeren was launched on the back of another apparent killing of a creature by a group of road builders. When the scientists arrived, however, the body had already disappeared.

The next major sighting in 1976 brought the wildman to worldwide public attention. On 14 May, six Chinese Communist local government officials were travelling home by jeep through southern Hubei Province in the early hours of the morning, when the driver suddenly saw a large hairy figure on the road ahead – 'strange, tail-less ... with reddish fur'. The driver blew the vehicle's horn, frightening the beast into attempting to escape, before putting his headlights to high beam. The group watched the creature as it began to climb an embankment. As it tried, however, it fell, landing in front of the jeep. Five of the group got out and surrounded the animal which stayed on all fours, apparently immobilized by the bright stare of the jeep's headlights.

One of the group, Zhou Zhongyi, then picked up a stone and threw it at the beast. He hit it on the buttocks, which made it stand up briefly. The group drew back, allowing the yeren to move off and make its escape up the embankment. Following the encounter the men gave a detailed description of the wildman: it had fine, soft hair somewhat like a camel's. There was a purple-red streak down its back. Its legs were long and thick, with heavy thighs. It had a large belly and protruding buttocks. The witnesses also said that the face was ape-like, long, broad across the brow but narrow at the chin. Its eyes, they said, were quite human.

A month later, in the Qiaoshang Commune in Hubei Province, a peasant woman named Gong Ylan had a very close wildman encounter. Gong had run out of grass for her pigs, and had decided to take her four-year-old son and search for a new supply up the nearby mountain. When the pair were crossing a pass they saw a red figure some 20 feet away. The woman stared, realizing that she was looking at a large hairy animal, scratching itself on a tree. Suddenly frightened, Gong picked up her child and ran. Unfortunately the beast had seen her; it tried to pursue her, crying 'Ya, ya!' She escaped the beast and ran a quarter of a mile to the house of her commune leader. The commune leader's wife answered the door: 'When Gong arrived at my house, the beads of sweat on her forehead were as big as soybeans. She kept saying "wild man".' When a group returned to the tree where the beast had been scratching itself, they managed to recover some samples of hair. These were later examined at the

Beijing Medical Institute. They confirmed that the hairs had not come from a bear, but resembled those 'of the higher primates, including man'.

These two important sightings of the yeren in 1976 in Hubei Province led to a major research expedition in March 1977 to try to find more conclusive evidence. Led by Zhou Guoxing of the Peking Museum of Natural History, the team of 110 contained zoologists, biologists and photographers as well as soldiers equipped with tranquilizer guns. The expedition searched for eight months and failed in its goal of capturing a live wildman. They did, however, see one of the creatures, and gathered some important evidence:

Many footprints, 12 to 16 inches long, were found. Faeces sometimes found beside the footprints and presumed to be from the creature, was analysed and found to be from neither a human nor a bear, according to Mr Zhou. Hair samples, believed to have come from the animal and found stuck to a tree bark, suggest that it is some sort of higher primate, he said.

From accumulated evidence, including purported witnesses, Mr Zhou described the creature as about six feet six inches tall, covered with wavy red hair, with the hair on its head falling nearly to its waist. It walks upright, he said, and its footprints show it to have no arch, hence a clumsy gait. The three smallest of its five toes are not completely separated, he said, and because of this it may have the ability to grasp things with its feet. No tail has been detected, but some witnesses said breasts were distinguishable.

The creature is believed to be omnivorous but is said to prefer walnuts and chestnuts, tender young leaves and roots, and insects. While no recording exists of its calls, those who have heard it say it emits one long and one short cry.

The team also collected statements from witnesses in the area where they studied. This description is typical of many others:

He was about seven foot tall, with shoulders wider than a man's, a sloping forehead, deep-set eyes and a bulbous nose with slightly upturned nostrils. He had sunken cheeks, ears like a man's but bigger, and round eyes, also bigger than a man's. His jaw jutted out and he had protruding lips. His front teeth were as broad as a horse's. His eyes were black. His hair was dark brown, more than a foot long and hung loosely over his shoulders. His whole face, except for the nose and ears, was covered with short hairs. His arms hung below his knees. He had big hands with fingers about six inches long and thumbs only slightly separated from the fingers. He didn't have a tail, and the hair on his body was short. He had thick thighs, shorter than the lower part of his leg. He walked upright with his legs apart. His feet were each about 12 inches long and half that broad – broader front and narrow behind, with splayed toes. He was male. That much I saw clearly.

More than 200 sightings like these have been recorded by Zhou Guoxing's team since they first started to collect evidence of the Chinese wildman. Apart from sightings, they have collected hair and faeces, although, so far, there have been no photographs or film. From the wealth of evidence Mr Zhou has developed a theory that there may in fact be two distinct types of wildman:

> There appear to be two types of yeren. A larger one of about two meters in height, and a smaller one, about one meter in height. Also there are two types of footprint: one is large, 30–40 cm, remarkably similar to that of man, with the four small toes held together and the largest one pointing slightly outwards. The other type is smaller, about 20 cm, and more similar to the footprint of an ape or monkey, with the largest toe evidently pointing outwards.

Zhou Guoxing believes that the ape-like creatures may have evolved from *Meganthropus*, an 'apeman that died out because it lacked sufficient intelligence to adapt to its environment.'

An expedition was launched in 1980 to capture a wildman in the province of Zhejiang. The expedition's first port of call was Zhou Shousong, the biology teacher who had preserved the hands and feet of the wildman killed by Xu Fudi and her comrades some 23 years earlier. The body parts were fortunately still in good condition: the hairy feet were about 7½ inches long, while the hands were some 5½ inches. The scientists came to the conclusion that the relatively small yeren was a primate, perhaps similar to a chimpanzee.

The expedition later accompanied a 60-year-old herb picker into the wooded hills. At an altitude of some 5,000 feet, they discovered a kind of nest, created from branches, leaves and grass, and 'wedged between trees and a rock'. The way that the nest had been constructed indicated great strength on the part of its creators. As the team climbed higher they found another 11 nests in an area called Fengshuyang. Some nests were on the ground, others were built in the trees. Around the nests, the scientists found footprints, droppings and some hair samples. More nests were found in the Nine Dragon Mountains region, as well as some 13-inch footprints. For the scientists the results came as a happy surprise; for the local people the wildman was just a normal part of the region's wildlife. A report from Zhang Qilin of Xikangli Village was typical:

For the past 30 years or more I have gone up to Nine Dragon Mountains every year, in September or October, to guard the maize crop against ape-men.

I saw an ape-man about 10 years ago. It approached from Fengshuyang. It was about as high as a house door and it was covered in reddish-brown hair with long hair falling around its shoulders and over its face. It walked upright.

On another occasion I saw an ape-man lying in a nest in a tree. It was quite relaxed and it clapped its hands when it saw me. Most of the time it just lay there, eating maize. There was a big pile of cobs on the ground.

In October 1994 the Chinese Government demonstrated the seriousness with which they now view the wildman and other rare creatures, by setting up the Committee for the Search of Strange and Rare Creatures. Its members included scientists from the Chinese Academy of Sciences. The committee has already studied eight hair specimens collected from throughout China as well as Tibet. None of these come from either a human source or a known animal source. The samples vary in colour from white, to black to the reddish brown of the so-called 'yeren'.

The committee's 1995 expedition comprised a 30-strong group led by their chairman Professor Yuan Zhengxin. To coincide with the expedition, the Hubei branch of the China Travel Service launched a major marketing exercise by announcing a set of substantial rewards for bounty hunters and evidence seekers; 500,000 yuan was offered for a live wildman (about £37,000 or $68,000), 50,000 yuan for a dead example, and 40,000 yuan for a video recording or photographic evidence. Hair and droppings were priced at a mere 10,000 yuan. Rewards or not, though, the expedition returned to Beijing without any major new evidence.

The lack of new evidence is unlikely to deter further research which has now, with more and more research money behind expeditions, gathered significant momentum. It may not be very long before the world sees an end to this mysterious Chinese puzzle.

ALIEN BIG CATS

The cat family holds a special fascination for the human race. From the times when the sabre-toothed tiger held sway at the top of the food chain, there has always been a respect and fear for the world's most powerful hunters. Their independence and calm self-possession has left its mark on the human psyche. Perhaps for these reasons the cat has been respected and revered by many of the world's pre-eminent cultures and religions. In Ancient Egypt cats were worshipped as goddesses: many hundreds of thousands were mummified as a mark of respect for their place not only in this world, but also in the next. So, when reports appear of 'alien big cats' – big cat species prowling the countryside, or, worse still, appearing in suburbia – it seems to stir distant genetic memories of uncertain times before modern civilization, before the cities engulfed the wilderness.

In the last 40 years sightings of pumas, leopards and other big cats have definitely been on the increase. When farmers find their animals killed, stripped of flesh, disemboweled in ways consistent with the feeding habits of big cats, questions are asked. While the frequency of big-cat sightings has risen in many parts of the world, it is in the UK, particularly since the early 1980s, that the resurgence has threatened to become a metaphorical plague – at least if all the reports are to be believed. There has been a beast of Moray, a Beast of the Isle of Wight, an Earlston Puma, a Welsh Puma, a Chiltern Puma, even a Cuffley Lion.

The beast that really started the alien big cat phenomenon was the 'Surrey Puma' which first broke cover in 1962, and which was most visible in and after 1964. Altogether, from September 1964 to August 1966, the official records show 362 sightings, and there were many more, possibly as many again, claimed but not officially reported. In other words this animal (*Felis concolor* – the puma), declared by American experts to be 'rarely seen by man', was showing itself on average once every two days for a period of two years.

At the time, the Godalming police, based at the epicentre of events, believed that around 50 of the 362 sightings could be considered 'solid'. Yet soon the beast was starting to appear across the whole of southern England, before spreading to the

North and into Scotland. In one week alone it appeared in ten different places.

In the 1980s it was the so called 'Beast of Bodmin' – claimed to roam the wild areas of Exmoor in Devon – that attracted the most attention. The search for the Beast of Bodmin in the far south-west of England provoked a government report after farmers had reported 77 incidences of sighting, livestock kills and injuries in an 18-month period up to June 1995. They believed the events were due to alien big cats (ABCs). When the government report was published on the 19 July 1995 it concluded that there was no verifiable evidence for the big-cat phenomenon, and that there was 'no significant threat' to farmers' livestock. This did not convince many who had experienced first-hand encounters with something very real. A typical reaction came from farmer John Goodenough, aged 66, who had already lost ten ewes and three calves on Common Moor, part of Exmoor. He said that the government report was a farce. He had tripled the number of workers on his farm in order to protect his livestock. 'We are in one hell of a position,' he said, 'because they are breeding fast.'

Five days later three teenagers found the skull of a big cat in the River Fowey, and the media went berserk. An expert from London Zoo examined it and said it came from the panther family, and had been dead about a year. A fully funded expedition was suggested . . .

Two weeks later events took a rather different turn. A second report on the skull from the Natural History Museum revealed a rather different story. The skull was from a young male leopard, possibly from India. Since its death the animal had been kept 'either in a warm country or stored in a building where it was exposed to the attentions of tropical cockroaches'. The back of the cranium had also been cut off – a technique used when a leopard's head was mounted on a leopard skin rug! The source of the skull has yet to come forward.

Nevertheless 1995 brought further reports. One local Cornish sceptic named David Byrne became an overnight believer when he and his wife caught a long, black slender creature in their headlights. 'It was freaky,' he said. 'I was a non-believer until last night.' He returned the next morning to search for paw marks, but none could be found.

Back in Surrey, 'Puma' country, a Winchester police officer named Stephen Challis was called out after a sighting by a pensioner, Walter Clarke. He too saw the black beast in a field. It was about the size of a springer spaniel or fox, but it was black like a domestic cat. He estimated the creature's size at two feet high and three feet long. 'I am convinced it was a large cat.' Mr Clarke agreed: 'It just looked like a very big cat. It wasn't enormous but it was about three or four times the size of a normal cat.'

'Alien Big Cat' (ABC) theories fall into two or three main groups. If the big cats are really *big* cats, then there are two central possibilities: the first is that they are escaped zoo or circus animals that have managed to establish a population, possibly by cross-breeding with the domestic cat, or the wild 'feral' cat. The second, and less likely, explanation is that they are an ancient species that has managed to survive the advances of our technological age. Both theories suffer from a general weakness that a puma, panther or any similar cat needs to eat great quantities of meat to survive (up to one roe deer a day) – and up to now none of the cases that have been examined have shown that the cat in question is really taking deer, sheep or cattle of the required amount.

The third theory is the very simple notion that big-cat sightings are all misidentifications: that the animal is either a large domestic cat, or – in the case of attacks on stock – that the attacker in question is simply a different animal, a dog for instance.

In the UK the Dangerous Animals Act of 1976 outlawed the keeping of certain animals as domestic pets. This has meant that some isolated big cats kept as pets may have been released into the wild by irresponsible owners, but the evidence for genuine populations of the beasts is still scant. Recent breeding experiments in the USA, though, have shown that escaped jungle cats have the ability to breed with domestic cats. The results of these experiments are known as 'chausies' after the Asian jungle cat's Latin name *Felis chaus*. These hybrids are fertile, and capable of mating with either of their parental species. They are also very large: some measure 15 inches to the shoulder, and weigh in at 30 pounds. This discovery has added weight to the side of those who believe that many ABCs are the result of escaped cats breeding with domestic cats.

In the United States sightings of black panthers and lion-like animals are surprisingly common. There are certain areas where the puma is conventionally known to reside – Northern California is a good example. The wilds of Florida are also home to the southern panther. Yet what surprises observers is the increase in sightings of big cats on suburban streets.

In 1994 Lower Michigan developed a panther problem with three or four panthers believed to be stalking the communities of Coloma, Grand Rapids, Manchester and Wixom. The first sightings described the big cat as black with pointed ears. Its tail was some two to three feet long and it appeared to weigh about 100 to 150 pounds. Early attempts to trap the cat failed. On 12 July, Ken St Jean, a loader at a paving company, had a clear view of a beast from a high vantage point:

> I've got a 360-degree view. I happened to be looking straight forward when it ran across the driveway in a slow stance, kind of prancing. I only saw it for six or seven seconds. The cat loped past, made an easy leap over a fence that is nearly eight feet high, if you count the barbed wire at the top, and then it moved on into the woods.

The wildlife authorities in these areas receive reports regularly. They admit that they do not act on them, as they generally do not believe them. Sightings do not tend to involve the taking of animals – unless the data for disappearing pets can be put together. Also, given some 615 reports of panthers between 1983 and 1990, there are still no clear photos of the beasts, nor indeed any skins or skeletons.

In Australia, where the entire fauna has followed a distinct and unique course, the big cat is a stranger notion. The beast that most commonly appears to fill this gap in the popular imagination is the Tasmanian tiger, or *Thylacinus cynocephalus*, which is in fact a marsupial cousin of the kangaroo. Many people claim that the Tasmanian tiger has been extinct since the beginning of the 20th century, but this strange striped beast still attracts sightings. One Australian big cat – which many people thought to be a surviving Tasmanian tiger – was blamed for 340 livestock killings in 1957, and despite large hunting parties was never caught.

Rumours of a 'Queensland tiger' are still regular, and have hotted up since 1995 when a *thylacinus*-like creature started to be reported around the Buderim area. Lance Mesh, a Buderim resident, reported seeing a 'peculiar' animal that was 'goldy, brindly in colour, had a doggish shape and a prominent bump on its head above its eyes'. Mesh was also struck by the animal's markings: black stripes all along its back: 'I could not take my eyes off them.' Cryptozoologist Steve Rushton is a supporter of the Tasmanian tiger theory: 'I don't believe someone is painting stripes on dogs just to fool people. I think they are out there and there are a lot of them.' In August 1995, the *Sunday Mail* newspaper carried a report from a Mr Swaby, who claimed to have had a night-time sighting of a beast chasing two kangaroos across a road:

This incredible sandy-coloured striped animal leapt out from the side of the road a full 15 feet and into the glare of my 100-watt halogen spots and four headlights. It stopped on the road, turned to look at me and fell back onto its huge hindquarters, its large green-yellow eyes glowing in the light, and then it opened its jaws like a crocodile, like a mantrap. It took two steps and then suddenly crouched and sprang again, 15 to 20 feet, this time into the scrub. I was 20 metres away from it and my lights lit up the road and the creature like it was daylight. I could even see its whiskers . . . I drove back home shaking. I am almost six feet tall and about as much again across and not prone to fear, but whatever it was I saw that night had me white and jelly-like.

Mr Swaby supplied a drawing of the animal he, his wife Beryl and two neighbours had seen, as well as a photograph he had taken the morning after the sighting. The photograph showed large paw-prints left by the beast. In the photograph the paw-mark, which is shown alongside an empty 35 mm film canister, measures five inches long and four inches wide:

The animal was four to five feet long and its huge tail was another two to three feet. The stripes started halfway down its back. I thought it was like someone had cut a dingo in half and a 'roo in half and joined them together. Except for those massive teeth and jaws. And it was sleek and healthy looking.

Mr Swaby, keen to establish his status as a credible witness, added that he had not touched a drink for 20 years, nor had he smoked any 'funny weed'. 'On the Thursday following I went to Bundaberg to try to check in the library what it was I'd seen and I found a lithograph of a Tasmanian tiger. There is absolutely no doubt that is what I saw.' Legends tend to grow with age, and some Tasmanian tiger reports have developed lance-like claws and protruding fangs. Nevertheless, with the growing wealth of well-attested encounters, it may only be a matter of time before an example is caught, and one alien big cat crosses from myth into science.

VAMPIRES

The fans, the vampire groupies, love the idea of this androgynous, preternatural figure stalking the night, and craving aesthetic pleasure just as he craves blood, wearing only the best velvet clothes, and savoring red roses.

Anne Rice, the author of *Interview With the Vampire*, captured the appeal of the vampire in describing its modern manifestation, yet, she acknowledges, its source lies deeper: 'It takes us back to primitive times when we worshipped dark gods as well as light gods. And it's a powerful metaphor for the outcast – and monster in all of us.'

The vampire is the ultimate creature of the dark. In our subconscious minds the vampire is epitomized by the cinematic and literary creations of the 20th century – of Count Dracula, blood dripping from his fangs, drinking the venous blood of beautiful virgins, before escaping by transformation into a bat. Yet this wing-flapping image is only a recent creation. The central vampire myth has always focused on the unconsecrated souls of the dead who, though buried, refuse to pass over into the spiritual world. These are lost souls who inhabit their coffin-bound bodies by day, and who nightly leave the grave to steal the very life-force of their helpless victims.

In the Middle Ages, and up until the 16th century, the vampire legend was taken very seriously by many parts of European society – particularly the Church, who argued over the exact causes of vampirism. Some believed that vampires were demons, the devil's emissaries, inhabiting a human disguise. Others held that vampires were the souls of the sinful and dispossessed. Information collected over the centuries helped to identify those most likely to become vampires following their deaths. Suicides, victims of murder and violent death, witches, the excommunicated, the stillborn, those who had not been buried in hallowed ground were all considered dangerous to the living.

When these people died, special precautions were taken to ensure their proper departure to purgatory. In many cultures it became common practice to nail into their coffins the bodies of murderers, suicide victims and those who had been excom-municated from the Church. In Romania a nail was ham-mered through the head of the victim. Also, special objects and powerful foods were buried with the dead: a piece of holy bread, a lemon or the famous clove of garlic – all intended to stop the vampire from returning to the body after its nightly wanderings.

If blood-sucking corpses were believed to be rampaging, graves would be opened to see whether bodies remained strangely intact, still filled with lifeblood from their victims. These bodies would be exhumed, pierced by swords or stakes, decapitated, cut into pieces or burned – whatever it took to expel the vampire's soul. The piercing of the heart was often a key to ending the vampire's occupation of the body. Sometimes this was done with a wooden stake – often made of aspen wood, the wood of Christ's cross. Otherwise a sanctified dagger might be used. If the corpse did not immedi-ately turn to dust – which was considered a possibility – then the head should be decapitated, the rest of the body burned, and the ashes scattered to the four winds.

These practices were by no means the preserve of the Middle Ages. On 5 February 1870, in the Polish town of Kantrzyno, a man named Franz von Poblocki died of con-sumption. He was buried by his family in the churchyard at Roslasin. Within two weeks Poblocki's son Anton died of 'Galoppierende Schwindsucht' – galloping consumption. As Anton's body was being prepared for burial other members of the family started to have symptoms of serious illness, as well as suffering from terrifying nightmares.

When they got together to discuss the situation, the remain-ing members of the family soon came to the conclusion that Franz von Poblocki had become a vampire, and was now trying to claim the souls of the living. The family brought in the local vampire expert, Johann Dzigielski, to deal with the problem quickly and effectively. As a first step, Dzigielski beheaded Anton's corpse before it was buried. He next went to the churchyard with the aim of getting the undertaker to dig up Franz von Poblocki's corpse. The undertaker refused to help the vampire hunter, and told the local priest what was about to happen in his churchyard. The priest, Father Block, wrote to the Poblocki family, insisting that they stop their vampire hunting.

That night, with their blood up, Dzigielski and the Poblocki family took to the churchyard, opened Franz von Poblocki's grave and decapitated him. The next day the law caught up with them. They were put on trial: Dzigielski was sentenced to four months in jail; the Poblocki family, grateful for Dzigielski's help, appealed to a higher court, pleading that their lives had been in danger from their vampire father. They had acted, they claimed, in self-defence. The judges agreed, and on 15 May 1892, all charges against these Polish vampire hunters were dropped.

Where have these myths of vampires come from? Bram Stoker's *Dracula* was published in 1897, and portrayed the caped, toothsome count who came to virgins' windows in the night. Before he wrote the story, Stoker had been strongly influenced by the classic vampire legends that preceded him. He had a fascination with fantasy novels, as well as a strong interest in the occult: he was, in fact, a member of the esoteric Order of the Golden Dawn. These influences were catalysed into a creative form by an encounter with Arminius Vamberry, a professor of Eastern languages at the University of Budapest. It was Vamberry who told Stoker the horrific tale of Vlad Dracul, Vlad son of the dragon, Vlad the Impaler, the character who was to burn into Stoker's mind, and who would form the model for Count Dracula, the vampire who must slake his thirst for human blood.

Vlad the Impaler was born in 1431, a prince of an ancient kingdom now part of Romania. Vlad actually had two surnames: Tepes (the Impaler) and Dracula (Vlad's father's name, meaning 'dragon'). His reputation as a cruel, bloodthirsty tyrant grew from the merciless impalings and dismemberments of tens of thousands of Ottoman enemy prisoners, as well as the murder of many more of his own people. It has often been recounted that Vlad killed solely for his own pleasure.

The German chronicles that record his terrible deeds rank him 'even among the most bloodthirsty tyrants of history, such as Herod, Nero and Diocletian'. History might now add Hitler and Stalin. It is the shared sense of gluttonous self-satisfaction at the death of their many victims that has marked out those who have formed and sustained the vampire legend. For Vlad was not alone.

The trial of Erzebet Bathory in the Hungary of 1611 brought to light the barbaric cruelty of a woman who is believed to have murdered as many as 300 young girls. All the accounts of her atrocities reveal that she drank her victims' blood, and even bathed in it to maintain her youth. In less than ten years her dungeons played host to one of humanity's worst crimes, as dozens of young women were hideously tortured and then bled to death, following the use of sharp needles.

Bathory was only halted when a small army, led by one of her cousins, broke into her castle in the midst of one of her blood orgies. At her trial she was found guilty, but ironically her aristocratic 'blood' saved her from death: her uncle was a Transylvanian prince. Instead she was imprisoned for the rest of her life in a room where doors and windows were closed and no light ever shone.

The castle of Csejthe, where Bathory perpetrated her crimes along with a small band of misfits and black magicians, eventually became the model for Bram Stoker's castle in *Dracula*. There is little doubt too that the terrible acts of Bathory, while not supernatural, formed the basis for much of today's vampire legend.

Even before Countess Bathory, another 'Blood Countess' had terrorized a community with her evil. This French comtesse occupied the Château of Deux-Forts, a castle in the Auvergne region in the 12th century. Her story tells that one night as she was preparing for bed she found a brown spot on her belly. Her servants were ordered to scrub it off, first with cold water, then with hot. When she awoke the next morning the spot was still there. She called her doctor, who, perhaps unwisely in hindsight, told her that the spot was the first sign of leprosy. At this, she grabbed the doctor and advised him, in the most threatening way possible, that if he did not find her a cure she would make sure he was skinned alive. The doctor, for whatever reason, came up with a solution that would prove costly for the local community. He told the comtesse that only one thing would cure her of leprosy: to bathe in human blood.

Within days children from the local region started to disappear. Soon the comtesse had a reputation as a fairy tale ogress who loved to eat children. With her reputation spreading it wasn't too long before the Count of Auvergne had reported the disappearance of children to the king, and the comtesse was brought to trial. The doctor and the servants were hanged, while the comtesse herself was 'quartered' – pulled apart by four horses. The place of her execution is now marked with a cross.

It may seem strange that in the 20th century, a time of such technological progress, that there should have been such a fascination with the vampire legend. Nonetheless the legend seems to have grown in the collective psyche of the Western world. Over 20 major feature films have developed the qualities and powers of the vampire – from the German epic of 1922, *Nosferatu, A Symphony of Horror*, to the 1994 success for Tom Cruise, *Interview With The Vampire*, from the novel by Anne Rice. In 1967 Roman Polanski's spoof, but scary version, *The Fearless Vampire Killers* starred his then wife Sharon Tate, who was to fall victim, only a few years later, to the mass murderer and satanist Charles Manson. The Dracula story has even attracted the talent of Francis Ford Coppola, director of *The Godfather*. His 1992 film *Bram Stoker's Dracula*, starring Gary Oldman, inspired a new fervour in vampire admirers the world over.

In these films the heroes have pitted their goodness against the temptation of Dracula's darkness. The vampire hunters, often Christian, have seen the powers of light stretched to their limits, in order to overcome the darkest threats to life itself. These films have spawned new fans and fanatics – those who take the legend very seriously, and even believe themselves to be un-dead creatures of the night.

In 1995 journalist Chris Webb, from the UK's *Encounters* magazine, arranged a meeting with a group calling themselves the Vetala. The eight members of the clan appeared to be convinced that they were actually vampires.

They left me with no doubt in my mind that I had witnessed the closest thing we have in this country to a conventional vampire – people who seek out human or animal blood for consumption. I witnessed the drinking of blood from two sources, blood kept in bottles and the blood from a live animal. Whether the former was taken without the owner's permission I wouldn't like to say. I watched intently as a female from the troupe produced a single silver chalice which was bent out of shape and well worn, I suppose it may have all been an act for my benefit, but they had insisted that I not take any pictures of their faces. I cannot see how they could get any attention if they weren't prepared to be seen. Up to this point I was convincing myself they were good actors or role-players, showing me up to be a gullible reporter.

The blood they gulped so fervently could have easily belonged to a special effects kit, which I certainly hoped was the case. What they did next was more than enough to turn the situation from strange to macabre. They brought a live pheasant from a box in their van . . . and took turns to bite its neck and drink its blood.

Webb went on to interview the self-proclaimed vampire:

Why do you drink blood? What does it offer you?
Blood is the life that flows through the bodies of all animals. By stealing life from others we revitalise our own, we become

155

stronger and more powerful with every drop of blood we consume.

Do you ever forcibly take blood from humans?

Human blood is the most potent of all. Sometimes it is necessary to take human blood to be sure of survival and immortality.

So you attack other humans?

I am no more human than the pheasant who sacrificed itself to us this evening. We are not murderers, Mr Webb, we never kill those we steal from. We have the power to take life, but that makes us no more dangerous than any human or animal on the planet. Show me a human that lacks the strength or skill to kill another and I will show you a vampire who lacks the same.

You think the animal sacrificed itself to you? Did it not have the right to live?

Just as humans are placed higher than animals on the food chain, we vampires are placed above humans. Just be glad that we are restrained enough not to attack and kill you as well.

Is that a threat?

Hardly, I was speaking metaphorically. The days of slaughtering people in their sleep have long since passed. We would not survive long if we took so much as a single life. We can provide sufficient sustenance from animals and the occasional quick drink from a willing human.

So what you're saying is the only reason you don't kill humans is because you'd never get away with it?

Roughly speaking, yes. None of us have ever taken a human life, and we hope that none of us ever will. We move around the country a great deal, it is dangerous for us to stay in the same place too long.

A new phenomenon in the vampire repertoire emerged with terrifying results in March 1995. Residents of Orocovis and Morovis – two Puerto Rican municipalities – began to discover the corpses of animals which appeared to have died in an apparently unique way. Goats, chickens, rabbits: they had all succumbed to the unknown killer which sucked all the blood from their veins – usually through a single puncture mark. Soon the mysterious killer had been given a name: *chupacabra*, which translates literally from the Spanish as 'goatsucker'.

Six months into the epidemic of slayings, the first eye-witness descriptions began to appear. Around 15 residents of Canovanas – a city to the east of Puerto Rico's capital San Juan – claim to have had close encounters with the beast. Typical is the description offered by 25-year-old college student Michael Negron:

> I was looking off the balcony one night, and I saw it step out of a bright light in the back yard. It was about three or four feet tall with skin like that of a dinosaur. It had bright red eyes the size of hen's eggs, long fangs and multi-coloured spikes down its head and back.

The strange beast then disembowelled the Negron family's goat, and drained the blood from its neck. Other descriptions have likened it to an alien-looking kangaroo.

In 1996 the phenomenon migrated to the Hispanic communities of Miami with as many as 50 animals found with the tell-tale puncture marks. This prompted sceptics to theorize that the *chupacabra*'s origins lay in the myths and beliefs of the Hispanic religious tradition of evil spirits. Other theorists have put the animal killings down to cult activity or other religious rituals. Nevertheless the eye witnesses keep coming forward. When six animals were found dead in south Florida, the woman owner claimed to have seen two beasts fly down out of the sky. She described the beast as having large black eyes, prominent fangs, a huge pair of wings and a row of thorn-like spines all the way down its back and tail. At the end of the tail was a kind of hook with which the beast grabbed her animals before sucking the blood from their helpless bodies.

Meanwhile back in Puerto Rico the mayor of Canovanas has vowed to rid the city of the troublesome *chupacabra*.

Chemo 'Jones' Soto, who models himself on Indiana Jones, has assembled a crack team of *chupacabra* hunters. Chemo has prepared himself for the possibility that the *chupacabra* is a vampire: he carries a 12-inch crucifix, and breathes a killer dose of garlic, after extensive overeating of the protective vegetable. He carries a further weapon, with which he expects to deliver the final blow: a water pistol filled with holy water.

WEREWOLVES

The werewolf – the transformation of a man or woman into a wolf – has a history that reaches back as far as Ancient Greece and beyond. Paulus Aegineta, writing in 7th-century Alexandria, was the first practitioner to describe the medical condition of 'melancholic lycanthropy'. Sufferers were said to have ulcerated legs from moving about on four legs; they were drawn to wander the night howling until daybreak. The illness was believed to be caused by an excess of black bile, one of the four elements in the body, an ailment also known as melancholy.

The werewolf featured in the legends of the Romans, and accounts of people transformed into wolves appear in Virgil, Petronius and Ovid. Herodotus wrote of the 'Neuri' people that '[they] are sorcerers, if one is to believe the Scythians . . . for each Neurian changes himself, once in the year, into the form of a wolf, and he continues in that form for several days, after which he resumes his former shape.' In Norwegian and Icelandic cultures, it was said of certain people that they were 'not of one skin' – originally a pagan idea that they could take on the form and nature of any being they chose: 'if he has taken the form of a wolf, or if he goes on a wolf's ride, he is full of the rage and malignity of the creatures whose powers and passions he has assumed.' In early Christian times it was said that Saint Patrick changed Vereticus, King of Wales, into a wolf. Saint Natalis, another Christian saint, pronounced an 'anathema', a kind of justifiable curse, on a family in Ireland, with the result that each one of them took the form of a wolf for seven years, and was forced to live in the forests, howling mournfully and feeding on the peasants' sheep.

In the popular imagination, werewolves are inextricably linked to the world of the un-dead – the souls of those poor, or sinful souls, whose bodies did not decompose, and who would leave their tombs to go rampaging at night. Through-out the Europe of the Middle Ages, these wandering souls were often called *vrykolakas*, which means 'werewolf' in the Slavonic language. *Vrykolaka* usually referred to a person who had not been buried in consecrated ground for whatever reason – he may have been excommunicated by the Church for some crime, or he may even have committed suicide.

By the 16th century *vrykolaka* was used throughout Eastern Europe to mean the living dead as well as the bloodthirsty werewolf. The level of concern about the phenomenon within the Roman Catholic Church was so high that for 200 years an investigation continued: during this time around 30,000 cases of humans adopting the forms of wolves – classic 'lycanthropy' – surfaced.

One of the most shocking stories of a convicted werewolf is that of the 16th-century German Peter Stubbe. We know of Peter Stubbe's story from a report translated by George Bores in the London Chapbook of 1590. The introduction sets the tone:

A true Discourse
Declaring the damnable life and death of one Stubbe Peeter, a
most
wicked sorcerer, who in the likeness of a
Wolf committed many murders, continuing this
devilish practice 25 Years, killing and devouring Men, Women, and
Children.
Who for the same fact was taken and executed the 31st October

last past in the town of Bedbur (Bedburg)
near the City of Collin (Cologne)
in Germany

The report goes on to describe how Stubbe fell to the terrible acts he was to be remembered for:

> In the towns of Cperadt and Bedbur near Collin in high Germany, there was continually brought up and nourished one Stubbe Peeter, who from his youth was greatly inclined to evil and practising of wicked arts even from twelve years of age till twenty, and so forwards till his dying day, insomuch that surfeiting in the damnable desire of magic, necromancy, and sorcery, acquainting himself with many infernal spirits and fiends, insomuch that forgetting the God that made him, and that Savior that shed his blood for man's redemption.

At his trial he was convicted of a series of terrible murders, and acts of cruelty and immorality. It was said that he made a pact with the devil in which he was given a wolf-skin belt, which he only need wear to transform himself into a blood-thirsty wolf:

> The Devil, who saw him a fit instrument to perform mischief as a wicked fiend pleased with the desire of wrong and destruction, gave unto him a girdle which, being put around him, he was straight transformed into the likeness of a greedy, devouring wolf, strong and mighty, with eyes great and large, which in the night sparkled like unto brands of fire, a mouth great and wide, with most sharp and cruel teeth, a huge body and mighty paws. And no sooner should he put off the same girdle, but presently he should appear in his former shape, according to the proportion of a man, as if he had never been changed.
> ... Yea, often it came to pass that as he walked abroad in the fields, if he chanced to spy a company of maidens playing together or else a milking their kine, in his wolfish shape he

160

would incontinent run among them, and while the rest escaped by flight, he would be sure to lay hold of one, and after his filthy lust fulfilled, he would murder her presently ... and so much he had practised this wickedness that the whole province was feared by the cruelty of this bloody and devouring wolf.

For 25 years Stubbe roamed the area around Cologne, killing and eating cattle and sheep, murdering, raping and even eating women and young girls. His own family did not escape his immorality: he is said to have sodomized his daughter and his sister, and violated and killed his own son before eating his brains. Stubbe was apparently captured as he turned himself back into human form – throwing away his wolf-pelt, which was never found. He was tortured on the rack and confessed – as most victims of the rack eventually did – to the crimes he was accused of: 16 murders and his pact with the devil. Convicted of his crimes, his end was to be as violent as the murders he had supposedly committed:

> Stubbe Peeter as principal malefactor, was judged first to have his body laid on a wheel, and with red hot burning pincers in ten several places to have the flesh pulled off from the bones, after that, his legs and arms to be broken with a wooden ax or hatchet, afterwards to have his head struck from his body, then to have his carcass burned to ashes.

On 31 October 1589, the sentence was carried out, along with the burning of his daughter and 'gossip' (mistress) who had, it was claimed, been accessories to the terrible crimes. After the execution

> ... there was by the advice of the magistrates of the town of Bedbur a high pole set up and strongly framed, which first went through the wheel whereon he was broken, whereunto also it was fastened; after that a little above the wheel the likeness of a wolf was framed in wood, to show unto all men the shape wherein he executed those cruelties. Over that on

the top of the stake the sorceror's head itself was set up, and round about the wheel there was hung as it were sixteen pieces of wood about a yard in length with represented the sixteen persons that was perfectly known to be murdered by him.

Another classic case of lycanthropy was recorded by folklorist Sabine Baring-Gould in the 19th century. The story tells of the late-16th-century French werewolf Jean Grenier:

Jean Grenier was the son of a poor labourer in the village of S. Antoine de Pizon ... The story he related of himself before the court was as follows:

'When I was ten or eleven years old, my neighbour, Duthillaire, introduced me, in the depths of the forest to a M. de la Forest, a black man, who signed me with his nail, and then gave to me and Duthillaire a salve and a wolf-skin. From that time I have run about as a wolf.'

... In the parish of S. Antoine de Pizon he had attacked a little girl, as she was keeping sheep. She was dressed in a black frock; he did not know her name. He tore her with his nails and teeth, and ate her ... Jean said that he had the wolf-skin in his possession, and that he went out hunting for children, at the command of his master, the Lord of the Forest. Before transformation he smeared himself with the salve, which he preserved in a small pot, and hid his clothes in the thicket.

He usually ran his courses from one or two hours in the day, when the moon was at its wane, but very often he made his expeditions at night. On one occasion he had accompanied Duthillaire, but they had killed no one ... he added that the Lord of the Forest had strictly forbidden him to bite the thumbnail of his left hand, which nail was thicker and longer than the others, and had warned him never to lose sight of it, as long as he was in his were-wolf disguise.

In 1603 Jean Grenier was tried as werewolf, found guilty and sentenced to the, then lenient, term of life imprisonment. He died in prison seven years later.

Over the next two or three centuries werewolf trials in Europe continued, often ending in the execution or imprisonment of the supposedly guilty parties. Lycanthropy was seen to be the result of sin, witchcraft, or a pack with dark forces, but modern theories have focused on medical explanations. One medical source for the belief in 'wolf people' may stem from the kind of genetic disorders which cause excessive facial hair – in both men and women. A classic East European case was that of Petrus Gonsalvus whose excess of hair led to his being nicknamed 'the wolf-man of Bavaria'. A portrait of Gonsalvus' daughter, her face covered with furry hair, was even presented to the King of Bohemia by William Duke of Bavaria.

With cases of lycanthropy, there is often a confusion about the extent of the transformation. Legends focus on the 'shape-shifting' transformation of man into wolf. In some cases, however, there is simply the belief, or self-delusion that a person is becoming a wolf. In recent years science has shown us that there may be real, chemical reasons behind the idea of lycanthropy as self-delusion.

It has been discovered that a particular fungus, known as 'ergot' fungus, or *claviceps*, can induce delusions of wolf-identity, and can even produce wolf-like behaviour: howling, uncontrollable rage, salivation and running around on four legs. Some experts now believe that grain contaminated with the ergot fungus could have been responsible for a number of mass outbreaks of lycanthropy. One well-documented outbreak of mass lycanthropy took place in Devon, England, during the 12th century. Gervase of Tilbury, writing in his 1212 *Otia Imperialia* described the 1195 event: 'frequently . . . men in England transformed into wolves for the space of a month.'

The most recently recorded outbreak of mass attacks dates from about 1700. A Dr Friend reported that many villages close to Exmoor in Devon '. . . were taken with frequent barking and howling like wolves and foaming at the mouth.'

Even in the 20th century, cases of lycanthropy, still persist, with patients insisting that they turn into wolves under certain conditions. A British man committed suicide because he believed he was becoming a wolf. In another case a US Army soldier became convinced he was a werewolf after taking LSD and strychnine while in a German forest. He believed that hair appeared on his hands and face, and was overcome by a strong desire to eat live rabbits. LSD is, in fact, chemically very close to the active ingredient in the ergot fungus – providing some confirmation of the theory that drug-induced illusions may have formed the basis for historical cases of lycanthropy.

ZOMBIES

Battalions of 'zombies' have been formed in Haiti – to halt the threat of an American invasion. The military junta claims to have created a force of men once dead, but brought back to half-life to serve voodoo priests.

So ran a 1994 story in Britain's *Daily Mail* newspaper, just prior to the American military invasion of Haiti. The original sources of this story obviously hoped that an idea such as this would strike fear into the American forces. It may, however, only have reinforced the fears of the native Haitians, whose belief in the power of voodoo is literally a matter of life and death.

Voodoo, like many religions, is organized around a group of powerful priests – priests who have powers which can be used either to help or threaten the 'non-priests', the ordinary people who follow their leaders. On Haiti these powerful priests – known as 'houngans' or 'bokers' – are believed to be able to raise the dead. The houngan steals the person's soul, only to reanimate the corpse as his mindless slave – the zombie. Ordinary people in Haiti live in fear that the bodies and souls of their departed relatives will be stolen from their graves. They take special precautions to avert this terrible possibility, such as weighting the coffin lid with a large rock, waiting over the grave until putrefaction sets in, or providing the departed soul with beads and string to help it resist the calls of the priest.

In 1930, French anthropologist Georges de Rouquet had the dubious privilege of meeting four zombies. De Rouquet recorded the encounter in his journal:

Toward evening we encountered a group of four male figures coming from the nearby cotton field where they had been toiling. I was struck by their peculiar shambling gait, most unlike the lithe walk of other natives. The overseer with them stopped their progress, enabling me to observe them closely for some minutes. They were clothed in rags made from sacking. Their arms hung down by their sides, dangling in a curiously lifeless fashion. Their faces and hands appeared devoid of flesh, the skin adhering to the bones like wrinkled brown parchment. I also noticed that they did not sweat, although they had been working and the sun was still very hot. I was unable to judge even their approximate ages. They may have been young men or quite elderly. The most arresting feature about them was their gaze. They all stared straight ahead, their eyes dull and unfocused as if blind. They did not show a spark of awareness of my presence, even when I approached them closely. To test the reflexes of one I made a stabbing gesture toward his eyes with my pointed fingers. He did not blink or shrink back. But when I attempted to touch his hand the overseer prevented me, saying this was not permitted.

My immediate impression was that these creatures were imbeciles made to work for their keep. Baptiste [the guide], however, assured me that they were indeed the zombies; that is dead persons resurrected by sorcery and employed as unpaid labourers.

De Rouquet then looked on as the four zombies were locked away in a dark shed without any windows. When he suggested to Baptiste, his guide, that they go and investigate the prison, Baptiste became frightened and suggested very firmly that they leave.

Alfred Métraux was another French anthropologist who made a detailed study of the zombie phenomenon. When he first went to Haiti, Métraux had been very sceptical of the evidence for zombies, particularly when one supposed zombie turned out simply to be a mentally retarded woman. A number of cases, however, impressed him: the first was the very sad story of a young betrothed woman who had died a few days after refusing the unwelcome advances of a houngan. Her family prepared for the funeral, but found that they had, unfortunately, ordered a coffin too small for their daughter's body. In order to make her body fit it was necessary to twist her neck. At the wake someone dropped a cigarette onto the girl's foot, leaving a small burn mark. Eventually she was buried, and mourned.

A few months later reports started to circulate that the girl had been seen alive with the houngan she had rejected. The family searched for confirmation, but no more was discovered. Then, after some years had passed, the girl arrived back at her home. Apparently the houngan had been seized with an attack of conscience and had released all his zombies. Members of the girl's family positively identified their daughter, remarking on her bent neck, and a small burn mark on her foot.

Generally it is the poorer people of Haiti who take voodoo most seriously: members of the educated classes tend to look down on voodoo sorcery and the existence of zombies as ancient superstition. Alfred Métraux, however, told a story of an educated 'Monsieur' who may not have taken as much care with voodoo as he should. The man was driving near a small village when his tyre got a puncture. Getting out of his car he looked for help from a local villager. He was met by an old white-haired man, who offered him coffee at his house while the tyre was mended. The white-haired man confessed to the 'Monsieur' that he was, in fact, a houngan sorcerer, that he had caused the flat tyre with a spell, and that his car contained an evil charm, known as a *wanga*. When the Monsieur started to dismiss these ideas with suspicious amusement, the houngan became angry: 'Had the visitor known a Monsieur Celestin?' 'Why, yes. Monsieur Celestin had died only six months before,' the visitor confirmed. 'Would the Monsieur like to see Celestin?' the houngan asked. The houngan suddenly cracked his whip six times, and in immediate response a man entered the room, shuffling backwards. When the houngan commanded, the figure turned to face the visiting Monsieur. It was his old friend Celestin – but not the man he had known. The previously lively gentleman was now a limp shadow of his former self – expressionless eyes, head hung down, and seemingly devoid of all emotion or humanity. The Monsieur was now in shock.

The houngan told the Monsieur that Celestin had been 'killed' by a sorcerer who had then turned him into a zombie. The houngan had bought him for $12.

The fact that Métraux heard this report is, presumably, confirmation that the Monsieur did get his flat tyre fixed.

Zombies are conventionally thought of, by voodoo believers, as 'reanimated' people – captured, body and soul, from their graves before the spirit can pass over to the 'other side'. The voodoo sorcerer's aim is to build up an army of zombies to do his work, or be sold on to others for a profit. These mechanical slaves may serve to make the zombie master rich, working his plantation from dawn to dusk for no money, and, some believe, for no food either.

The most popular theory to explain zombies has a basis in medicine rather than sorcery. Ethnobiologist Wade Davis has suggested that a deep coma can be brought about by certain poisons found in the puffer fish and a particular kind of toad. While some medical doctors may recognize the symptoms of such poisons, there may be some voodoo followers who do not. In these cases people may be buried 'alive' only to be 'resurrected' by the bokor with an antidote some days later. The side effects of the drugs may well cause an appearance of 'zombification', which may indeed be permanent, or may possibly require the victim to be continuously sedated by the zombie masters.

One of the most convincing cases of zombification points to an explanation of this kind. On 30 April 1962, Clairvius Narcisse was taken to the Albert Schweitzer Memorial Hospital in Deschabelle, Haiti, with a high fever. Over the next day or two his condition deteriorated, and on 2 May, with his sister Angelina at his bedside, he was declared dead. The following day he was buried close to L'Estere, his family's home village.

Eighteen years later a man approached Angelina in the local marketplace, claiming to be Clairvius Narcisse. Angelina was unsure whether to believe him, even when he told the story of his life as a zombie:

> [In the hospital] I couldn't get enough air in my lungs. My heart was running out of strength. My stomach was burning.
> Then I felt myself freeze up. I heard the doctor tell my sister, 'I'm sorry he's dead.' I wanted to cry out, to tell her that I was alive, but I was unable to move.

When his relatives and friends came to pay their last respects, Narcisse said that he could see them and hear them, but he felt nothing, and could do nothing about his predicament. After his burial the next thing he could remember was when he was standing next to his grave in a zombified state. Two men covered his grave over, tied him by the wrists, and took him to a farm where he was kept as a slave worker with around a hundred others.

Narcisse claimed that he had been kept enslaved for two years until their slavemaster failed to keep his captives properly drugged. A number of the zombies – including Narcisse – returned to full consciousness, attacked and killed their slavemaster and escaped. Though free, Narcisse decided not to return to his family village: he believed that his brother had organized his zombification with the help of a voodoo sorcerer. When he finally heard in 1980 that his brother had died he felt safe to make his reappearance to the friends and relatives who thought they had mourned his loss 18 years before. To confirm his identity Narcisse was subjected to a number of tests and questions: by the end of them, more than 200 residents of l'Estere, including his sister Angelina, declared their conviction that he was indeed the man they had buried in 1962.

Voodoo is taken so seriously in Haiti, that there is even a law against creating zombies:

> Also shall be qualified as attempted murder the employment which may be made against any person of substances which, without causing actual death, produce a lethargic coma more or less prolonged. If, after the administering of such substances, the person has been buried, the act shall be considered murder no matter what result follows.

Despite the legislation, however, a report from 1959 shows how the law has not always been able to stand up to the power of voodoo. When a zombie arrived in a village one day he was tied by the hands and taken to the police station. He claimed he had an aunt in the village, and, indeed the woman identified him as the nephew she had buried some four years before. He told the police that he was only one of many zombies working for a houngan. The police were so scared of this local houngan that they immediately offered to return the zombie. But he died two days later, killed, it was presumed, by the sorcerer's powers. Now the police decided to act – arresting the houngan for the murder of the zombie. The police were not able to free the other zombies though: the houngan's wife had escaped with them all and taken them with her into the hills.

Haiti's interweaving of voodoo and legal power became institutionalized with the rise of Francois 'Papa Doc' Duvalier. Duvalier came to power in 1957 with the proclaimed intention of rehabilitating voodoo as both the political and spiritual heart of the Haitian people. He claimed to defend the black, African roots of the former slave culture which had been oppressed by the Catholic Church for nearly 300 years. Yet Papa Doc brought his own form of ruthless dictatorship which was to make slaves of the Haitian people: he had soon taken control of many voodoo networks, which he then used as a secret police force, modelled on the Nazis. These violent bands – called the Tonton-macoutes – embarked on a reign of terror intended to wipe out all opposition. Using the methods of voodoo, Duvalier wielded a combination of threat and propaganda to bring the entire nation under his power.

By 1986 Papa Doc had passed the reins of power to his son Jean-Claude 'Baby Doc' Duvalier. On 7 February, however, a raging mob of ordinary Haitian people reclaimed their country from the Duvalier tyranny, and started to dismantle the regime's terrible legacy. Voodoo priests who had worked for the Duvaliers were killed or imprisoned. By 1987 a new constitution was ratified which gave a freer reign to the practice of the authentic African voodoo.

Today reports still emerge of zombies appearing many years after the death of the person they claim to be. Some of these have no basis in truth, and may simply be an attempt to take advantage of a family's grief. For others though, the stories they have to tell may yet convince many that zombies are not simply the invention of 1950s B-movies.

ANGELS

What idea is more beguiling than the notion of lightsome spirits, free of time and space and human weakness, hovering between us and all harm? To believe in angels is to allow the universe to be at once mysterious and benign. Even people who refuse to believe in them may long to be proved wrong.

According to a *Time* magazine headline from 1993, 69 per cent of Americans believe in angels. More recently, research has put the figure as high as 90 per cent. In a supposedly secular world, this level of belief in the supernatural force of angels may seem extraordinary, yet perhaps more remarkable is the number of people worldwide who are openly reporting angel encounters. Some reports describe the huge winged figures of biblical angelology, while others are reported as 'modern' angels: contemporary characters in modern clothing, who may appear in times of trouble, only to disappear just as mysteriously. Other angels may only make their presence felt through a disembodied, or even an 'internal' voice which provides guidance and comfort in times of need.

In December 1991, 76-year-old Norah Threader was in Manchester Royal Infirmary, in the UK. She was waiting to have a major operation, a procedure which she feared might bring her death:

> An eight-foot-tall angel appeared in the hospital room, with beautiful ash blond hair. In his right hand he held a huge sword, which he wielded from left to right, as if it weighed no more than a feather. It was an enormous sword with a round guard on the handle. I think he was St Michael. His wings were beautiful, like the softest down, cream coloured, edged with apricot. He opened his wings slightly and closed them around me, sheltering me from all the evils of the world and I knew I was safe. He had the most beautiful face I have ever seen, but he was not at all feminine. He was totally masculine and there was such strength about him.

The effect of Norah Threader's angelic encounter was dramatic. Her daughter, Catherine, says it changed Norah's life forever: instead of being anxious she was joyful. Even though she was not well, and knew, deep down, that she was dying, Norah told her daughter that she was happier than she had ever been in her life. She died four months later, in a peaceful, happy state. Her daughter remembers: 'I was privileged to be with her when she died – she smiled.'

*

Martin Israel, who leads religious retreats, records many angel encounters in his book *Angels: Messengers of Grace*. He questions the reason why the popular image of the angel has been so consistent:

> A frequent visual form of an angel is that of a tall being with a human face, well over six feet tall, which may envelop a person or else stand a little distance away from them. There is a distinctive aura of light around the angel, and it seems to act as a protective presence, particularly when peril is sensed as being afoot. Sometimes there is no personification, but simply a focus of light. Usually there are the characteristic wings so well depicted in medieval and renaissance Christian painting, but these are usually additions that have been conjured up by the mind of the beholder. This brings us to the important point as to whether angels are as they appear to us because they really look like this, or because our minds have translated the formless, non-material nature of an angel into a form that we can recognise and communicate with in confidence.
>
> ... I was somewhat amused recently when a lady who had attended one of my retreats told a friend that she had seen just such a winged angle alongside me as I spoke inspirationally ...
>
> Angels can assume forms other than the classical winged apparition. Among the most convincing are angels that appear as completely human, sometimes as personable young men aiding stranded motorists in appalling weather conditions or helping people in near danger of drowning. Sometimes they avert apparently inevitable traffic accidents. On the other hand, the appearance may be that of an older man who guides strangers to an unknown destination. The essential features of all these encounters is the sudden disappearance once the work has been done. One may look around wanting to thank or pay the helpful stranger, only to find nobody there.

One story of 'ordinary angels' was recorded by Robert J. Grant, in his book *Are We Listening to Angels?* An American woman named Marie Utterman, from Richmond, Virginia, was on her way to visit her daugher Jenny who was due to give birth in a few weeks time. Marie had been feeling anxious about her daughter all morning and had decided to visit her even though the telephone answer machine indicated she was out. Unfortunately today was the day that her car's transmission chose to give out as shc travelled the 50 or so miles down the Interstate highway. She pulled the dying car over to the side of the road feeling very lost and worried. She prayed for help to start the car. To no avail: it needed to be repaired, just as her garage had warned her it would. If only she had done something before. Just then a white van pulled up and three handsome young men jumped out dressed in white windbreakers and white trousers:

'*Maybe they're interns at the hospital,*' Marie thought as she rolled her window down. The blond man smiled reassuringly at Marie. 'Ma'am, if you'll step out of the car, we'll see if we can get it going again.' Marie didn't hesitate. 'I can't begin to thank you,' she said, stepping out of the car. 'I've got to get to my daughter. She's going to have a baby, and . . .'

Marie told her story as the three men pulled tool-box and hydraulic jack from the back of the van. The car jack was shining and new. They smiled at Marie and nodded as she cxplained her dilemma. They didn't hesitate in beginning their work . . . *Why, they'll get grease all over their clothes*, Marie thought.

After five minutes of careful, almost surgeon-like work on the car, one of them tried the ignition – it started perfectly. Marie could not thank them enough. They refused her offer of a 50 dollar bill, saying it was what they were there for. It was at this point that she noticed something very strange: their pristine white clothes were still white – even after rolling around under the car, and checking under the hood. One of the men then suggested, perhaps a little hastily, that she had better get on her way to her daughter. The van sped off up the hill. It didn't even reach the horizon, for in Marie Utterman's description it simply vanished.

When Marie arrived at her daughter's home she found Jenny sitting in a pool of blood – she had haemorrhaged, and her blood pressure was close to critical. Fortunately with good medical care both baby and new mother came through fine. But not, in Marie Utterman's mind at least, without the help of her guardian angel mechanics.

Kelsey Tyler's book *There's an Angel on Your Shoulder* describes 22 accounts of angel encounters in contemporary America – all describing a modern belief that angels are just as likely to appear in the guise of an ordinary person or child, as they are with wings and shining light. Tyler says that 'often the percipients only reflect on the divine origin of their helpers, guides and confidants with hindsight.' One story describes a depressed woman who was grieving for her recently deceased father, when he appeared to her, and comforted her. She did not take this to be his departed spirit, but rather an angel who had taken his form. Another case described a child who flagged down a passing motorist and appealed to the driver for help for a crashed school bus. When the driver was helping to recover the injured he discovered the body of a child – the very boy who had stopped him on the road.

Whether these are stories of angels or of some other manifestation is obviously hard to discern: many angelologists claim that the signature of angels is that they always leave a sense of peace and joy when they depart. The same is not always said about the presence of spirits of the dead or 'loved ones in spirit' as they are often called by mediums. From early times the mystics of the Catholic Church taught that every human is possessed of an angel who guides and guards the individual soul. The great medieval mystic Bernard of Clairveaux gave some advice to his monks on the Guardian Angel and on its power for good in their lives:

In whatever place you may be, in whatever secret recess you may hide, think of your Guardian Angel ... If we truly love our Guardian Angel, we cannot fail to have boundless confidence in his powerful intercession with God and firm faith in his willingness to help us ... Many of the saints made it a practice never to undertake anything without first seeking the advice of their Guardain Angel.

Modern-day guitarist and composer Carlos Santana attributes his creativity and success to the inspiration of the angelic realms and, particularly, to his guardian angels. Interviewed by the author Terry Lynn Taylor, Santana told of one particular experience that left an enduring mark on him. The singer Julio Iglesias had requested permission to record a version of 'Europa', one of Santana's songs, and to have Santana play on the record. Santana, sensing a huge difference in their musical approaches, had declined the invitation: 'I am a street guy. I just don't get along with the system ... I'm still a hippie . . .'

That evening Santana was preparing to play tennis. He threw the ball into the air and it disappeared. A voice then asked him: 'Who gave you this song?' Santana, who already acknowledged the influence of the angels in his music, had to admit that the angel *had* given him the song. Santana asked the voice what it wanted done with the song. 'I want you to record the song with Julio, and all the money that you get from it, I want you to pledge it to the children of Tijuana. You don't need it.'

Santana did as he was told and recorded the song with Iglesias. He claimed his life was changed that day. 'To me, it is all a lesson in humility. I have to be wise and follow the voice. It has got me this far.'

Many people who experience angel encounters report that the angel has appeared in response to a prayer, or at a time of great stress or great need. Perhaps the most famous stories of angels appearing as saviours in a time of great need have emerged from the tragedy of wartime.

In 1914 the Belgian, French and British forces were being swept out of Belgium by a powerful and merciless assault by a large German force. The British forces were taking the main brunt of a wide German front, and, since they were seriously outnumbered, it seemed that defeat and annihilation were inevitable. At home in Britain, the churches had been filled with people, called to a National Day of Prayer, even though many of them knew the likely outcome. The newspapers had already announced the destruction of the British force at Mons.

Yet events were to transpire, which would be remembered and discussed for many decades. The many descriptions are not necessarily consistent: indeed there seem to be two sets of events described. The first set of reports say that the angelic form of Saint George, the patron saint of England, appeared with an army of 'bowmen' – as if from the medieval battle of Agincourt. This report was later enshrined in a story by Arthur Machen, called *The Bowmen*, and at first Machen claimed that the story was purely fiction. However, a report had appeared in April 1915 in the Roman Catholic newspaper *The Universe*, of just such an encounter. Its writer was a soldier, a Catholic officer, who told the story in simple but moving words:

> A party of about thirty men was cut off in a trench, when the officer said to his men, 'Look here, we must either stay here and be caught like rats in a trap, or make a sortie against the enemy. We haven't much of a chance, but personally I don't want to be caught here.' The men all agreed with him, and with a yell of 'St George for England!' they dashed out into the open. The officer tells how, as they ran on, he became aware of a large company of men with bows and arrows going along with them, and even leading them on against the enemy's trenches, and afterwards when he was talking to a German prisoner, the man asked him who was the officer on a great

176

white horse who led them, for although he was such a conspicuous figure, they had none of them been able to hit him. I must also add that the German dead appeared to have no wounds on them. The officer who told the story was a friend of ours. He did not see St George on the white horse, but he saw the archers with his own eyes.

A captured German soldier reported that his army had to retreat when a large army of white clothed figures, armed with bows and arrows, appeared, led by an officer on a white horse. They had fired on the officer, but nothing had stopped him.

Another story emerging from the battle was quite different. Instead of Saint George and the bowmen, several officers and men had reported that a group of angels had stood between the British and German forces:

The British expected annihilation, as we were almost helpless, when to our amazement the Germans stood like dazed men, never so much as touched their guns, nor stirred till we had turned round and escaped by some cross-roads. One man said he saw 'a troop of angels' between us and the enemy. He has been a changed man ever since. Another man was asked if he had heard the wonderful stories of angels. He said he had SEEN them himself. When he and his company were retreating, they heard the German cavalry tearing after them. They saw a place where they thought a stand might be made, with sure hope of safety; but before they could reach it, the German cavalry were upon them. They therefore turned round and faced the enemy, expecting nothing but instant death, when to their wonder they saw, between them and the enemy, a whole troop of angels. The German horses turned round terrified and regularly stampeded. The men tugged at their bridles, while the poor beasts tore away in every direction from our men.

Other soldiers reported seeing the figures of Joan of Arc, Saint Michael the Archangel and Saint George the patron saint of England. A number of British soldiers sat and watched for half an hour as the three huge celestial figures hovered in the sky, Saint Michael apparently protecting them with out-stretched wings. Eighty years on, the full truth is hard to investigate with any clarity, yet the sheer number of individual accounts, albeit that they vary in what they describe, offer many researchers some convincing evidence for the intervention of angels at Mons.

Hope Price is a British woman who trained as a nurse and a health visitor before embarking on missionary work in Africa. As a Christian she knew of the Mons incident, and of other reported angelic appearances which went back to biblical times. In the early 1990s the question of whether angels still existed arose in conversation, and soon she found the topic occurring in many separate and unconnected conversations. A meeting with a publisher convinced her that perhaps she might be the person to bring together a book on the subject, despite her lack of writing experience. She placed adverts in papers and magazines: 'Have you seen an angel?' was the simple question.

In the next year or so she received thousands of accounts of angelic encounters. She was overwhelmed, but also inspired, by the torrent of stories, often told for the first time. Certain factors characterized the accounts: they were nearly always 'one-off' experiences that had never been repeated; they had left a mark on the person that meant the experience was as fresh as the day it had occurred; and that the people concerned, while they may have felt initially frightened by the experience, were always left with a sense of peace and comfort. The stories record appearances which have given warning of impending difficulties, saved adults and children from disaster, and offered protection in times of danger, again, often in wartime.

In 1941 London was the victim of the German 'blitzkrieg' – 60 consecutive nights of intense bombing. Donovan and Doris Cox were prepared for the worst, and had sent their son away to a boarding school. One night Donovan told his wife that there was going to be some disturbance that night, but that they were going to be OK. Doris asked how he could be so sure with all the bombing. 'I can see an angel over our house protecting us,' replied Donovan. He had seen a huge, angelic figure floating over their house in a horizontal, protective position. He knew for sure that something would happen that night, but that they would be protected.

They went to sleep, but were awoken in the night by a terrific explosion above the house. Doors were blown open and a pressure wave threatened to blow the windows in. But nothing was damaged. When the warden arrived in the morning he told them that they had been the victims of a parachute bomb. Normally these bombs exploded on impact with the ground, causing terrible damage over a significant area. But the warden had seen the bomb explode – very unusually – in mid-air, right over their house, before it had time to reach the ground. Donovan Cox was convinced that the angel he had seen had protected him.

The cult of angels has collected so much momentum, particularly in the United States, that it is threatening to become a religion all of its own. What is so fascinating about the phenomenon is that it is based on personal experiences, rather than any particular dogma or belief system. As such it is hard to argue with – those who are convinced are unlikely to become unconvinced. The question that many people ask, though, is whether angel encounters are on the increase? Or is it simply the open reporting of them that is multiplying? Have high proportions of people always had these experiences, keeping them to themselves in times of persecution? Or are these encounters another harbinger of millennial changes?

NATURE SPIRITS AND FAIRIES

The fairy folk, the little people, the good folk, the spirits that live in the woods, sylphs, salamanders, undines, gnomes and trolls. To most of us, the beings from the fairy world are the creations of imagination, the stuff of fairy tales: their cheeky, mysterious, and sometimes threatening personalities are nothing but simple entertainment for children. For an increasing number of people though the realm of fairies and nature spirits is as real as ours – an invisible world that interpenetrates our own. The spiritualist medium Mrs Osborn Leonard was categoric in her support for this world's reality:

> Yes they do exist. They are the nature spirits and there are many classes of fairies. Clairvoyance is needed to see them. They belong to another vibration. They don't have quite the same soul as we do. But they have spirits. All forms of life are used again. Nature spirits don't die like us. Some are created out of earth or fire or friction. They are all activity and movement.

To believers the world of 'faerie' exists in a different dimension: a dimension that can sometimes become visible to those who seek it out – and even to others who do not.

A typical, unbidden fairy encounter occurred to a London woman named Mary Treadgold. In April 1973, Ms Treadgold was travelling through the Highlands of Scotland on a coach trip. On the Island of Mull, she was gazing out of the coach window when, to her surprise, she saw something very unusual:

> ... a small figure, about 18 inches high, a young man with his foot on a spade, arrested (frozen like a bird or a squirrel on the approach of something alien) in the act of digging ... He had a thin, keen face (which I would know again), tight, brown, curly hair, was dressed in bright blue bib and braces, with a very white shirt, with rolled-up sleeves. An open sack, also miniature, stood at his side. He was emphatically not a dwarf, nor a child, nor (last desperate suggestion of a sceptic) a plastic garden gnome. He was a perfectly formed living being like any of us, only in miniature.

Scotland is one of the natural homes for such strange meetings – meetings which seem to go back many hundreds of years.

Robert Kirk was an Episcopalian minister from the Highlands of Scotland who became convinced of the reality of the fairy folk. In his famous work of 1691 *The Secret Common-Wealth*, Kirk preserved the fairy lore of his region, describing fairies as a 'middle nature between man and angel', and possessing bodies which were 'somewhat of the nature of a condensed cloud, and best seen in twilight. These bodies are so pliable through the subtlety of the spirits that agitate them, that they can appear or disappear at pleasure.' There is a myth that Robert Kirk himself did not die, but passed into the fairy realm at a hill in Aberfoyle which still bears his name. It is also claimed that this extraordinary minister is still active in the fairy realm, available to all those who seek him out.

Other Celtic countries, like Wales and Ireland, have been the most regular source for experiences of nature spirits. One of the most famous collections of fairy lore and stories of fairy sightings was put together by the American scholar of the early 20th century W.Y. Evans-Wentz. In his 1911 book, *The Fairy Faith in Celtic Countries*, he quotes an Irish account:

I have never seen a man fairy nor a woman fairy, but my mother saw a troop of them. She herself and the other maidens of the townland were once out upon the summer sheiling [grazing]. They were milking the cows, in the evening gloaming, when they observed a flock of fairies reeling and setting upon the green plain in front of the knoll. And, oh King! but it was they the fairies themselves that had the right to the dancing, and not the children of men! Bell helmets of blue silk covered their heads, and garments of green satin covered their bodies, and sandals of yellow membrane covered their feet. Their heavy brown hair was streaming down their waist, and its lustre was of the fair golden sun of summer. Their sun was as white as the swan of the wave, and their voice was as melodious as the mavis of the wood, and they themselves were as beauteous of feature and as lithe of form as a picture, while their step was as light and stately and their minds as sportive as the little red hind of the hill.

Such definitive reports of the fairy world go back much further in history to less scientific, less sceptical times when the little people were accepted as part of the normal culture. Descriptions of their world formed a normal part of some people's everyday reality. In his book *The Living World of Faery*, R.J. Stewart drew on an 18th-century journal he had discovered, describing the faery world's own cultural life:

> There are many classes or orders of the People of Light, with their own habits, lives, structures of tribe, family and the like. Some are well known to mortal men and women, others are invisible and hidden away, yet they will emerge at certain times or if bidden appropriately. It is mainly of these hidden orders that I shall treat here in detail, as those commonplace brownies, helpers, grain and cattle wards and well keepers are widely known and still have intercourse with country people. Yet there is a more secret art by which the hidden orders are found and this shall be the core, the Pearl, of my account.
>
> This art I learned at first in confused then clear dreams, as did the prophets and sibyls of old, but also from an aged woman cottager in Devonshire, and some Irish-Scottish seers in Virginia in the Colonies. Thereafter it is given to converse and learn direct with the People in their own manner, according to their realm, element, hive or tribe.
>
> By this deep art one may reach through pools, enter hills and trees, meld with stones, and come at last to the halls of the People of Light, who are within the body of Land. And they may also come to you, for the threshold once opened may be crossed in either direction. You may also see with their eyes and they likewise shall see with yours for mutual learning.

Another documenter of faery lore was Sabine Baring-Gould, the Victorian priest, folklorist and historian. He claimed that when he was four he had a sighting of fairy folk as he was travelling in a carriage with his parents: 'I saw legions of dwarfs of about two feet high running along beside the horses; some sat laughing on the pole, some were scrambling up the harness to get on the back of the horses.' Baring-Gould's wife also claimed to have seen a fairy person when she was 15. He was 'a little green man, perfectly well made, who looked at her with beady black eyes. She was so frightened that she ran home.' The third sighting in the family was by one of their sons, who, on being asked to fetch some peas from the garden, returned saying he had been surprised by a 'little man wearing a red cap, a green jacket, and brown knee-breeches, whose face was old and wan, and who had a grey beard and eyes as black and hard as sloes. He stared so intently at the boy that the latter took to his heels.'

Sightings of fairies are surprisingly common among children, although the great majority of these reports are not taken seriously by adults. Edgar Cayce, the remarkable American psychic known as 'The Sleeping Prophet', appeared to have had clairvoyant experiences almost from birth. In early childhood he would play in his garden with boys and girls who, to his school friends, were completely invisible and 'imaginary'. These 'nature playmates', as his mother called them, became a secret between the two of them after Cayce was ridiculed by his fellow schoolmates. It was only some years later that Cayce read about nature spirits and realized that what was described in books as myth was, for him, the reality he had perceived quite naturally.

The story that has attracted the most attention to fairy encounters in the 20th century involves two young English girls and their attempts to take photographs of the fairies they say they saw at Cottingley Glen in Yorkshire. In July 1917 Frances Griffiths and her cousin Elsie Wright decided to take pictures of the fairies that they had seen. Using a 'Midg' camera belonging to Elsie's father, they took a photograph that would start a 60-year controversy. This famous first photograph shows Frances with four cavorting fairy figures, one of which is playing a pipe. Two months later they took another photo of Elsie with a gnome. Having shown the photographs to Frances' and Elsie's parents, the girls' story might have ended there.

In 1920, however, Elsie's mother attended a lecture on folklore, ending up showing the photos to the lecturer. Via a chain of connections, the original photographs, along with a further three taken in 1920, were circulated amongst theosophical and esoteric circles. They came to the attention of Sir Arthur Conan Doyle, author of the Sherlock Holmes stories and a prominent voice in the Spiritualist movement. Late in 1920 he wrote an article about the photographs for *The Strand* magazine, and the fame of the photographs began to spread. In 1922 Conan Doyle wrote the book *The Coming of the Fairies* in which he expressed the idea that the fairies might be thought-forms which had been created by the 'associated auras of the two girls'.

Despite the fact that controversy raged for 60 years, and that many people still believe that the photographs really depict fairies, they *are* fakes. The 'fairies' in the photos were made up from cut-out figures from a 1915 picture book called *Princess Mary's Gift Book*. This is not merely theory, for, in 1983 Elsie wrote to Geoffrey Crawley, the editor of *The British Journal of Photography*, admitting that the Cottingley fairy photographs were a practical joke. The motivation for the hoax came from an event when Frances had been punished by her father after getting wet in a nearby pond. She had said that she had been playing with the fairies, but her father disbelieved her. In order to get her own back on him she determined to *make* him believe her. The original intention had been to reveal the trick as soon as they had convinced him, but the joke just kept on going.

The two girls were so embarrassed by all the attention that they both decided, once Conan Doyle had become involved, that they could not confess their hoax until his death, or indeed until the death of two further advocates of the photos. Despite the two women's admissions, both still maintained, some 70 years later, that they had indeed seen fairies at the Glen.

Fairies and nature spirits do not seem to be limited to the world's Celtic countries. Almost all native traditions talk of nature spirits of some kind. The folklore of Greece was studied by John Cuthbert Lawson at the beginning of the 20th century, and resulted in a close encounter of his own with a female fairy known as a Nereid:

> I myself once had a Nereid pointed out to me by my guide, and there certainly was the semblance of a female figure draped in white and tall beyond human stature sitting in the dusk between the gnarled and twisted boles of an old olive yard. What the apparition was, I had no leisure to investigate; for my guide with many signs of the cross and muttered invocations of the Virgin ordered my mule to perilous haste along the rough mountain path.

Since the 1960s, there has been a growing movement of interest in nature spirits, which has been supported by the parallel concern over the world's environment and the consequences of man's destructive activities. One of the pioneers in this field of study has been the Findhorn Foundation community, based near Inverness in Scotland. Since 1963 members of the spiritual community claim to have had regular and continuous communication with many different aspects of the fairy and nature-spirit worlds. They have, in effect, resurrected the ancient notion that nature spirits, or 'Devas', are the archetypal forces behind the creation and growth of trees, flowers and even animals. By attuning to these forces, by listening psychically to their messages, and by applying their understanding, the Findhorn community members say that we all have a chance to develop a new and more fruitful relationship with the natural world. Through this improved relationship we can start to harmonize and heal the Earth, and nature's damaged areas. To add practical action to these idealistic claims, members of the community have won conservation awards for their reforestation of some of Scotland's depleted woodlands.

The community's belief that plants and trees grow and unfold under the influence of invisible energies challenges every scientific notion we might have. That we can influence the rate and quality of plant growth is, perhaps, less challenging. There have always been those with green fingers, and the notion that plants have sensory and sympathetic abilities has been shown in laboratory experiments. Nevertheless, we are still talking about listening and talking to fairies!

In the 1960s and 1970s the gardens at the Findhorn Caravan Park became famous for the massive vegetables grown on impossibly poor sandy soil. One of the community's founders was Dorothy Maclean, a trained psychic, who was genuinely surprised when she started to receive messages from the 'Devas' of different plants such as the pea and the cabbage. These messages were intended, she said, both for her illumination, and for the practical application of work in the garden. One of the early messages came from the Deva of the golden Lily:

> The theory of evolution that puts man at the apex of life on Earth is only correct when viewed from certain angles. It leaves out the fact that God, universal consciousness, is working out the forms of life. For example, according to generally accepted regulations, I am a lowly lily unable to be aware of most things and certainly not able to talk with you. But somehow, somewhere is the intelligence that made us fair and continues to do so, just as somehow, somewhere is the intelligence that produced your intricate physical body.

Dorothy Maclean's sense of these nature spirits was not of small winged creatures. Rather she viewed 'Devas' as swirling patterns of energy, quite cloud-like, yet luminous. Another of the community's founders, though, had more 'literal' visions of these characters. Scotsman Robert Ogilvie Crombie was originally a folklorist and academic. After a number of strange spiritual apparitions he started to see a vast figure of Pan, complete with hairy hoofs and his famous pipes. His first encounter, however, occurred in the Edinburgh Botanical Gardens:

> I saw something moving from the corner of my eye, something that distracted me. I looked and saw a figure dancing around a tree some twenty five yards away. And then I looked again. It was quite startling. It was a beautiful figure, about three feet tall. I thought: something's happened. I must be going mad. I can't believe this!

Inspired in part by the gardens at Findhorn, American Machaelle (pronounced Michelle) Small Wright developed her own garden called Perelandra near Jeffersonton, Virginia, where she claims to garden with the 'guidance' of nature spirits. In her book *Behaving As If The God In All Life Mattered* she describes her experiences of the nature spirits she works with in her garden:

> Thanks to centuries of tradition, fairy tales and folklore most people think of nature spirits in terms of elves, gnomes, fairies ... the 'little people' of the woods. I experience nature spirits as swirling spheres of light energy. I have walked through the woods with one of these 'balls of energy' moving beside me, and, when necessary, I've moved around a tree while the 'ball of energy' continued to move straight through the tree, coming out the other side. My personal inner vision lies in the area of energy. I tend to see waves of energy, energy dynamics and interplay; in fact, I tend to see the reality around me as energy first, then five-senses form. So, I'm comfortable with the concept of energy reality. I was not familiar with or comfortable with the concept of fairies, elves and gnomes.
>
> Having read horse books during my childhood, I simply didn't have a background steeped in fairy tales and folklore. So out of consideration for me, when the nature spirits chose to

be visible, they chose a context with which I was comfortable – energy. Had I seen an elf or a gnome come toward me, I definitely would have checked into a rubber room.

Most modern promoters of contact with nature spirits – like Machaelle Small Wright and the Findhorn community – do not claim their experiences to be exclusive to them, or the result of any special powers or abilities. Communication, they say, can be learnt. Contemporary author and teacher Ted Andrews claims that we are all able to make contact with the 'Faerie Realm'. In books and articles he describes the kinds of experiences he says await those who are willing to call on the presence of the nature kingdoms. He claims that he has always been aware of the fairy people – that there has never been a time when they were not with him. Andrews says that the first time he actually saw a fairy spirit was when he used to read fairy tales as a child.

On many occasions I could feel the presence of others, although I could not always see them. Sometimes slight indentations would appear on the bed around me, as if others were settling in to enjoy the stories as well. The first sights were of flickering lights and of a little bearded man lighting a pipe as he leaned against the wall at the head of my bed frame.

He would nod as if to tell me to keep on reading, and as I read he seemed to hear my thoughts as words, just as if I were reading aloud to him. Rarely did he speak, but he made his thoughts well known. For the most part, he seemed content to just listen, although his rugged features could change sharply if elves or dwarfs were described within the stories in a manner that was obviously offensive and false. At such times he would snort and look disgusted. Then he would motion with a wave of his hand for me to continue.

Sometimes I did read aloud – using a whispered voice – and on those occasions the lights would grow stronger around me, and there would always seem to be more of a crowd . . . I have seen this little man many times in my life; I consider him my 'good luck dwarf'. Although this term tends to make him seem like some kind of mascot, he is anything but. He is a wonderful teacher and friend who accepts me as I am. He has shared his magic over the years and opened the mysteries of the faerie realm to me. Whenever I am feeling down or am not sure how things are going, he shows up and the wheels begin moving in my direction. Were it not for him, I would not know that magic and miracles are supposed to happen – that life is supposed to work out.

Can we really believe such messages, such experiences? Can we risk the ridicule of the majority – as Prince Charles and many others have done – to experiment with 'nature com-munication', If a tiny figure did ever appear to us, would we really be able to believe our eyes, or would we dismiss such an experience as hallucination? Until it happens, we may never know what surprises the nature realm has in store for humanity.

PSYCHIC ANIMALS

In spite of scientific advances many people believe that the relationship between man and the animal kingdom is just as mysterious now as it ever has been. In the modern world it is often easy to lose sight of our interdependence with animals. While we rely so much on animals to feed us, we are also indebted to them for the work they do, and for their com-panionship as domestic pets. So, perhaps we should not be so surprised when we hear of the extraordinary acts of ordinary animals: of their loyalty, their selflessness, their intelligence and their supposed psychic skills. We look first at just some of the many stories that testify to the often heroic qualities of the animal kingdom, and at the courageous acts that have actually saved human life.

In December 1991 Jack Fyfe, aged 75, was paralysed by a stroke at his home in Sydney, Australia. As he lay helpless on the floor, only his sheep-dog, Trixie, was aware of his plight. For nine days the faithful dog kept her master alive by bringing him towels soaked in water from her drinking bowl. When the drinking bowl was emptied Trixie resorted to the water from the toilet. Each time that Fyfe needed some more water he simply called to Trixie for help. Nine days after the stroke, both were found by Fyfe's daughter after he failed to turn up for a family meal. He had lost four stone in weight.

Another lifesaving feat was accomplished by Roy, a pet Alsation dog, in May 1977. Roy's owner, Leif Rongemo, lives in Malmo, Sweden, with his wife and two-year-old daughter Anneli. One day Mr Rongemo left his daughter and the dog in the living room of their fourth-floor flat while he attended to some housework in the kitchen. When he returned a few minutes later he was shocked to find that both his daughter and the dog had gone, and that the window to the street was open. Racing to the window he looked down to the street 36 feet below. Nothing. To his left, though, on the narrow ledge that ran around the building, his daughter was crawling on all fours: Roy the dog, obviously distressed, was trying, tentatively to follow her. Mr Rongemo was unwilling to follow them, fearing that any false move might send them all to their deaths. Instead he called the fire service and rushed down to the street with a blanket. Together with a neighbour he held the blanket below the tiny child. Back in the flat Mrs Rongemo could hardly look as the child crawled further and further from her reach.

Then, very suddenly, Roy took heroic action: he quickly and carefully closed his jaws on the little girl's nappy. Lifting her in his mouth, he shuffled his way backwards for a full three minutes before delivering her to the waiting Mrs Rongemo. Once Anneli was safely in her mother's arms, Roy jumped back into the room, enthusiastically wagging his tail. Ironically, prior to the incident, the Rongemos had been thinking of selling Roy as they felt he was too boisterous to have in the same house as their baby daughter. If the incident had happened a few weeks later the people of Malmo might have been hearing of a tragedy rather than a miracle.

While the loyalty of dogs might be anticipated, birds do not have the same reputation: perhaps we underrate their potential. Miss Rachel Flynn, a native of Cape Cod, New England, was walking along a cliff edge in 1980 when she fell 30 feet to the deserted beach below. The 82 year old was too seriously hurt to move, and had almost resigned herself to a slow death. She had not counted on the intelligent actions of a seagull, which, she believed, was the very creature that she and her sister regularly fed outside their home, and which they had nicknamed Nancy. Later, Miss Flynn remembered saying to the bird: 'For God's sake, Nancy, get help.'

Rachel Flynn's sister June was in her kitchen, when a seagull arrived and started making a commotion at the window. It was tapping on the glass with its beak, and flapping its wings wildly. It was, in June's words, 'making more noise than a wild turkey'. After 15 minutes of trying to get the bird to go away, June decided that the bird might be trying to alert her to something. She followed the gull, which would stop to make sure she was still close behind, and ended up at the edge of the cliff. When June looked down she saw Rachel, her sister, lying injured on the beach. The fire service was called and took Rachel to hospital where she was treated for bruising and a twisted knee.

After the incident they both firmly believed that Nancy the gull had saved Rachel's life: 'it was incredible, the way she came to the window and caused all that racket.' Maybe it is worth putting something out for the birds after all.

When people move home, or go on long journeys, the family pet usually comes pretty far down the list of priorities. But cats and dogs often have their own agendas: it might be to stay with their owner, it might be to stay in the place that they know. Whatever it is, they can, quite literally go to extraordinary lengths to get there. In 1977 a 15-year-old boy named Kirsten Hicks was leaving Adelaide, Australia, to go on a long journey overseas with his parents. He had to leave his Persian cat Howie with his grandparents some 1,000 miles from Adelaide on the Queensland Coast. Unfortunately, while Kirsten was abroad, the cat ran away from the grandparents' house. The grandparents tried to trace the cat, but to no avail, and when Kirsten returned home to Adelaide they had to break the bad news of cat's disappearance. Kirsten was understandably upset, as he had a close bond with Howie.

One year later Howie the cat arrived at the family home in Adelaide: he was in a poor state, with a filthy coat, and sore, bleeding paws. On his thousand miles of incredible journeying, Howie had crossed rivers, deserts and large tracts of wilderness area. It's still far from clear how the cat was able to accomplish such an extraordinary feat of homing and endurance.

Howie's story is not the only example of such an achievement. Another Persian cat called Sugar took over a year to track its owners 1,500 miles from California to Oklahoma, crossing both the Rocky Mountains and the Great American Desert. In France a family took their cat Gringo to their holiday cottage, some 350 miles from their family home. When they got back the cat seemed to go into a sulk, and then, suddenly disappeared. He reappeared, six months later at the family's holiday cottage. Some people thought that maybe he simply preferred the holiday atmosphere. A twist in the tail of these cat stories comes from another French example; the Ehmig family were moving from Paris to a village some 400 miles away in the country. When they got there, their white cat Blanchette could not seem to settle down and soon disappeared. Five months later she arrived at the old family home in Paris. As she scratched at the door of her old home she was spotted by a neighbour who took pity on her. Eventually the cat was settled with the Ehmig's parents in Paris. Once a city cat . . .

A number of pet dogs have endured and survived similar, and even more remarkable, journeys. The current, unofficial record for the single longest 'homing' journey for a dog is held by Bobbie, the dog immortalized in Charles Alexander's book, *Bobbie: A Great Collie of Oregon*. Bobbie's owner was a man named Brazier, who owned a restaurant in Silverton, Oregon. In August 1923, Bobbie had gone on a trip with his owner to stay with relatives in Wolcott, Indiana. When Mr Brazier was filling up with petrol at a garage, Bobbie disappeared after being chased away by a pack of other dogs. To Mr Brazier's sadness there seemed no way to get him back.

It was six months later that Bobbie arrived back in Silverton, Oregon, some 3,000 miles away, exhausted and emaciated. On his journey he had crossed the White River, the Wabash River and the Tippecanoe River; he had also traversed Iowa, Nebraska, the Great Plains and the Rocky Mountains. Later statements from people who had seen him on his journey indicated that he had initially searched over a wide area of around 1,000 miles, before finding his bearings for home. When he first arrived back he headed for the farmhouse where he had initially been raised: he was found asleep on the grave of his puppy-hood friend, a fox terrier. Once fed, he raced to his owner's restaurant where he leapt onto the bed of the snoozing Mr Brazier. Needless to say Mr Brazier was more than a little surprised, but was immediately convinced of Bobbie's identity from a tell-tale scar and an injured hip. After his extraordinary adventure Bobbie became something of a hero, and would receive visitors, admirers and gifts for the next 12 years of his life.

While dogs and cats now occupy a special place in the relationship between human and animal kingdoms, the horse has filled a practical working role in man's life for many thousands of years. It should not be forgotten that until a hundred years ago, the horse was still the majority form of transport power, and had been responsible for ploughing and other agricultural work since early civilization. This special bond is, for the most part, based on man's respect for the horse, and the horse's trust of its master. Without either, there is, surely, no 'special relationship'. The horse has often been attributed with great intelligence, with an understanding, that some experts believe comes more from 'psychic knowing' than from simple use of the ordinary senses.

The story of the intelligent horse known as 'Clever Hans' has become a classic in the literature of parapsychology, and still remains a subject of considerable controversy. Willem von Osten, of Eberfield, Germany, was a 19th-century 'horse fancier': in plainer words he liked horses and believed them to be intelligent and sensitive creatures. According to von Osten, he decided that he would train his horses to solve problems and to give answers by tapping on the ground with their hooves. Hans, it seems, learned to count out numbers, and to tap out letters, using a code based on one for 'a', two for 'b' and so on. The horse seemed to progress quickly, and was soon able to answer sums presented to it on a blackboard: 30 plus 10 was greeted with 40 taps on the floor.

When the German Kaiser heard of the clever horse he initiated an enquiry: animal trainers, zoologists and other researchers studied von Osten and Clever Hans closely and thoroughly. They came to the conclusion that somehow von Osten was giving Hans invisible but effective signals. It is known now, as it was then, that animals can be trained to tap the ground to order. Traditionally this was done by first teaching them to paw the ground when they smelt food. This action was then conditioned by rewards of food. They could next be taught to stop tapping at the ground, again by conditioning – perhaps by the threat of a whip. This threat can be associated with a gradually smaller action – such as the slight (unnoticeable to most observers) movement of a whip, or even a change in the trainer's angle of gaze. Through this training, then, the horse's master has (with the aid of a carrot and a stick) taught the horse to start and stop the tapping of its hoof without anyone noticing how it is done. So was Clever Hans just such a trained horse? The answer appears to be 'no', since Hans' feats – unlike similar circus horses – did not stop at these simple tappings.

After two years of training, Clever Hans was indicating the day and date of the month, was solving mathematical equations, and could read simple musical notation. Von Osten came under increasing criticism from, some say, those who feared for the continued supremacy of the human race. As he neared death, von Osten, determined that his experiments should continue, passed all his methods on to a friend named Karl Krall. Krall trained a further two horses, Muhamed and Zarif, who, together with Hans, became known as the Eberfield Horses.

Krall tried to improve the methods by which the horses demonstrated their skills: he designed a 49-square chart containing the letters, vowels and dipthongs of the German language. The horse would now put its hoof on the appropriate square on the chart to make up its answer. A Swiss psychologist named Clarparede studied Krall's methods, and wrote extensive reports on the achievements of the Eberfield Horses. In one session Clarparede watched as Krall drew on the blackboard the following sum: multiply the square root of 49 by the square root of 36. Muhamed first indicated 52 before correcting himself and giving the correct answer 42. Clarparede then asked his own question of Krall, which was written on the board: the square root of the square root of 614,656. According to Clarparede, Muhamed answered swiftly, and correctly: 28.

Clarparede was completely convinced: not only of the intelligence of the horses, but also of Krall's integrity and trustworthiness. Even after prolonged periods of time with the horses and their trainer, the psychologist remained convinced that fraud was not a possibility. Another contemporary who took the horses' intelligence very seriously was the Belgian Nobel Peace Prize winner Maurice Maeterlinck. In his book *The Unknown Guest*, Maeterlinck describes his long sessions with one of the horses which, he claims, actually spoke:

One day, Krall and his collaborator, Dr Scholler, thought they would try and teach Muhamed to express himself in speech. The horse, a docile and eager pupil, made touching and fruitless efforts to reproduce human sounds. Suddenly he

195

stopped, and in his strange phonetic spelling, declared, by striking his foot on the springboard: 'Ig hb kein gud sdim' – 'I have not a good voice.'

Observing that he did not open his mouth, they strove to make him understand, by the examples of a dog, with pictures, and so on, that in order to speak it is necessary to separate the jaws. They next asked him: 'What must you do to speak?' He replied, by striking with his foot, 'Open mouth'. 'Why, then, don't you open yours?' his questioners next asked. His reply (again by taps) was 'Weil kan nigid' – 'because I can't'.

There were, and quite naturally still are, sceptics who believe that all the performances of the Eberfield Horses were simply conditioned responses. Maeterlinck came to a very different conclusion: 'There is probably in the horse, and probably in all that lives on earth, a psychic power similar to that which is hidden beneath the well of our reason.'

Another remarkable horse was Lady Wonder, whose psychic and telepathic talents were studied by the famous ESP theorist J.B. Rhine in his early days at Duke University before the Duke laboratory had been formally established. Lady Wonder originally came to Rhine's notice after reports that she could do mathematical sums, and would act as a kind of oracle, by answering questions posed to her. The mechanism via which she gave her answers was a rather strange, horse-sized typewriter, comprising letters and numbers, which Lady Wonder's owner Mrs Claudia Fonda had designed for her. Rhine's researches were an experimental advance on those of the Eberfield Horses, since Rhine was able to persuade Mrs Fonda to be absent from the room when he was giving the horse questions. During these experiments Lady Wonder seems to have had a deal of success, although Rhine never laboured her attainments. Perhaps her greatest success came later when she was brought in to help on a murder enquiry. Asked about a missing boy, Lady Wonder spelled out the words: 'Pittsfield Water Wheel'. A local police captain was able to turn these into 'Field and Wilde Water Pitt', the name of an abandoned quarry. When the police searched the quarry the boy's dead body was found. While this relied on the police captain's interpretation, it still makes for an extraordinary coincidence. After all, the horse could have tapped in simply anything, and, we must presume, its trainer had no prior knowledge of the body's location.

Intelligence is a quality that Susan Chernak McElroy, author of *Animals as Teachers and Healers*, would claim for the dog that appeared following the death of her 17-year-old son in a diving accident. Other qualities she could add might include compassion, sensitivity and the ability to induce emotional healing:

My seventeen year old son was killed in a diving accident. Only a parent who has lost a child can understand the personal devastation. The evening before the accident, I happened to drive past our local cemetery. Sitting next to the fence was a stray dog. She sat on a small knoll between two trees, seemingly waiting for someone. She looked like a bedraggled red fox. Little did I know that three days later I would be burying my son on the exact spot where the little dog waited.

On the day of my son's funeral service, I saw the little dog again. She was standing a short distance away from where we gathered at the cemetery. The next morning, just before dawn, I went to visit my son's grave for the first time. And sitting beside the mound of flowers at his graveside was the little red dog. As I approached, she rose and stepped back a few feet, as if in respect. When I sat on the ground by the grave, she came back and sat beside me, not touching me or asking for attention for herself. She seemed to just 'be there' for me. Together we watched the sun rise, and I felt a slight touch of peace. I arose and she walked me back to my car, then returned to my son's grave and lay down on it. The next morning was a repeat of the first. There she was, nestled beside the flowers. As she sat beside me, I ran my hand down along her back. She was slightly wet, as if from night dew. 'You been here all night?' I asked. She answered with a slight wag of her tail. 'What are you? Some kind of a guardian angel?' She turned toward me and looked at me with eyes that seemed to reach my very soul. I began to cry and tell her of my terrible pain, and she sat and listened.

The next morning, there she was. Beginning to think of someone besides myself, I had brought a bowl of food and some water for her. Apparently someone else had noticed that the little dog was doing twenty-four-hour duty, because there was a bowl of water by the grave. Knowing that my son wasn't alone, that he had this small dog with him, began to give me comfort. I remembered that several years before, my son and a friend had rescued a small red dog that had been shot with an arrow. My son named her Callie, and she stayed on as a beloved pet until an untimely accident took her life.

After about a week, I took the cemetery dog home with me. Strangely enough, she was quiet and subdued. I couldn't think of a name for her. Then one day, I said, 'you know something? You look just like old Callie.' It was as if I'd hit a magic switch. 'Callie' stood up and, tail wagging furiously, ran over to me and put her paw on my knee. It was as if she had finally 'come home'.

Who is this dog who showed me my son's cemetery plot, and then did round-the-clock sentry duty when my son was laid to rest there? Who is this dog who was there to help me through the greatest trauma of my life, who now shares my home and helps fill the lonely moments? Is there such a thing as reincarnation, and are dogs reincarnated? I don't know. I just know that she came into my life in a very mysterious way. My other dogs couldn't give me the comfort that this little red dog did, and still does.

As we study more about animals we find that their senses are heightened in ways that ours are not. Their intelligence can express itself in very different ways to our own. If we are to fully appreciate animals, and their place in the pattern of all species, we may need to see things more from their perspective, as well as simply from our own. From the simple facts that different animals can far exceed our sensory abilities, it should be clear that we do not hold the monopoly on 'good-quality' sensory inputs. Nor, perhaps, should we be sure that the five senses that we use are the only ones available to the animal kingdom. We talk of a sixth sense, which animals are often suspected of possessing. In times to come we may not stop at six.

WILD CHILDREN

In 1195 two green children appeared in the Suffolk village of Woolpit, close to Bury St Edmunds in England. A boy and a girl, they were found by workmen in the pits intended to catch wolves. They were dressed in green clothing, and their skin was coloured a profound green. They spoke initially in a strange, incomprehensible dialect. Later, when they had learned to speak English as the local people, they told how they came from a Christian land known as St Martins. The enduring story was recorded by two historians, some 15 years after the event: Ralph of Coggeshall gave perhaps the most thorough and detailed report of the green children:

> Another wonderful thing happened in Suffolk, at St Mary's of the Wolfpits. A boy and his sister were found by the inhabitants of that place near the mouth of a pit which is there, who had the form of all their limbs like to those of other men, but they differed in the colour of their skin from all the people of our habitable world; for the whole surface of their skin was tinged of a green colour. No one could understand their speech. When they were brought as curiosities to the house of a certain knight, Sir Richard de Calne, at Wikes, they wept bitterly. Bread and other victuals were set before them, but they would touch none of them, though they were tormented by great hunger, as the girl afterwards acknowledged. At length, when some beans just cut, with their stalks, were brought into the

house, they made signs, with great avidity, that they should be given to them. When they were brought, they opened the stalks instead of the pods, thinking that beans were in the hollow of them; but not finding them there, they began to weep anew. When those who were present saw this, they opened the pods, and showed them the naked beans. They fed on these with great delight, and for a long time tasted no other food. The boy, however was always languid and depressed, and he died within a short time. The girl enjoyed continual good health; and becoming accustomed to various kinds of food, lost completely that green colour, and gradually recovered the sanguine habit of her entire body. She was afterwards regenerated by the laver of holy baptism, and lived for many years in the service of that knight (as I have frequently heard from him and his family) and was rather loose and wanton in her conduct. Being frequently asked about the people of her country, she asserted that the inhabitants, and all they had in that country, were of a green colour; and that they saw no sun, but enjoyed a degree of light like what is after sunset. Being asked how she came into this country with the aforesaid boy, she replied that, as they were following their flocks, they came to a certain cavern, on entering which they heard a delightful sound of bells; ravished by whose sweetness, they went on for a long time wandering on through the cavern, until they came to its mouth. When they came out of it, they were struck senseless by the excessive light of the sun, and the unusual temperature of the air; and thus they lay for a long time. Being terrified by the noise of those who came on them, they wished to fly, but they could not find the entrance of the cavern before they were caught.

Theories about a 'Middle Kingdom' – a world within the world – have existed for hundreds, possibly thousands of years, and the Green Children of Woolpit quite naturally provide evidence for this idea. A similar encounter occurred in Spain, when two children were found at a cave outside Banjos in Spain in August 1887. Their skin was also green, like the

Woolpit children, and their clothes were said to be of an 'unfamiliar' material. Their eyes, it was reported, were of an oriental cast. They were unable to speak the native Spanish. In another echo of the Woolpit story, the boy soon died, while the girl seemed to thrive. She learned Spanish and was able to answer many of the questions put to her: they had come from a 'sunless' land, and had come into this upper world when a whirlwind had deposited them in the cave. The girl died five years later, with the location of her true origin still unknown.

These cases are linked to, although different from, the cases of feral, or wild, children who appear to have been brought up by animals, particularly wolves, in the wilderness, and who are then introduced to civilization. These stories resonate with one of the most famous legends of all: Romulus and Remus, the two twins who were suckled by wolves, and who were eventually responsible for the founding of modern Rome.

The first case of a feral child to be recorded 'as fact' was of a wolf-boy captured in the German principality of Hesse in 1344. The first detailed account, however, dates from 1724, when a boy was captured near the German town of Hameln. 'Wild Peter', as he became known, was believed to have been about 12 years old, although he was incapable of speech, and ate only grass and vegetables, and sucked at green stalks. When King George I of England and Hannover came to know of the boy's discovery, he brought the child to the English court, where he became something of a favourite. Although he was never able to speak properly, he would address the King as 'ki scho' and his Queen Caroline as 'qui ca'.

Wild Peter's case attracted much attention, as he symbolized 'natural man' – untainted by civilization. As such he became the object of research into the development of man. The Scottish Lord Monboddo wrote of Peter: 'I consider his history as a brief chronicle or abstract of the progress of human nature, from the mere animal to the first stage of civilised life.'

*

In the 20th century a case of wild children appeared which provided an even more extraordinary insight into the development of the child. The Rev J.A.L. Singh was in charge of an orphanage and church school in the Midnapore district of India. In 1920 he heard stories of *manush-baghas*, or man beasts, reputed to be living among a family of wolves who lived in a termite mound. One night he saw the wolves and returned in the morning to excavate the mound. Two wolves ran away, but the third, a female, was shot by the group. Inside, Singh found four creatures: two small wolf cubs and two human girls – one about eight, the other two.

Singh took the girls to his orphanage and started what he felt to be his Christian duty – the civilizing of the two poor savage beasts, whom he had named Amala and Kamala. At first they behaved like wolves: walking and running on all fours; keeping away from daylight; howling through the night; eating raw meat and even carrion. Despite Singh's care and attention Amala, the younger girl, died within a year of being found. Kamala lived on for nine years, during which time she learned to walk upright and to speak some phrases in Bengali.

Since 1920 the case has been extensively investigated, and has been found to be genuine in its details. In 1959, however, the psychoanalyst and writer Bruno Bettleheim published a paper suggesting that the wild girls were autistic, and that they had been abandoned by their parents because of their condition. Despite continuous research, though, it is likely that their true origins will remain a mystery forever.

With the improved communications of the 20th century more and more cases of wild children have appeared over the last 50 years, particularly in Asia, Africa and some of the less developed parts of the world. One boy, Ramu the wolf-boy, was found naked in a third class waiting room at Lucknow railway station, in India, in 1954. He was around ten years old and had deformed limbs. His cries were like those of an animal. His eating habits, too, were those of an animal, snatching and tearing with his sharp teeth. Again, his origins were unknown, but it seems possible that his parents had abandoned him at an early age. His story is typical of many children abandoned, only to be suckled by dogs, wolves or monkeys.

A particularly unusual case was reported by the French anthropologist Jean-Claude Armen in 1970. In the Spanish Sahara, Armen spotted what he called a 'gazelle-boy': 'a naked human form ... slender and with long black hair, galloping in gigantic bounds among a long cavalcade of white gazelles'. The boy left distinctive tracks: 'the weight resting on the front part of the foot and hardly making any impression on the sand, revealing a rare suppleness.' Armen's first-hand report put the age of the boy at about ten. It seemed that not only had he been accepted into the herd, but that he had also learned the ways of the gazelle, licking and sniffing just as they did. The boy was never caught, leaving Armen wondering about the boy's fate: 'How could a retarded child, even though "aided" by animals, continue to exist in the harsh environment of the desert?'

It is unusual that a child is allowed to become wild while still within its parent's care, but this seems to have happened in the case of a Chinese girl discovered living like a pig in 1984. The ten-year-old peasant girl, known as Cho-Lee, was suckled by the sows, ate from their swill, and even slept in their sty at night. The report from a Chinese newspaper explained: 'The pigs never bite her and, in fact, the temperamental porkers had only to hear her cry and they would come running to her side.' Cho-Lee had become so attached to the pigs that when neighbours tried to remove her from their sty she would scream. She could not speak properly as other children: instead she would make grunting noises, and when hungry would simply snort. Nevertheless she refused all but the leftovers given to the other pigs. She was investigated by an animal-behaviour expert called Dr Chou Lai-Myung. He maintained that she was of at least normal intelligence. It was his belief that she thought and acted like a pig out of choice.

Her father claimed that Cho-Lee had been fascinated by pigs as a baby, and as soon as she could get around on her own, she would end up in the pig sty. After some time the pigs became possessive of her, and it became impossible to get her out. From this time until she was five she lived entirely on sow's milk. Later she weaned herself on to pig swill. Her father was aware that the neighbours were concerned, but all attempts to get her away from the pigs had been unsuccessful. When last heard of, she was still in the hands of the animal-behaviour experts.

These stories of children brought up by animals demonstrate a bond between child and animal which we, as adults, may be incapable of maintaining. To some it may even indicate a tolerance, or even a compassion on behalf of the animal – a compassion which, in these cases, may even exceed that of the children's own parents.

3

INCREDIBLE HAPPENINGS

Whatever hasn't happened will happen, and no one will be safe from it.

J.B.S. Haldane

What are the Laws of Nature? Do phenomena provide our model of the universe or are restrictive, scientific models trying to discriminate between what is 'allowed' to happen and what is 'simply impossible'? The question for science at the end of the 20th century is just how we will build our new model of the universe.

Einstein's Theory of Relativity was just that – a theory, a model. Einstein was humble enough to know he had made only a model. He proposed the speed of light to be a constant. Experiments now indicate that the speed of light varies. Einstein would not have been upset: if someone breaks your model you can always build another one, a 'better' one, a model that is closer to the truth. As David Hume, the Scottish philosopher, observed, just because the sun came up this morning, and has done for the last few billion mornings, it does not guarantee it is going to do it again tomorrow morning.

Perhaps there is such a thing as 'phenomenal jealousy' among scientists. This is how it might work: if I, as a scientist, have not seen something, witnessed something, tested it with my own experimental apparatus, then it cannot be true. It is a kind of scientific hubris. Do I really have the right to reject the possibility of any event, any phenomenon? Surely this is the most anti-scientific position of all. Science is based on phenomena. And when enough reports, sightings, encounters mount up around the existence of new, yet *incredible* happenings, then the open-minded scientist can step in and review the evidence.

Just because we do not know, does not mean it is not true. We do not have to decide just yet. Because an event does not fit our current world picture, does not mean that the picture will not, one day, change. After all, if there is one certainty above all others, it is *un*certainty – the knowledge that today's paradigm will become tomorrow's old ideas ... Hey! Didn't that light just change its speed?

SYNCHRONICITY AND COINCIDENCE

Everyone loves a coincidence, a synchronicity. When a small miracle occurs, unbidden, it can make us feel that all is right with the universe, and that we are, after all, somehow taken care of ... at least that's the theory. Yet not all coincidences are pleasant, nor do they always appear to express the benevolence of a universal deity.

The concept of synchronicity – an 'acausal' link between events – was first proposed by the psychologist Carl Gustav Jung. Jung did not believe in the randomness of the universe, and expressed in scientific terms the idea that events can be linked by meaning. In his own words Jung described synchronicity as 'the equal significance of parallel events'. An archetypal story from Jung's own life expresses his understanding of the concept very clearly:

> A young woman I was treating had, at a critical moment, a dream in which she was given a golden scarab. While she was telling me this dream I sat with my back to the closed window. Suddenly I heard a noise behind me, like a gentle tapping. I turned around and saw a flying insect knocking against the window pane from the outside. I opened the window and caught the creature in the air as it flew in. It was the nearest analogy to a golden scarab that one finds in our latitudes, a

scaraeid beetle, the common rose-chafer (*Cetonia aurata*), which contrary to its usual habits had evidently felt an urge to get into a dark room at this particular moment . . .

There . . . seems to be an archetypal foundation to the . . . case. It was an extraordinarily difficult case to treat, and up to the time of the dream little or no progress had been made. I should explain that the main reason for this was my patient's animus, which . . . clung so rigidly to its own idea of reality that three doctors – I was the third – had not been able to weaken it. Evidently something quite irrational was needed which was beyond my own power to produce. The dream alone was enough to disturb ever so slightly the rationalistic attitude of my patient. But when the 'scarab' came flying in through the window in actual fact, her natural being could burst through the armour of her animus possession and the process of transformation could at last begin to move. Any essential change of attitude signifies a psychic renewal which is usually accompanied by symbols of rebirth in the patients' dreams and fantasies. The scarab is a classic example of a rebirth symbol.

Jung's key work on the subject of synchronicity was entitled *Synchronicity: an Acausal Connecting Principle*. By using the word 'acausal' Jung was careful not to imply an intelligence behind the happenings in the world. The shadow of Sigmund Freud's atheism was very long, and even in 1960, many years after Jung's split from his mentor, Freud, Jung was careful not to imply the presence of a father figure – human or Universal.

Another scientific definition of coincidence was provided by Dr Tom Leonard, a professor of statistics at the University of Warwick, England. His definition, and a story which amply demonstrates it, were told to the author and champion of the paranormal Arthur Koestler in 1974.

A particular coincidental event has, by definition, an infinitesimally small probability of occurring. However, there are infinitely many events which might possibly occur coinciden-tally to a particular person but, as it happens, do not occur. If we summed over all possible coincidental events, then we would find the probability of at least one of them occurring during the person's lifetime to be quite sizeable. I would indeed be surprised if many people could say that they had never experienced an extreme coincidence.

The best coincidence yarn that I know of runs as follows. In his first lecture at this university, a new professor of statistics was describing the laws of probability to his students. To illustrate them, he removed a coin from his pocket and tossed it in the air. It landed on a polished floor, spun around a few times, and to thunderous applause came to rest – vertically on its edge! The point is that this was one of many coincidences that might have happened.

This is not just an unlikely coincidence – one mathematician calculated its probability as one billion to one. It also has the wonderful trademark of the great coincidence: a sense of irony, a sign that the cosmic joker is at play.

The author J.B. Priestly had a fascination with synchron-icity and time, which often featured in his novels and plays. Knowing of Arthur Koestler's interest in the subject, Priestly wrote to him in 1972 to tell him of a peculiar recent experience which had impressed Priestly and his wife Jac-quetta Hawkes:

My wife bought three large lithographs by Graham Sutherland. When they arrived here from London she took them up to her bedroom, to hang them up in the morning. They were leaning against a chair and the one on the outside, facing the room, was a lithograph of a grasshopper. When Jacquetta got into bed that night, she felt some sort of twittering movement going on, so she got out and pulled back the clothes. There was a grasshopper in the bed. No grasshopper had been seen in that room before, nor has been seen since. No grasshopper has been seen at any other time in this house.

The appearance of particular people at a remarkable time has formed the basis for many extraordinary synchronicities. Allan Falby was captain of the El Paso County Highway Patrol in 1930s' Texas when he was involved in an accident that left him seriously injured from a ruptured artery in his leg. If it had not been for a passing motorist named Alfred Smith and his first-aid skills with a tourniquet, Falby would probably have died. Thanks to Smith, though, Falby recovered and was able to return to work some months later.

Five years later Falby was on patrol when a radio message came through to attend a serious accident: the car had hit a tree and its driver was in a critical condition. He arrived before the ambulance and attended to the unconscious driver, applying a tourniquet to a severed artery in the injured man's leg. Having stopped the bleeding, Falby checked the victim's face: it was Alfred Smith.

In the early 1970s the British Oscar-winning actor Anthony Hopkins agreed to appear in a film version of a story called *The Girl from Petrovka* by the author George Feifer. As part of his preparation for the role Hopkins needed to get hold of a copy of Feifer's original novel, so he searched through the bookshops in London's Charing Cross Road, but without success. Frustrated he headed for Leicester Square Underground station. As he waited for his train he noticed a book lying on a seat in the station: a copy of *The Girl from Petrovka*.

Two years later when the story was being filmed in Vienna, George Feifer visited the filmset, and, while he was talking with Hopkins about the story of the film, the author admitted that he no longer had a copy of his own book. He had lent it to a friend in London who had managed to lose it. Hopkins produced his copy: 'Is this the one with the notes scribbled in the margins?' The well-travelled book had managed to find its way home.

Another author who has experienced synchronicities on a regular basis is Richard Bach. The author of *Jonathan Livingston Seagull*, *Illusions* and many other best-selling books Bach told of one particularly remarkable coincidence in his book *Nothing by Chance.* An enthusiastic aeroplane pilot, Bach was flying his 1929 Detroit-Parks P-2A Speedster – a biplane so rare, only eight were made – through the midwest of America. In Palmyra, Wisconsin, Bach lent the plane to another pilot who damaged it in a poor landing. On closer inspection Bach found that everything could be mended except for one vital part – a wing strut. Where was he going to find a wing strut for a plane of which only eight had ever been built in the history of aviation? Things looked pretty hopeless. Then a man walked over from the nearby hangar, keen to see if he might be of help. Bach told him the problem. The man pointed to a pile of parts. There was the strut:

> The odds against our breaking the biplane in a little town that happened to be home to a man with the forty-year-old part to repair it; the odds that he would be on the scene when the event happened; the odds that we'd push the plane right next to his hangar, within ten feet of the part we needed – the odds were so high that coincidence was a foolish answer.

Another benign example of coincidence goes back to 1967 when Peter Moscardi, a police officer working in London, was told by a friend that he had not been able to get through to him on his phone line at work. Moscardi told his friend that in fact his telephone number had been changed: he gave his friend what he thought was the new number. Unfortunately he had given his friend the wrong number, ending in 116, rather than the correct 166. Later the same week Moscardi was on night patrol. Noticing an unsecured door he entered the premises of a light industrial unit. Within moments the telephone rang and Moscardi decided to pick it up. To Moscardi's amazement it was his friend – ringing the incorrect number that Moscardi had given him.

It is the precision of the story that impresses: Moscardi's timing and initiative seem to have been perfect. The event also takes the common occurrence of the 'I was just thinking about you' telephone call to an extraordinary extreme.

Being in the right place at the right time seems to be an essential ingredient of many synchronicitous events. When Camille Flammarion, the 19th-century astronomer and researcher of the occult, was writing his book *L'Atmosphere* something happened that seemed to bring together at least two elements of strangeness. As he wrote a chapter about the wind, a gale blew his window open and wafted the pages of his manuscript straight out into the street. Some days later Flammarion was more than slightly surprised to receive the proofs of the missing chapter from his publisher. The publisher's porter, who knew Flammarion quite well, had found the papers in the street, and had taken them straight back to the publisher as normal.

On 5 May 1974, *The Sunday Times* of London published the winner of a competition for the most remarkable coincidence. Over 2,000 letters were sent to the paper – including one from a Mr Page:

About the month of July, 1940, I was a young soldier in the service of his Majesty at the time somewhere in England. I was to discover that my long awaited wedding photographs had been opened by mistake by a soldier in another troop (A), my troop being 'B'. He was most apologetic, having opened the letter, and, realising his error, which was not surprising, seeing that our names and numbers were so similar. His name being Pape No. 1509322 and my name being Page No. 1509321. This mix up in the mail being frequent until I was posted to another Battery. Some time after the war had ended I was employed as a driver with London Transport at the Merton depot, Colliers Wood, S. W. London. One particular pay day I'd noticed that the tax deducation was very heavy, and duly presented myself to the superintendent's office ... Imagine my amazement when I discovered that my wages had been mixed up with a driver who had been transferred to the garage, not so surprising when I found out that his name was Pape, yes the very same chap ... the weirdest thing of all, our PSV licence numbers were – mine 299222, Mr Pape 299223.

Stories of coincidence do not always bring smiles: there are darker stories that reveal a different kind of meaning, and, perhaps, some kind of warning. When a Dr Reisneren and a Mr Armstrong met earlier this century they discovered a number of strange coincidences: not only did they look astonishingly alike, they also shared the same birth-date. Their link lasted until their deaths. They died on the same day, at the same time: their cars crashed into each other and they were both fatally injured.

Two of the greatest tragedies in American history are linked by a set of extraordinary coincidences. The assassinations of Presidents J.F. Kennedy and Abraham Lincoln have been studied as closely as any events, and have yielded some unlikely comparisons:

1 Lincoln was elected President in 1860, Kennedy in 1960, exactly 100 years later.

2 Both were assassinated on a Friday, while they were with their wives.

3 Both wives suffered the loss of a son while living at the White House.

4 Both men were killed by a bullet that entered the back of the head.

5 Lincoln was killed in Ford's Theater, while Kennedy was killed while riding in a Lincoln convertible made by Ford.

6 Both were succeeded by vice-presidents named Johnson, who had been democrat senators from the southern states.

7 Lyndon Johnson was born in 1908, while Andrew Johnson was born in 1808, 100 years earlier.

8 Both Lincoln and Kennedy had been highly involved in the issue of civil rights for Afro-Caribbean people.

9 The first name of Lincoln's private secretary was John, the surname of Kennedy's secretary was Lincoln.

If Lee Harvey Oswald can still be considered Kennedy's assassin, there are a number of further coincidences that relate to the two killers.

1 John Wilkes Booth was born in 1839, while Lee Harvey Oswald was born in 1939.

2 Both were southerners who held extremist views.

3 Booth shot Lincoln in a theatre and then escaped to a barn. Oswald shot Kennedy from a disused warehouse, and then escaped into a movie theatre.

4 Both were murdered before they came to trial.

Whether kind or cruel, coincidences and synchronicities will continue to fascinate. The cosmic joker personifies this dual-sided nature: seeming to work with endless subtlety to concoct mystery and fascination, while challenging our sense of a fair and just universe. The joker reminds us that a supernatural or superconscious mind may just be working behind the apparent randomness of life.

THE FACE ON MARS

In 1976 two Viking probes entered orbit around Mars at an altitude of 1,000 feet. The images they were to send back of an area called Cydonia appeared to show a sculpted face, 15 miles long and 1.2 miles wide. On release to the public NASA immediately denied the idea that there was any intelligence behind the formation of these shapes. They were simply random shapes made sensible by some trick of the light. A pretty coincidence. For some researchers, though, these explanations were simply not credible.

Greg Molenaar and Vince DePietro were two computer experts and researchers who would not let the subject rest. In the years following the Viking mission they started to trawl through the 60,000 images stored at the National Space Library. They discovered more pictures of the same area – from different angles and in different lighting condition. They put the images through a computer enhancement process which revealed more features of the face: 1,640 feet high, it seemed to have deep eye sockets, teeth, and some kind of helmet, or head dress around it.

In 1983, on the strength of their enhanced images, the pair managed to involve Dr Richard Hoagland, a scientist and an ex-NASA consultant. Inspired by the face image, he started to analyse pictures of the area close to the face. If the face were artificial, then there might be other evidence of 'constructions'. When he found a collection of pyramid-like structures within miles of the face, Hoagland believed he had struck gold. One of the most impressive structures was a five-sided pyramid shape (now called the D&M pyramid after DiPietro and Molenaar), which, though not wholly regular, was strikingly smooth. He started to speculate that these were part of some Martian city. Hoagland now gave the shapes 'man-made' names: the Fortress, the Cliff, the Tholus, the Spiral. To Hoagland and his team at the 'Mars Mission', it seemed impossible that natural erosion and landforming processes could have created such 'synthetic' shapes as a face-like hill, and geometric pyramids with regular, smooth sides. It simply was not scientifically possible.

Further analysis of the shapes, and their arrangements, revealed a geometry which, for some, has strengthened the case for intelligent creators. Particular emphasis has been placed on findings that 'the designers' of the structures appear to have employed the mathematical constants 'e' and 'pi' in the relationships between different dimensions. When SETI – the Search for Extra-Terrestrial Intelligence – was set up, one of its key criteria used for assessing the 'intelligence' of any received radio signal was a use of such universal constant numbers as 'e' and 'pi'. A study of the mathematics has also led to a complex theory that there are correspondences between the location of the face on Mars, and the location of certain sacred sites on Earth – particularly the Gizeh pyramids and Avebury in southern England. Avebury is a focus for crop circle and UFO activity and research, but this new 'angle' on its significance takes it into a new realm. Hoagland has posited that the Mars City has a layout design which – if scaled down – mirrors the key landscape features of the Avebury complex with an astonishingly accurate 'fit'.

With the weight of their evidence behind them, the Mars Mission team were now convinced that the 'artefacts' had been constructed by intelligent beings. If this were so, who were these beings? Had some technologically advanced race built and lived in these buildings? At what time? Had they died out, or were they a race capable of moving through the solar system? Were they, indeed, our ancestors? Did they know that these buildings would one day be seen by their galactic cousins on Earth? Had they left the face and the pyramids as a message about themselves and their civilization? Was there a connection with the pyramids and the sphinx at Gizeh in Egypt? The questions flow on and on from the basic premise that the features on Mars were not 'natural', but built. There was another important question that Hoagland wanted answered: why didn't NASA believe these theories to be significant?

To answer at least some of these questions required more information – information that could only be gleaned from more pictures with better resolution. In 1992 Hoagland and his team started some serious lobbying: they petitioned the UN to persuade NASA to commit the Mars Orbiter (due to launch that autumn, and arrive at Mars by autumn 1993) to take the pictures of Cydonia that they wanted. With Orbiter's superior imaging equipment, here was the chance to put an end to all the speculation.

NASA seemed to resist the idea, or at least to come up with obstacles that made people suspicious of their motives. Even when they were persuaded to look at the potential for taking more pictures, it seemed that they would not allow live transmission of any images, and that the public would have to wait for around six months to see what Orbiter had discovered. This naturally led to conspiracy theories that any photographs of the face and the rest of the Cydonia area would somehow be doctored or changed.

Even as the Mars Orbiter was launched these arguments had not been resolved. The craft entered Mars's orbit in the autumn of 1993 as expected. To the consternation of Hoagland's team, though, the entire mission suffered technical failure, just as it was about to start returning images to Earth. In the aftermath NASA claimed that they had lost all contact with the craft. Even though they tried to regain control, they said, it had proved impossible. This only served to strengthen the conspiracy theory that information about Cydonia and the face is being suppressed. An 'official' investigation by a Professor McDaniels strengthened Hoagland's case when it found that there was some kind of cover-up being perpetrated by NASA. McDaniels went on to uncover a report allegedly commissioned by NASA. The report is lengthily entitled: 'The need to investigate the possible social consequences of an extra-terrestrial discovery, and to consider whether such a discovery should be kept from the public in order to avoid political change . . .' Questions over the report's provenance remain, and have only served to further conspiracy theories around this issue. Hoagland summed up his attitude in a recent interview with *Fate* magazine:

There are apparently two space programs. There's the space program we've all seen. And then there's the space program that the Brookings Institution warned NASA they shouldn't tell us about if they found certain things because it would destroy civilization. The Brookings Institution is a major think tank in Washington. It's been there for decades. It's composed of academics.

According to the paperwork, which we have, in 1959 when it was formed NASA turned to Brookings to basically lay out the outline of the space program. Brookings took a year and did an extremely extensive survey of all the areas that NASA might make discoveries in, ranging from weather modification to extraterrestrial life. In every area except one, Brookings recommended to NASA that it proceed full speed ahead.

With regard to extraterrestrial life – Brookings recommends to NASA that it probably could find, in the coming years, evidence of other intelligent life in the solar system, either in the form of ruins or signals – they were talking about radio signals at that point. They then recommended that NASA give serious consideration to not telling anybody.

On December 15, 1960, the *New York Times* picked this story up and made it a full-page headline: 'Government Report Warns That Discoveries May Topple Civilization'. It is our belief now, compounded by additional evidence which comes in every day, that at that point the space program bifurcated – it became two programs, one in public that would keep us little kiddies sleeping quietly, and the other space program that only a handful of the inner, inner sanctum ever got to see.

In a strange twist to the tale, a man named Joe McMoneagle came forward to claim that NASA had used his psychic abilities to investigate the Cydonia region. McMoneagle had worked for the American Intelligence Services for some 20 years as a 'remote viewer'. In other words he claims to use a psychic gift to provide detailed factual information about distant locations. In many cases he works with the briefest of information, such as co-ordinates of longitude and latitude. In this particular case McMoneagle was given map co-ordinates by NASA. Focusing on the target information McMoneagle drew a sphinx-like figure and five pyramids. He believed that he had been focusing on an earthbound target: in fact, he was told, the co-ordinates were for a site on Mars known as Cydonia! Joe's psychic session provided him with some further information:

> Towards the end of the session I became aware of something else and it turned out it had a lot to do with who constructed the pyramids. I had a perception that it was a race of beings or humanoids that were sort of passing through at the time. My sense was they were moving through the solar system and had to move on to a different location and it's possible they moved there.

Further missions to Mars are now underway or planned – including a manned flight. Whether these missions provide the conclusive evidence that Hoagland and his colleagues seek remains to be seen. Whatever happens, the face on Mars has provided one of the 20th century's most fascinating enigmas. The words of astronomer Carl Sagan neatly sum up the dilemma the face poses: 'Despite our shortness of breath and beating of our hearts, the Martian sphinx looks natural – not artificial, not a dead ringer for a human face ... But I might be wrong.'

BALL LIGHTNING

Ball lightning has a stunning reputation as one of Nature's most exotic creations: it comes in different colours, sizes and strengths. Some say it burns, others that it merely fizzes, and a minority that it can go through walls, windows and even people. It is certainly no ordinary lightning, and there are many researchers who have linked its appearances to both crop-circle phenomena and UFO sightings.

Until as recently as 1970 ball lightning was not a subject for serious scientific discussion: it was not considered a real phenomenon and only occurred as an hallucinatory experience in the minds of a demented few. This was the prevailing view despite a number of well-evidenced reports of 'fireballs' dating back many hundreds of years: in the 16th century fireballs were witnessed, hovering in the sky over the city of Basle in Switzerland. In the 19th century the French writer W. de Fonville described how, on 10 September 1845, a fireball rolled into a French country kitchen in a village called Salagnac. One of the cooks shouted to another man to kick it from the room, or stamp it out: the gentleman wisely let it roll on to a nearby stable where a pig took a sniff at it and it exploded – killing the unfortunate pig and causing significant damage to the stable.

The phenomenon moved from apocryphal story to real science when ball lightning was first witnessed by a respected scientist. R.C. Jennison, a British university professor, was travelling on an airliner from New York to Washington on 19 March 1963. The plane had just been struck by lightning, when a small glowing ball emerged from the pilot's cabin and floated down the aisle – witnessed by Jennison and many of the aircraft's passengers. Jennison said that the eight-inch globe was about as bright as a ten-watt bulb, and gave off no perceptible heat. The scientist was particularly interested to note that the ball appeared perfectly spherical and 'almost solid in appearance'. Professor Jennison's scientific paper on the phenomenon was published over six years later in the prestigious scientific journal *Nature* and opened the way for further reports of the anomalous phenomenon.

One of the most startling examples of ball lightning behaviour was described by a woman in Smethwick, England, in the 1970s. In a scientific paper published in *Nature* in 1976 she described how a purple-blue, four-inch ball with a flame-coloured halo around it, appeared above her cooker during a thunderstorm. She tried to brush it away but it seemed to pass right through her. From other descriptions of ball lightning this contact might have been fatal, but the mysterious ball only seemed to 'burn' a two-by-four inch hole in her dress and tights. She reported that the material around the hole was shrivelled but not charred. The print pattern on the dress was faded. She also had burns from where her wedding ring had heated up as it passed through the mysterious ball. Perhaps remarkably, no other negative effects were reported.

With the increasing number of sightings in the past 30 years, interest has grown in this previously esoteric form of energy. Ball lightning has become an area of serious study for conventional scientists as well as those who believe that there may be some intelligent force behind its appearance. With the arrival of the first harvest of crop circles in southern England in the mid-1980s, a number of reports have indicated that the presence of ball lightning may be linked to their formation.

Despite speculations that alien landings or UFO activity might be the cause of these often remarkable patterns in the crops, there were also persistent and well-documented reports like that of Tom Gwinnett, a local farmer from Gloucestershire. Gwinnett had been driving past a field on a warm summer's evening in July 1988 when the electrics in his car suddenly failed. He got out to investigate the problem, and was still trying to restart the car when he heard a 'strange whirring sound'. When he looked at a nearby wheat field he saw a dull red ball – about the size of a football. It was not a solid form, but seemed to be made up of a cluster of red sparks – fed by a supply of sparks coming from the top of the wheat. The farmer continued to watch the strange sphere for a minute or two, while the same distinctive sound continued. It then, very suddenly, disappeared. At the same time the car's electrics were restored to full health. Gwinnett drove off without inspecting the field, but when he returned in the morning he discovered a simple 20-foot crop circle where he had seen the phenomenon.

In Russia research into ball lightning is now taken very seriously, and the Information Centre on Ball Lightning in Moscow now carries a database of around 2,000 sightings.

Analysis of the reports show that ball lightning can vary significantly in size, with about two-thirds measuring somewhere between 4 and 20 inches. Only a few per cent of the sample appeared to be greater than two feet in size. Its colour can also vary greatly: the most common colour is bright white, although yellow, red and orange are often reported, with blue and purple showing up less often. Only very occasionally, it seems, are green examples seen.

Another Russian research organization at the Yaroslavl State University has published 43 sightings of ball lightning in which the phenomenon has been seen to pass directly through matter: the report contains examples of the ball passing straight through glass without causing it to crack or break, as well as revealing its ability to appear from light and power sockets.

In many reports there seems to be a strong connection between ball lightning and other weather phenomena – particularly with storms and tornadoes. A mysterious phenomenon was held responsible for digging a trench across a clay tennis court in Mauritius on 24 May 1948:

A trench running in a north–south direction, 60 feet long and 1 to 2½ feet wide, was cut in the bare surface of the court to a depth varying from one to four inches. The material lifted from the trench was all thrown to the west to a distance of 50 feet; pieces weighing about one pound were thrown as far as 30 feet. The surface material was slightly blackened as if by heating, and a crackling like that of a sugar-cane fire was heard for two or three minutes ... One witness claims to have seen a ball of fire about two feet in diameter which crossed from a football pitch to the tennis court through a wire-netting fence without leaving any evidence of its passage.

The link between ball lightning and tornadoes also appears in a report told by the survivors of an incident in Toledo, Ohio, in the 1960s:

We were shaken up and our trailer along with others was dented badly from hail the size of baseballs. The beautiful electric blue light that was around the tornado was something to see, and balls of orange and lightning came from the cone point of the tornado. The cone or tail of the tornado reminded me of an elephant trunk. It would dip down as if to get food then rise up again as if the trunk of an elephant would put the food in his mouth. While the trunk was up the tornado was not dangerous, just when the point came down is when the damage started. My son and I watched the orange balls of fire roll down the Race Way Park then it lifted and roof came off one of the horse barns.

There seems little doubt that certain forms of ball lightning are associated with high levels of electrical energy in the atmosphere. Some scientists believe that if we understood ball lightning more fully that we might be able to tap into a new source of electrical energy. Nikola Tesla, the great inventor and developer of AC current in the earlier part of the 20th century, tried to extract electrical power from lightning. As far as we know he was not successful, although he did manage to blow up the local electrical distribution station on a night of high electrical activity. Current research into tapping electricity from lightning phenomena has focused on the replication of ball lightning in the laboratory. Dr Yoshi Hiko Ohtsuki has led this research at Waseda University in Japan: his attempts to recreate ball lightning have had some marked success – creating small glowing balls a few milli-metres across. However they die away quickly and have so far not yielded up any usable power. Interestingly though, they seem to leave small circular imprints on the metal plates used in the experiments. Could these be miniature crop circles?

As knowledge grows of ball lightning it seems likely that we will come to know more about how it forms – both naturally and synthetically in controlled laboratory con-ditions. The story of ball lightning has shown how, in some 30 years, a 'fringe' subject, worthy of ridicule in the orthodox scientific community, can become a respectable, mainstream area of study. Perhaps the ball lightning story offers some hope to those researchers who find themselves struggling in the wilderness.

SPONTANEOUS HUMAN COMBUSTION

Over four centuries around 200 cases of Spontaneous Human Combustion have been documented, although many more unexplained deaths from bodily fire are known to have occurred. In many of these cases there seems to be no external cause of ignition, and, perhaps most amazingly, while a person's body is almost fully burnt to ashes, the surrounding environment is left relatively unscathed. The cause or causes of this strange enigma continue to defy logic, even though there is no lack of detail in the evidence.

The first celebrated case that benefits from a clear first-hand account describes the death of Countess di Bandi of Cesena, Italy. The case was reported by a priest, the Reverend Joseph Bianchini of Verona in 1731:

The Countess Cornelia (di) Bandi, in the sixty-second year of her age, was all day as well as she used to be; but at night was observed, when at supper, dull and heavy. She retired, was put to bed, where she passed three hours and more in familiar discourses with her maid, and in some prayers; at last, falling asleep, the door was shut. In the morning, the maid, taking notice that her mistress did not wake at the usual hour, went into the bed-chamber, and called her, but not being answer'd, doubting some ill accident, open'd the window, and saw the corpse of her mistress in this deplorable condition.

Four feet distance from the bed there was a heap of ashes, two legs untouch'd, from the foot to the knee, with their stockings on; between them was the lady's head; whose brains, half of the back-part of the scull [sic] and the whole chin were

223

burnt to ashes; amongst which were found three fingers blacken'd. All the rest was ashes, which had this particular quality, that they left in the hand, when taken up, a greasy and stinking moisture.

The air in the room was also observed cumber'd with soot floating in it: A small oil-lamp on the floor was cover'd with ashes, but no oil in it. Two candles in candlesticks upon a table stood upright; the cotton [wick] was left in both, but the tallow was gone and vanished ... The bed receiv'd no damage; the blankets and sheets were only raised on one side, as when a person rises up from it, or goes in: The whole furniture, as well as the bed, were spread over with moist and ash-coloured soot, which had penetrated into the chest-of-drawers, even to foul the linnens [sic]: Nay the soot was also gone into a neighbouring kitchen, and hung on the walls, moveables (furniture), and utensils of it. From the pantry a piece of bread cover'd with that soot, and grown black, was given to several dogs, all of which refused to eat it. In the room above it was moreover taken notice, that from the lower part of the windows trickled down a greasy, loathsome, yellowish liquor; and thereabout they smelt a stink, without knowing of what; and saw the soot fly around.

It was remarkable, that the floor of the chamber was so thick smear'd with a gluish moisture, that it could not be taken off; and the stink spread more and more through the other chambers.

The Countess was a lady of good reputation, and not known for overindulgence with alcohol, so it is unlikely that this was a factor in her combustion. She was known, however, to wash her body with camphorated spirits of wine when she was feeling poorly, and it was suspected that she had done so the night before her death. Nevertheless the medical authorities of the time, dismissing lightning as a cause, attributed her death to an internal combustion that had consumed her body from the inside out, without setting alight any furniture or fabric in her room. Particularly her combustion resulted from

... inflamed effluvia of her blood, by juices and fermentation of the stomach, by the many combustible matters which are abundant in living bodies for the uses of life; and, finally, by the fiery evaporations which exhale from the settlings of spirit of wine, brandies, and other hot liquors in the tunica villosa of the stomach, and other adipose or fat membranes; within which (as chemists observe) those spirits ingender a kind of camphire; which in the night time, in sleep, by a full breathing and respiration, are put in a stronger motion, and, consequently, more apt to be set afire.

This typical and thoroughly documented case was one of many researched and studied by Charles Dickens, the great English novelist of the Victorian era. Dickens became fascinated with the Spontaneous Human Combustion phenomena and could justifiably claim to be the world's first serious 'SHC' researcher. In *Bleak House* Dickens bestowed the dubious honour of such a death on Krook, one of the story's main antagonists. Dickens used all his knowledge of the phenomenon to paint an accurate and disturbing picture of this fitting end to a rotten life – a fate that was thought deserving for all that was corrupt in Victorian England. Most people of the time had no idea that the manner of Krook's leaving was anything more than a fancy of Dickens' own mind. In the chapter describing Krook's death, Dickens urges the reader to take the symbolism of such a terrible death seriously:

Call the death by any name [you] will, attribute it to whom you will, or say it might have been prevented how you will, it is the same death eternally – inborn, inbred, engendered in the corrupted humours of the vicious body itself, and that only – Spontaneous Combustion, and none other of all the deaths that can be died.

The death in 1951 of Mrs Mary Hardy Reeser, of St Petersburg, Florida, has been a key case in the modern search for an answer to the riddle of Spontaneous Human Combustion.

When the few remains of Mrs Reeser were found in her otherwise undamaged apartment, virtually every possible medical and technical test was applied to the evidence in an effort to determine the cause of her death. In spite of the efforts of pathologists, arson researchers, fire officials and the FBI, the St Petersburg police announced they were no closer to a solution over a year after the event:

> Our investigation has turned up nothing that could be singled out as proving, beyond a doubt, what actually happened. The case is still open. We are still as far from establishing any logical cause for the death as we were when we first entered Mrs Reeser's apartment.

Dr Wilton Krogman, an expert in the effects of fire on the human body at the University of Pennsylvania's School of Medicine, was similarly baffled: 'I regard it as the most amazing thing I've ever seen. As I review it, the short hairs on my neck bristle with vague fear. Were I living in the Middle Ages, I'd mutter something about black magic.' Mrs Reeser was a widow of 67 living in a four-apartment block belonging to a Mrs Pansy Carpenter, who also lived in the block. On the night of 1 July 1951 Mrs Carpenter visited Mary Reeser briefly at about 9pm. Reeser was sitting in a chair, smoking a cigarette. She wore a night-gown, a housecoat and black satin slippers. Her bedclothes were folded back ready for her to get into bed.

At 5am Mrs Carpenter woke up: she soon noticed a faint smell of smoke, which she took to be a water pump in the garage that had been overheating recently. After turning the pump off she returned to bed. Getting up an hour later the smell of smoke had disappeared.

At 8am a telegram arrived for Mrs Reeser. Mrs Carpenter signed for it and took it along to Mrs Reeser's apartment. When she grasped the doorknob Mrs Carpenter found it to be hot. She took a step back and called for help. Two painters who were working across the street ran over to assist. One of them entered the flat and immediately felt a blast of hot air.

He looked around, hoping to rescue Mrs Reeser. He could not find her. The bed was empty and some smoke lingered. A small flame still burned on a wooden beam. Firemen soon arrived and put out the fire. The Assistant Fire Chief started to inspect the premises. What he saw shocked him: in the centre of the room there was a burned area about four feet across. In this small area he found chair springs and all that remained of Mary Reeser's body: her left foot still wearing her satin slipper; her skull, considerably shrunken; her liver and a part of her spine; and a pile of ashes. She had been reduced from 175 pounds to a collection of parts weighing just 10 pounds, and yet nowhere was the considerable smoke that would have been expected. Perhaps the most extraordinary thing to those investigating was that none of the objects in the nearby area had been burned up at all. The FBI records, though, show there were some curious effects:

> The ceiling, draperies and walls, from a point exactly four feet above the floor, were coated with smelly, oily soot. Below this four-foot mark there was none. The wall paint, adjacent to the chair was faintly browned, but the carpet where the chair had rested was not even burned through. A wall mirror 10 feet away had cracked, probably from heat . . . Plastic wall outlets above the four-foot mark were melted, but the fuses were not blown and the current was on . . . An electric clock plugged into one of the fused fixtures had stopped at precisely 4.20 . . .
>
> Newspapers nearby on a table and draperies and linens on the daybed close at hand – all flammable – were not damaged. And though the painters and Mrs Carpenter had felt a wave of heat when they opened the door, no one had noted smoke or burning odor and there were no embers or flames in the ashes.

While the search for the cause of Mrs Reeser's demise was intense, the conclusions were less than clear: the FBI's laboratory could only say that no chemicals or accelerants were involved, and that the case was 'unusual and improbable'; an arson specialist from the National Board of Underwriters – an insurance man trained to detect foul play – was unable to say anymore than 'died from fire'.

Dr Wilton Krogman, who had made a speciality of the way the human body could or could not resist the effects of fire, was brought in to shed light on this baffling case. From previous experience he knew that it required enormous heat – something around 3,000 degrees Fahrenheit – for the skeleton to be consumed, leaving only ashes. The theory that a cigarette could have caused such a conflagration was not tenable: there simply was not enough material burned up in the fire to create such intense heat. Lightning was ruled out. As was some form of electrical problem: the fuse had not even blown. Murder and suicide were also ruled out: there were not the motives, and, in any case the facts of the case simply did not fit. Krogman was defeated: he had no answer to the riddle. 'I have posed the problem to myself again and again of why Mrs Reeser could have been so thoroughly destroyed, even to the bones, and yet leave nearby objects materially unaffected. I always end up rejecting it in theory but facing it in apparent fact.' The condition of Mrs Reeser's skull only added to the mystery which Krogman was left with:

> . . . the head is not left complete in ordinary burning cases. Certainly it does not shrivel or symmetrically reduce to a much smaller size. In presence of heat sufficient to destroy soft tissues, the skull would literally explode in many pieces. I . . . have never known any exception to this rule. Never have I seen a skull so shrunken or a body so completely consumed by heat.

Research into the Mary Reeser case has continued since the tragic happenings of 1951, and further cases have at least provided additional information, if not any real answer to SHC's engimatic causation.

A hundred or so cases of death from inexplicable fires are recorded around the world each year, but, in the UK at least, a death of this kind has never been formally recorded as

Spontaneous Human Combustion – it is, merely, an inexplicable death. Typical of these cases was the death of 19-year-old Maybelle Andrews in the late 1950s. Andrews was in a London discothèque with her boyfriend when she burst into flames. The fire started on her back and upper body, engulfing her head, and setting light to her hair. Her boyfriend Billy Clifford and others tried to put the fire out, but were unable to save her and she died in an ambulance on her way to hospital. Clifford confirmed that there were no obvious triggers for the fire: 'I saw no one smoking on the dance floor. There were no candles on the tables and I did not see her dress catch fire from anything. I know it sounds incredible, but it appeared to me that the flames burst outwards, as if they originated within her body.' On Maybelle Andrews' death certificate, the cause of death was given as 'death by misadventure, caused by a fire of unknown origin.'

It has often been thought that alcohol abuse plays a part in SHC cases. People who have soaked their internal organs in alcohol may well be more inflammable than most but, taking the research as a whole, there is little evidence that there is a causal link with drink. It is, however, relatively common that victims are older people living alone.

In a similar case to that of Mary Reeser, reported in 1966, a meter reader named Don Gosnell called to check the electricity reading at the home of John Irving Bentley, a 92-year-old retired doctor, living in Coudersport, Pennsylvania. Knocking on the door, Mr Gosnell received no reply, and decided to go in through the unlocked front door to check the reading in the basement anyway. He became aware of a 'light-blue smoke ... like that of starting up a new central heating system'. In one part of the basement he saw a pile of ash – about 14 inches around, and 5 inches high. Not thinking it to be anything particular he kicked it casually, distributing it a little around the room. While in the basement he failed to notice a hole in the ceiling about 2½ feet wide and 4 feet long, with burned edges. Once he had read the meter he went back up to the ground floor to see if he could find Dr

Bentley. Some more smoke was apparent, and he followed it to its source in the bathroom: there he was met by a shocking sight. Apart from Dr Bentley's walking frame, all that was left around the hole in the floor leading to the basement was the old man's lower right leg, still wearing a slipper. The shocked meter reader ran from the house, screaming to the world: 'Dr Bentley burnt up!'

The coroner was thoroughly mystified. One theory said that the doctor had set light to his bathrobe while lighting his pipe, and had then tried to get to the bathroom to put the fire out. The doctor's robe had been found in the bathtub, but was only slightly singed. Yet even a flaming robe could not set a human body on fire. Again virtually nothing around the completely consumed body had been affected. In the end the coroner's verdict was clear, yet gave scant sense of the causes: 'Asphyxiation and 90 per cent burning'.

While older victims predominate, it is not unknown for children to be at the centre of unexplained fires. In 1973 a seven-month-old baby named Parvinder Kaur was sitting in his baby carriage when he and the carriage went up in flames. The child survived the ordeal after treatment at Birmingham Hospital's Burns Unit. A year or so later a six-month-old child named Lisa Tipton was found burned to death in a confined room at her parent's home in Staffordshire. The fire did not seem to have affected any other rooms, and there was no apparent cause.

It was not until the 1980s that a strong, scientific theory to explain SHC was proposed – by Scottish expert on combustion Dr Doug Drysdale. The 'wick' or 'candle' theory proposed that in cases of human combustion the body is like a candle – with the skeleton acting as a wick, and the muscle and fat around the skeleton burning like the wax of a candle. A high-profile BBC science documentary shown in 1989 tried to fit the facts of various cases to this theory. For many viewers it offered a clear rational explanation of Spontaneous Human Combustion, and seemed to remove the supernatural or mysterious aspects of the phenomenon. Nevertheless many experts who appeared in the programme were unhappy that it had over-simplified the reality of SHC, and that there were many cases in which combustion had occurred too quickly to fit with this 'slow-burn' model.

Theories continue to multiply: some experts now believe that it occurs as a result of unexplained nuclear reactions in the body's cells; others see a link with ball lightning, and there is some evidence that lightning is often recorded around the times of these mysterious deaths. Another piece of research, published by two German scientists in 1993, has suggested that highly inflammable phosphane can build up in the human system. Some SHC researchers have extrapolated that if the phosphane were triggered, it could lead to an internal combustion of the body.

One case which may show how 'spontaneous' the combustion can be, occurred in 1985 to Paul Hayes, a 19-year-old computer operator living and working in London. Walking down a road in Stepney Green on the night of 25 May, Hayes inexplicably burst into flames. From the waist upwards flames surrounded his body as if he had been doused in petrol and set light to:

It was indescribable ... like being plunged into the heat of a furnace ... My arms felt as though they were being prodded by red hot pokers, from my shoulders to my wrists. My cheeks were red-hot, my ears were numb. My chest felt like boiling water had been poured over it. I thought I could hear my brains bubbling ... I tried to run, stupidly thinking I could race ahead of the flames.

Hayes collapsed on the pavement, curling into a ball: 'I thought I was dying. Images of my parents, my friends, my girlfriend, came to mind.' Then, quite suddenly, the flames died away: 'I opened my eyes. There was no flame, no smoke. For a few minutes I lay still, terrified. I began to shiver with shock. I was numb in some spots, white hot in others.' Hayes managed to stumble to the nearby casualty department of a London hospital, where he was successfully treated for his burns. To this day though, non-smoker Paul is no nearer to understanding the cause of his spontaneous combustion.

Research will, of course, go on. Hopefully further cases will yield up more to explain this enigmatic cause of death. A statement made by one of the officers investigating the Mary Reeser case, though, still sums up the mystery of spontaneous human combustion: 'As far as logical explanations go, this is one of those things that just couldn't have happened, but it did. The case is not closed and may never be to the satisfaction of all concerned.'

STRANGE RAINS

Since biblical times objects both animate and inanimate have been recorded falling to Earth. Fish, frogs, snakes, cats (and dogs), meat, stones, crosses, ingots, ice, jelly, cobwebs, meat, blood, mice, lemmings. If reports are to be believed all have fallen victim to gravity after, presumably, having succumbed to some form of levitation. In the conventional world view, what goes up must come down. While the passing of time may bring a ring of improbability to some ancient reports, the fact that strange rains are still reported regularly around the world should encourage us to look seriously at the evidence, however improbable it may sound.

Looking back as far as we can, the Bible reports a number of incidents of both benign and malign falls from the sky. In the Book of Exodus, 'manna' – a kind of superfood – fell from heaven to sustain the Israelites in the desert. Later, in the Book of Joshua, when Joshua and his army are pursuing the Armorite, they are assisted by some intervention from above:

> And as they fled before Israel, while they were going down the
> ascent of Beth-horon, the Lord threw down great stones from

heaven upon them as far as Azekah, and they died; there were more who died because of the hailstones than the men of Israel killed with the sword.

It was around AD 200 that the Greek historian Athaneus wrote of a three-day-long fall of fish:

I also know that it has very often rained fishes. At all events Phenias, in the second book of his Eresian Magistrates, says that in the Chersonesus (the place where this happened) it once rained fish uninterruptedly for three days; and Phylarchus in his fourth book, says that people had often seen it raining fish, and often also raining wheat, and that the same thing had happened with respect to frogs. At all events, Heraclides Lembus, in the 21st book of his History, says: 'In Paeonia and Dardania it has, they say, before now rained frogs: and so great has been the number of these frogs that the houses and the roads have been full of them; and at first, for some days, the inhabitants, endeavouring to kill them, and shutting up their houses, endured the pest; but when they did no good, but found that all their vessels were filled with them, and the frogs were found to be boiled up and roasted with everything they ate, and when besides all this, they could not make use of any water, nor put their feet on the ground for the heaps of frogs that were everywhere, and were annoyed also by the smell of those that died, they fled the country.'

Fishes, frogs and toads have featured regularly in reports over the past few hundred years. In 1653 at Acle in Norfolk, England, a deluge of small toads fell in such quantities that the townspeople had to collect them up in buckets to be burned. In 1794 toads made a bid to influence history when they fell on a section of Napoleon's army. They fell in such great numbers that an infantry group was forced to leave the safety of a depression in the land where they had hidden.

On 7 September 1953, frogs and toads 'of all descriptions' fell on Leicester, Massachusetts. Local children were delighted, and collected them into buckets with their bare hands. For those who thought they had arrived from an overflowing river there was some irrefutable evidence: the amphibians covered the roofs of houses, and even filled the gutters.

During a powerful thunderstorm in July 1841 hundreds of small fish and frogs fell – along with some ice – on Derby, England. The fish were mainly sticklebacks, about one to two inches long; the frogs were the size of large beans, and were still alive after landing on the pavement. In 1859 one of the best recorded fish falls landed on the small Welsh village of Mountain Ash. A key witness was a sawyer named John Lewis:

On Wednesday, February 9, I was getting out a piece of timber, for the purpose of setting it for the saw, when I was startled by something falling all over me – down my neck, on my head, and on my back. On putting my hand down my neck I was surprised to find they were little fish. By this time I saw the whole ground covered with them. I took off my hat, the bridge of which was full of them. They were jumping all about. They covered the ground in a long strip of about 80 yards by 12, as we measured afterwards. That shed [Lewis pointed to his workshop] was covered with them, and the shoots were quite full of them. My mate and I might have gathered bucketsfull of them, scraping with our hands. We did gather a great many, about a bucketful, and threw them into the rain pool, where some of them now are. There were two showers, with an interval of about ten minutes, and each shower lasted about two minutes or thereabouts. The time was 11 a.m. . . . it was not blowing very hard, but uncommon wet . . . They came down with the rain 'in a body, like'.

The largest fish was about five inches long and died soon after landing. Lewis sent some Mountain Ash fish to the London Zoo, but the scientists did not take his story seriously. J.E. Gray, an expert from the British Museum, wrote in the *Zoological Magazine*: 'On reading the evidence it appears to me most probably to be only a practical joke of the mates of John Lewis, who seems to have thrown a pailful of water with the fish in it over him.' This report appeared despite the well-attested accounts of many villagers – all providing first-hand information that thousands of fish had fallen.

One of the most torrential falls of fish was recorded over Singapore following a serious earthquake in 1861. The well-known naturalist Francis de Castelnau was able to give a first-hand eye-witness statement:

At 10 o'clock the sun lifted and from my window I saw a large number of Malays and Chinese filling baskets with fishes which they picked up in the pools of rain water which covered the ground. On being asked where the fishes came from the natives replied that they had fallen from the sky. Three days afterwards, when the pools had dried up, we found many dead fishes.

Having examined the animals, I recognized them as *Clarias batrachi* . . . a species of catfish which is very abundant in fresh water in Singapore, and in the Malay Peninsula . . . They were from 10 to 12 inches long . . .

An old Malay has since told me that in his youth he had seen a similar phenomenon.

In Yoro, Honduras, at the beginning of the country's rainy season, the local people gather with buckets, baskets and nets, waiting for fish to fall from the sky. This may sound like irrational behaviour, a ridiculous superstitious ritual, or the misguided result of some ancient belief. In fact, their behaviour is entirely practical. Every year, as far back as the people of Yoro can remember, great showers of sardines fall on grassy land near the town. The sardines are very much alive, and the people avidly fill their containers. Then, within hours of the fish's arrival, high winds and electrical storms hit the area, and the annual rains are underway.

*

235

The most popular theory to explain these strange rains suggests that waterspouts, tornadoes or whirlwinds pick up animals and other objects and transport them until their power subsides, when they are deposited randomly on land or sea. There is no doubt that these forces of nature have the power to carry great weights. Air speeds within the funnels of tornadoes can approach 300 miles an hour, and air pressures rise to 300 pounds per square foot. In a series of American observations, large objects have succumbed to the vortexian power of tornadoes: in 1883, a 675-pound metal screw from a cotton press flew 900 feet through the air with the help of a tornado; in an 1875 event, a 600-pound wooden beam travelled a quarter of a mile before returning to earth, while a lighter chicken house went for four miles; in 1877 a tornado carried a church spire for 17 miles. Waterspouts are known to have emptied, or nearly emptied, harbours and small lakes, and, in one case, witnesses have seen fish blown from a lake onto dry land.

While these forces of nature certainly possess the power to carry great weights, there are no clear witness reports describing the *collection* of shoals of fish, or huge colonies of frogs. While it seems likely that such natural phenomena may be behind some of the fafrotskies (as FAlls FROm The SKIES are sometimes known), there are still a number of unanswered questions. It is far from clear how such forces are able to be so selective in what they pick up. Rains often release animals of only one species, or one class of object. In the case of animals they also seem to deposit live bodies many miles from their natural source of life, such as water. How can these mechanisms be explained? Another problem is the number of reports that declare unequivocally that things have fallen not from the dark storm clouds that follow tornadoes, but from clear blue skies. It is these peculiarities that lead some researchers to postulate more supernatural explanations, such as parallel universes, poltergeist phenomena and the teleportation of objects from one place to another.

Charles Fort, the great investigator of the paranormal,

postulated a 'Supersargasso Sea' – a sea floating somewhere in the atmosphere from where such 'fafrotskies' might originate. He speculated that this surrogate sea might exchange objects and animals with the 'real' sea below. At times it would suck them from the sea below, and at others it would deposit its contents over the globe. While it is an unlikely hypothesis, such a theory had the benefit – at least at the time – of being virtually impossible to disprove. Fort's theory was typical of his approach to phenomena: there are some happenings which seem to defy all rational explanation. These phenomena may, quite simply, require a very new model of the universe.

It was October 1985 when Lynne Connolly was in her garden in Hull, England, hanging her washing out to dry. Nothing strange there: until she felt something land on her head. It was a small silver notecase, engraved with letters, possibly intials, a six-pointed star and the word 'Klaipeda'. By a strange synchronicity Klaipeda was the name of the Baltic town that experienced a special 'fall' of its own: in 1687 large flakes of black 'marsh paper' floated to earth. The marsh paper was damp and smelled of rotten seaweed. Some sheets were very large – large enough to cover a table. The same material fell again in 1839 in Silesia. Larger sheets were recorded: a reporter writing in the *Edinburgh Review* said he had a piece from a sheet of 200 square feet. He even claimed it was thick enough to make clothing from. When the original material from Klaipeda was analysed it was found to consist of vegetable matter, mainly *Conferva crispata*, (a thread-like algae), and partly of around 29 species of a small water-dwelling animal called an *Infusoria*.

Another unique manifestation that appears to defy all logic happened in 1957 when thousands of 1,000 franc notes fell on the town of Bourges in France. The year before a group of children in Bristol, England, had been hit by a shower of pennies and halfpennies that fell from the skies. In 1961 green peaches fell from a dense cloud onto the town of Shreveport,

Louisiana. The local weather bureau reported that there had not been any whirlwind or tornado activity which could have been responsible for their upliftment. In 1968 blood and flesh were scattered over an area of a third of a square mile near the Brazilian towns of Cacapava and Sao Jose dos Campos. The list goes on. Australasia alone has recorded an average of two inexplicable rains each year for the last 100 years. There seems no limit to the peculiarity of the matter that can fall from the skies.

Perhaps the strangest and most intriguing of all 'falls' involves a substance called 'angel hair'. Angel hair is made up of gauzy, web-like threads of white silky material. While it appears fragile, angel hair can be very tough, and may appear in strands as long as 50 feet. In October 1962, Mr R.H. Pape, the captain of a ship called the *Roxburgh Castle*, was walking on deck when he found thin hairy filaments on the vessel's railings:

> Calling the attention of the Chief Officer, I pulled one of these strands from a stanchion and found it to be quite tough and resilient. I stretched it but it would not break easily (as, for instance, a cobweb would have done) and after keeping it in my hand for three or four minutes it disappeared completely; in other words, it just vanished into nothing.
>
> Looking up [the captain continued] we could see small cocoons of the material floating down from the sky but as far as we could ascertain there was nothing . . . to account for this extraordinary occurence.

The conventional scientific response to this report was given by D.J. Clark of the Natural History Museum in London:

> Spiders are, I think, responsible for the phenomena you describe. The majority of these particular spiders belong to the family of Linyphiidae, and mature in the autumn. In the autumn, on fine, warm and sunny days, especially with a fairly

heavy early morning dew, the spiders begin to disperse and migrate in order to colonise new areas where the food supply is greater. The method they use is known as 'ballooning' ... The spiders sometimes are carried many miles ... I cannot explain the disappearance of these strands when held in the hand. It may be that the threads of the strand you describe were not so entangled and when handled broke up into individual threads, thus becoming very inconspicuous. Spider silk cannot melt because heat does not affect it, it is on the whole less soluble that true silk.

Alongside such prosaic explanations, others have theorized that angel hair is a kind of exhaust material from the motive forces of UFOs. A report by P.I. Lewis of Ontario, Canada, from 26 September 1948 makes this link very clearly:

This day was warm and the sky cloudless ... I was lying on my back on the lawn when I started to see an object resembling a star moving rapidly across the sky ...

At first it was easy to imagine that recent reports of 'Flying Saucers' had not been exaggerated. More of these objects came sailing into view over the ridge of the house, only to disappear when nearly overhead. With field glasses I was able to see that each was approximately spherical, the centre being rather brighter than the edges. The glasses also showed quite a number at such heights that they were invisible to the naked eye ...

Also visible now and then were long threads, apparently from spiders. Some of these were seen to reflect the light over a length of three or four yards, but any one piece may of course have been longer.

According to one modern scientist who has investigated the chemical make-up of angel hair:

My research had shown that angel hair is very unstable, and that it degrades in oxygen. Shortly after falling on the ground, it usually disappears. A few specimens have been preserved, when, shortly after falling, they have been sealed in air-tight containers. Analysis has shown that its structure contains silicon, magnesium, calcium and boron. The strands in our laboratories are therefore not alien to the earth, yet they are very strange indeed. I have not seen anything quite like this substance. I cannot say whether it comes from UFOs.

We have probably all seen, or even felt, hail fall to the ground in small pellets or balls. It does not take too much to imagine the damage that larger chunks of ice can do. Ice falls form a whole category of strange rains, and have gained a real notoriety since causing death on a number of occasions. In 1951, a carpenter working on the roof of his house near Dusseldorf, Germany, died when he was speared by a shaft of ice six foot long and six inches in diameter.

Reports of ice falls go back as far as 1552 when giant hail was described at Dordrecht, Holland:

[A Prodigiously Huge Hailstone]
In the year 1552 – Friday the 17th May between 4 and 5 o'clock in the afternoon – there was a particularly violent thunderstorm in a certain Dutch town called Dordrecht, driving the inhabitants in terror into their houses as if the world were coming to an end, because for more than half an hour there was a steady bombardment of horrible hailstones, so that every garden and orchard was destroyed. Some of the hailstones were of gigantic size and peculiar shape. Hundreds of people saw them, including a painter who sketched the hailstones ... Several hailstones had a natural shape of a sun. On others appeared a crown of thorns. Some weighed as much as half a pound. The water from these hailstones smelled as if there were boiling water. This hailstorm was followed by a foul-smelling cloud. It is a wonder what such signs may signify.

The French astronomer and scholar of the paranormal Camille Flammarion collected stories of ice falls in the mid-19th century. One of his reports documents a piece of ice 15 feet long and 11 feet thick. This could hardly be called hail, and it is far from clear how such a piece of ice could have formed in the skies. An even larger piece was recorded in 1849: an ice block 20 feet across and weighing nearly half a ton came to earth near Ord in Scotland. Fortunately there were no victims.

More recently, reports of ice blocks, or 'ice bombs' as they are sometimes known, appear to have been on the increase. Some experts now believe that contemporary ice falls can be explained by aircraft: ice builds up on wings, and subsequently falls to earth. There is a problem with this theory, though, since the de-icing capabilities of modern planes does not allow for large amounts of ice to form. A more likely link between ice and planes are their toilets. Some aircraft toilets are believed to have jettisoned their contents on a number of occasions and, in these cases, we could expect quite specific evidence – hard evidence that is not always apparent.

A major ice fall that occurred on 2 April 1973 over Manchester, England, was originally attributed to an aircraft, but analysis was to raise questions about this theory. Dr Richard Griffiths of Manchester University was walking down the road when he heard a loud clap of thunder. A few minutes later his walk was brought to an abrupt halt by the explosive impact of an ice bomb crashing to earth on the street in front of him. Griffiths rushed the largest chunk home to his freezer, before transferring it to the university laboratory for analysis. To establish whether the ice had come from an aeroplane flying over Manchester, Griffiths researched the flight plans of all aircraft in the area at the time. There were none that could have been responsible. In his laboratory he was to come up with even more interesting findings: first, the water from the ice bomb was of a type normally associated with clouds formations (ie not from an aeroplane); second, the piece of ice was formed out of layers, or strata, of ice. In fact there were

51 layers to the block, which could – like a hailstone – have added layer after layer as it plunged through the atmosphere. This analysis has strengthened the case that not all modern ice falls can be explained as the deposits of modern aircraft.

There is no reason why reports of strange rains should not continue and multiply. The events described represent just a tiny sample of the documented records, and there is no reason why we should not expect to see even stranger and more exotic falls from above. In the words of Bob Dylan, 'a hard rain's gonna fall.'

ANOMALOUS ARCHAEOLOGY

In June 1968 William J. Meister, a draughtsman and amateur fossil hunter, was looking for trilobites near Antelope Spring, Utah. Trilobites are the fossils of sea creatures which became extinct some 200 million years ago, and Mr Meister had become quite skilled at locating these rare objects. And yet when he broke open a piece of shale, hoping to find another trilobite, he was amazed to find the fossilized print of a human's shoe. The raised heel left an indent some eighth of an inch deeper than the sole, and showed the usual signs of wear consistent with a right-footed shoe: '. . . on one side the footprint of a human with trilobites right in the footprint itself. The other half of the rock slab showed an almost perfect mould of the footprint and fossils. Amazingly the human was wearing a sandal.' Meister returned to the site on 4 July with Dr Clarence Coombs of Columbia Union College, Tacoma, Maryland, and geologist Maurice Carlisle from the University of Colorado at Boulder. Carlisle examined the surrounding geology, and was able to confirm that the slab could have originally been on the exposed surface of the ground. Nevertheless it had only been on the surface for a relatively short geological period: the rock strata from which the print emerged was dated at over 500 million years old. Given that human presence on earth has so far been limited to the last one or two million years, and that shoes have only existed for a few thousand years, orthodox science found the implications of the 'discovery' too much to contemplate. Disbelief in the fossil's provenance was expressed at a news conference by James Madsen, curator of the Museum of Earth Science at the University of Utah: 'There were no men 600 million years ago. Neither were there monkeys or bears or ground sloths to make pseudo-human tracks. What man-thing could possibly have been walking about on this planet before vertebrates even evolved?' The site was examined further by a consulting geologist Dr Clifford Burdick a few weeks later on 20 July 1968. Burdick discovered another print – this time a child's:

> The impression was about six inches in length, with the toes spreading, as if the child had never yet worn shoes, which compress the toes. There does not appear to be much of an arch, and the big toe is not prominent ... Where the toes pressed into the soft material, the laminations were bowed downward, indicating a weight that had been pressed into the mud.

Sceptics like William Lee Stokes of the University of Utah, concluded that it was impossible for any of the prints to be genuine since they were solitary, and not a part of footprint sets: 'at the very least we would expect a true footprint to be one of a sequence showing right and left prints somewhat evenly spaced, of the same size and progressing regularly in one direction.'

The Antelope Spring 'shoe print' is not alone in the annals of anomalous archaeological research. The print of a hand-stitched leather shoe was found in Triassic limestone in Fisher Canyon, Nevada, in 1927, following on from a set of apparently shod tracks discovered in two-million-year-old sandstone in Carson City, Nevada, in 1882. While explanatory theories vary from hoax to mis-analysis, some researchers such as J.H. Brennan have gone as far as suggesting that the prints were left by time travellers visiting the prehistoric world:

A computer analysis of the [Antelope Spring] print ... found it deviated in no way from the type of print that would be left by a modern shoe, but if the shoe-print is genuine, we can no longer fall back on the idea of extraterrestrial visitors in Earth's distant past. What we have is an indication that a representative of the human race was strolling through Utah 500 million years ago.

The reason scientists are so resistant to the idea is that it is, in evolutionary terms, preposterous. The current picture of human evolution insists that the evolutionary ancestors of modern man, known as hominids, diverged from those of the apes somewhere between five and eight million years ago.

Another strand of research into anomalous archaeology focuses on the discovery of live animals – often reptiles – set deep inside rock and stone. A typical case occurred in 1865 when workmen excavating for a new waterworks in Durham, England, accidentally liberated a live toad from a piece of limestone 25 feet below the surface of the earth:

The cavity (in which the toad had been contained) was no larger than its body, and presented the appearance of being a cast of it. The toad's eyes shone with unusual brilliancy, and it was full of vivacity on its liberation. It appeared, when first discovered, desirous to perform the process of respiration, but evidently experienced some difficulty and the only sign of success consisted of a 'barking' noise, which it continues invariably to make at present on being touched. The toad is in the possession of Mr S. Horner, the president of the Natural History Society, and continues in a lively state as when found. On a minute examination its mouth is found to be completely closed, and the barking noise it makes proceeds from its nostrils. The claws of its fore feet are turned inwards, and its hind ones are of extraordinary length and unlike the present

English toad ... The toad, when first released, was of a pale colour and not readily distinguished from the stone, but shortly after its colour grew darker until it became a fine olive brown.

A local geologist and clergyman, the Reverend Robert Taylor, announced that he believed the toad to be 6,000 years old.

In a similar case recorded in France in 1851, a toad appeared from a solid piece of flint, when the rock was split by a worker's pickaxe. The toad immediately tried to escape, but was quickly replaced in his toad-shaped cavity and sent off to the Society of Sciences for examination. It was discovered that, if kept in the dark, the toad would remain in the lidless flint, but as soon as he was exposed to the light he would attempt to find shelter.

Many other toads have been found in rocks and pieces of coal – some when exposed to the heat of a log fire. Lizards and frogs have also been discovered in similar conditions. While it is known that frogs can hibernate in solid mud for many months, retaining a very low metabolic rate, it seems incredible that these creatures can really have been in the rock since it was formed many million years ago. That, though, is what many researchers into anomalous archaeology believe. There have been hundreds of such 'animal in stone' finds recorded over the past few hundred years, and many of them are curiously convincing. When living animals emerge from rock strata known to have been formed many million years ago, and it is not easy to find credible conventional explanations for their presence, alternative theories are bound to multiply. This is particularly true when the emerging creature seems to have been prehistoric.

Pterodactyls were flying reptile dinosaurs that became extinct some 100 million years ago. Yet in 1856 a creature identical to a pterodactyl emerged from the Jurassic limestone of a building project in France. With leathery wings over ten foot across, and a mouth full of sharp teeth, the beast gave a last flap before dying – all within minutes of appearing from

the stone. Its remains were positively identified as a pterodactyl by a fossil expert in the nearby town of Gray. He also
confirmed that the rock strata that had encased the animal
was consistent with the historical period of such a beast. On
closer inspection it was also clear that the rock contained a
perfect mould of the animal which, it appeared, had held it in
suspended animation for 100 million years.

One of the most unusual explanations for the phenomenon
of animals in stone emerges from a Tibetan report. In the late
19th century a Tibetan Buddhist Lama named Situ Pema
Wangyal Rinpoche was travelling to Lhasa, the Tibetan
capital, with some friends. On one particular day, to the
distress of his party, he became angry and disturbed. In a
change of plans, the venerable Lama abandoned the route to
Lhasa in favour of a direction that, as far as his respectful
companions could see, led nowhere.

After some hours, the party arrived at a large rock formation, which, the Lama announced, they were going to break
apart. The friends were aghast at the Lama's behaviour. They
looked at each other, starting to doubt his sanity. At this
moment, the Lama approached the rock and smote it with
one mighty blow of his walking stick. The rock cleaved open
to reveal a strange, black, salamander-like creature, which
struggled for breath. The Lama took it in his hands, placed it
on the ground and began to perform a yoga ritual known as
pho-wa over the creature. This particular ritual is normally
performed by lamas to assist in 'the transition of a human
soul from the earth body into the realms of Bardo' – or 'death'
as we more commonly call it in the West.

In this case the party witnessed a thin column of rainbow-
coloured light arise from the creature's head, moments before
it expired. The Lama went on to perform funeral rites, before
the body of the creature was burned. The friends were eager
to understand the significance of the event and asked the
Lama to explain. He said that his purpose had been to liberate
the animal – with which he had a previous life connection –
from what he described as one of the universe's 'occasional

hells'. In Tibetan Buddhism these occasional hells are states of existence which, while not in hell itself, are 'hellish'. The Lama believed that animals trapped inside rocks are, indeed, suffering a form of hell. By releasing it, the Lama had repaid his karmic debt to the creature and the universe.

Some inanimate objects found trapped in stone generate as much controversy as the animate creatures we have so far explored. When seemingly modern artefacts are found in rock strata many millions of years old, then questions start to be asked.

In 1961 Wally Lane, Virginia Maxey and Mike Mikesell from Olancha, California, headed in to the local Coso Mountains to search for interesting and unusual rocks and crystals. It was both their hobby and their work since together they owned a gem shop in Olancha. What they found, close to the peak of a 4,300-foot mountain, remains a subject of mystery to this day.

They often looked for geodes, ordinary-looking stones containing a 'micro-cave' full of crystals. Not only beautiful, they also sold well in their shop. Yet inside one geode was something that none of them had ever seen before. Instead of crystals, there was an object made of metal and a ceramic material. When it was examined by X-ray it seemed to closely resemble a spark-plug, with its metal core, ceramic insulation material, and a hexagonally shaped sleeve, now petrified. Although it appears not to have undergone a complete scientific analysis, one geologist has put the age of the object at some half a million years old. Some observers have wondered what kind of condition the car might be in . . .

EARTH ENERGIES

On a hot summer's afternoon in June 1921, a 65-year-old Englishman named Alfred Watkins had a profound revelation which changed the way many people now view the British landscape. On a walking trip through his native Herefordshire countryside, Watkins had stopped on a high hilltop to survey the view spread out before him. In one strange and profound moment 'a flood of ancestral memory' was released ... and a realization came to him that ancient sites throughout the land – mounds, crosses, hill peaks, churches and the like – are linked by a network of straight tracks, lines or 'leys':

> I had no theory when, out of what appeared to be a tangle, I got hold of the one right end of this string of facts, and found to my amazement that it unwound in an orderly fashion and complete logical sequence ... A visit to Blackwardine led me to note on the map a straight line starting from Croft Ambury ... over hill points, through Blackwardine, over Risbury Camp and through the high ground of Stretton Grandison where I surmised a Roman station. I followed up the clue of sighting ... the straight lines to my amazement passing over and over again through the same class of objects.

His son Allen, who often accompanied Watkins on his trips, adds to the story:

> A chance visit to Blackwardine caused him to look at the map for features of interest. He had no particular object in mind, but was just having a look around. He noticed on the map a straight line that passed over hill tops through various points of interest and these points of interest were all ancient. Then without warning it all happened suddenly. His mind was flooded with a rush of images forming one coherent plan. The scales fell from his eyes and he saw that over many long years of prehistory, all trackways were in straight lines marked out by experts on a sighting system. The whole plan of the Old Straight Track stood suddenly revealed.
>
> His lightning comprehension bore all the marks of being an ancestral memory of the Old Straight Track, just as John Bunyan's ancestral memory of the same thing was at work when he wrote 'The Pilgrim's Progress' ...

'The whole thing came to me in a flash,' he told me afterwards.

The work of Alfred Watkins and his son Allen inspired a whole new field of research called 'ley' hunting, a field which has confounded, confused and created controversy ever since. Ancient burial mounds, standing stones, wells, hills, trees and even churches – many of which are known to have been built on pre-Christian sites – seemed to be linked along perfectly straight lines. But why should ancient man mark out these straight lines?

While Alfred Watkins was content to think of 'leys' as straight tracks, roadways linking important places, many modern researchers have claimed that ley-lines mark measurable lines of earth energy which our ancestors were fully aware of. Indeed, the claims go further. Not only were earlier civilizations aware of the lines of energy, but their rituals and ceremonies were designed to activate and maintain flows of energy that move across and through the Earth. Some have likened the process to the way that a modern-day acupuncturist manipulates the energy in the physical body. For these ancient people, though, the need for such practice was threefold: to increase the fertility of the land and the helpfulness of the elements, and to maintain good relations with the source of these energies – whether the source came from above, below or both.

These controversial theories have gathered many detractors. Apart from those who claim that straight-line alignments of earthworks, stone circles and other significant sites are mere coincidences, there are also many who doubt the idea that English churches were built over pagan sites. Yet this overlaying process is even described in a letter, dated AD 604, from Pope Gregory to Abbot Mellitus who had been given the job of converting England to Christianity:

I have come to the conclusion that the temples of the idols in England should not on any account be destroyed. Augustine must smash the idols, but the temples themselves should be sprinkled with holy water and altars set up in them in which relics are to be enclosed ... I hope the people (seeing their temples are not destroyed) will leave their idolatry and yet continue to frequent the places as formerly, so coming to know and revere the true God.

It is, of course possible that, just as the Christians absorbed the previous pagan sites, so perhaps did the Celts and Druids adapt and change other even earlier sites, working with the energies that existed there. Author John Richards' assessment describes the process:

The activities of occultists and magicians often centre on Celtic sites such as tumuli, circles and snake-paths, and such places, which with or without the encouragement of ritual may suffer a psychic hangover from previous usage. This is particularly true of sites that have been desecrated. One theory is that stone circles, for instance, were constructed to attract energy, whether this is so remains a matter of opinion, but it does seem that such centres act as distribution points for occult forces which appear to run on power lines or 'leys' between each centre. The assessment by young people of a place by its good or bad 'vibes' [vibrations] and their willingness to spend hours at such sites as Glastonbury Tor, stems probably from an instinctive awareness of such things.

There is little doubt that there has been a flourishing renaissance of interest in earth energies. It seems to have coincided with the emergence of environmentalism, deep ecology and the 'nature consciousness' of the mid- to late-20th century. This growing movement has also involved the rediscovery of earth consciousness from other cultures: the shamanic work of the North American Indians and the Dreamtime of the Aboriginals are just two of its existing manifestations. In 1960 Charles Mountford went on a journey of 300 miles across the Central Australian Deserts with a group of Aboriginal men. The purpose of their journey was to stimulate the energies at a number of sacred sites along their straight-line paths. In his book *Winbaraku and the Myth of Jarapiri* he describes how each of the tribes is responsible for sections of these sacred lines. Each season the tribesmen visit the appropriate 'centres' and perform the rituals which keep the energies flowing as they should. These rituals involve the singing of particular songs, and together the different songs make up the 'songlines' that link the sacred sites of the Aboriginal landscape: 'It is an aboriginal belief that every food, plant and animal ... has an increase centre where a performance of the proper rituals will release the life essence or kurunba of that particular plant or animal, and thereby bring about its increase.'

Some of these points are marked with stones, or stone circles, a tradition that is repeated in the British and American landscape. In England the best-known and most thoroughly studied stone circle is Stonehenge. Thought to be some 5,500 years old – although its full construction may have taken 1,500 years – it remains one of the oldest constructions on the planet. Its famous 'bluestones' – 80 in number and weighing many tons each – were transported over 200 miles from the Presecelly Mountains in Wales. The larger sandstone megaliths, which still dominate the site today, weigh in at an average of 26 tons, and were brought from closer by.

While it seems clear from the work of astro-archaeologists that the henge was used as a sophisticated observatory, this does not explain the size and type of stones that were used in its construction. It is well known that generations of pre-Christian cultures carried out their rituals at the site, and many claim that the energies of the site are particularly powerful. Whether this might be as a result of the location, the continued practice of rituals there, or the energy in the stones themselves is less than clear. That there is power at the place is well reported: the dowser and earth-energy researcher

Tom Graves describes the experience of a colleague who tried to tap the power:

> A friend of mine, whom I'll call Peter, had an experiment of this type go wrong at Stonehenge, when he was using an *ankh*-shape as an aerial. The ankh was a big one, nearly two feet high, made out of cooker wire in outline form, to resemble a dipole aerial. The aim of the experiment was to see if the ankh could be used to pick up energy from the circle – and it succeeded rather too well.
>
> He climbed onto the roof of a car in the Stonehenge car park (he's not very tall) and, holding the ankh by the loop at the top, and pointing the open end away from him, he moved the ankh like a scanning radar aerial. The moment this aerial came into line with the stones he felt an enormous surge that seemed to burn his arm, and he lost consciousness for a moment. When he recovered from that, he found that he had been – as another friend put it – 'thrown bodily off the car', and his arm seemed to be paralysed. It took six months before he was able to use his arm fully again. Whether the paralysis was objective or subjective, it was still all too real from a practical point of view. So please don't play around with these energies: we don't yet know enough about them to know in detail what is safe and what is not.

One of the main methods researchers employ to detect earth energies is dowsing – using either rods, pendulums, or a host of other devices to amplify physical muscular reactions to any changing currents within the body. A great deal of dowsing research has been carried out since the discoveries of Alfred Watkins, in an effort to understand the invisible, parallel world that may echo the physically visible signs of Watkins' 'leys'. Dowser Tom Lethbridge has studied many of the large stones and stone circles in Great Britain and elsewhere, and has recorded many first-hand experiences of the energy that he has felt:

As soon as the pendulum started to swing, a strange thing happened. The hand resting on the stone received a strong tingling sensation like a mild electric shock and the pendulum itself shot out until it was circling nearly horizontally to the ground. The stone itself, which must have weighed over a ton, felt as if it were rocking and almost dancing about. This was quite alarming, but I stuck to my counting.

Another example of the power of the stones was recorded by Chris Barber and John G. Williams, authors of *Ancient Stones of Wales*:

Sensitive persons like dowsers sometimes detect different kinds of vibrations or powers at these sites if they are in their original positions. These are difficult to define but it is thought that there are seven different kinds of power bands of which three operate below ground level and the other four can be ascertained by some people on the sides of these stones above the ground . . . the fifth waveband up from the bottom of the stone, which has been called spiral power, is the easiest one for an open-minded person to experience.

Unfortunately many people through modern scientific teaching believe that these things are not possible and they make up their minds not to experience any reaction when it is explained to them how it is possible to contact this curious natural power . . . if the hands are placed firmly against the stone, after a short while a responsive person will experience a peculiar sensation of being pushed away from one side of the stone. But if either palm is taken away from the face of the stone, then this sensation ceases immediately.

This strange spiral power pushes a person away from the standing stone either to the right or to the left. If it pushes him away to the right and he then crosses over his hands and puts his palms flat on the face of the stone so that his hands swap positions, then the spiral will act in a reverse direction and push him away to the left. This is something like reversing an electrical circuit and indicates that the movement of the person away from the face of the upright stone is caused by some kind of power and is not the result of the person's imagination.

It has been found that this spiral power waxes and wanes in a 28-day cycle so there are times when the spiral power is less effective than at others. At the end of the cycle the power is reversed so that it moves a person to the right on one day then 28 days later it will move the same person to the left. Some people who experience this spiral power feel afraid of the unknown and just want to forget about it. Others, because of the variable factors mentioned above, think that they have been misled in some way because they may not be able to repeat the experience when the power potential has become low when approaching a change-over time.

On a number of occasions the authors found that photographs taken of standing stones have shown streaks and patches that appear to be light or energy of some kind:

It showed a white blur between the stone and John G. Williams, who was standing about 3 feet away. The blur of light extended from the bottom to the top of the stone, where it tapered slightly and this was seen against the background of the nearby hedge. This result would have been dismissed as a freak, because there was no sensible explanation for the white blur apart from camera or film fault, had it not been for two colour photographs taken at the same time by John G. Williams with a 35mm camera. They both showed a dark purple-blue around the base of the stone which faded away towards its top.

They were not alone in capturing something unusual on film close to the stones. In July 1977, when BBC Wales were filming for a children's programme at the Great Oak standing stone at Crickhowell, a 15-year-old boy called Richard Williams was demonstrating the effects of the stone's 'spiral power'. The filming first recorded young Williams placing his palms on the stone and being pushed away. Next John G.

Williams demonstrated the effect of a different 'energy band' from the top of the stone – being thrown back quite violently.

The results of the filming were screened on a programme called *Ty Bedd*. Within days at least five viewers had contact the BBC saying that they had seen an object emerging very quickly from a cloud above the stone. When the BBC analysed the high-speed film a 'small yellowish-white oval object' could clearly be seen. It was already quite distant when it flashed across a patch of blue sky only to disappear into clouds, close to the horizon. Estimates of its speed had the object travelling at 16,000 miles an hour.

While it is clear that not every photograph of a standing stone reveals some strange energetic phenomenon, the current evidence may offer the future hope of an objective method of recording the earth's energies. Efforts to reach an objective analysis of earth energies with dowsing equipment have proved elusive to 'ley-hunters'. While they may get reactions, not every dowser tends to receive similar reactions: a fact that has pleased the sceptics. If a more objective form of energy recording, or energy sensing, were possible, it could change the nature of earth-energy studies very significantly.

FENG SHUI

Feng shui (pronounced fung shway) means, literally, 'wind and water'. It is the name given to the ancient Chinese science of 'placement'. It is a practical science – though some might call it an art – aimed at bringing harmony to the environment in which we live. The ideas of feng shui can be applied to a room, a home, a town, a district, a country or even a planet: the same basic principles are in action, whatever scale the feng shui master works on. The aim is always the same: to bring increased harmony.

In China and Hong Kong, and a growing number of other countries, feng shui is used during the planning phases of large buildings to determine the most auspicious siting and orientation for the building's intended function. Feng shui masters are also employed by people who believe they can improve their existing home or office environment, by applying feng shui's mysterious principles.

Many feng shui masters use a complex compass to help them decide on the orientation and most beneficial alignments of a building and its contents. They will often hang one or more 'pak-kua' – an octagonal mirror which contains the eight trigrams from the *I-Ching* – intended to maintain good relations with the spirit realm. While this may all seem very strange to Western minds, its wide acceptance in the East, and our increasingly global osmosis of ideas, has brought feng shui some popularity in the West where it is now being used by both private individuals and commercial organizations. Feng shui believers claim that the successful application of the science has potentially limitless benefits: from increased happiness and well-being, to increasing the child-bearing capacities of couples and the wealth-creation of individuals or businesses.

The debate about feng shui between East and West goes far back in history. When the Western powers went East to trade in the 18th and 19th centuries, they found a culture that regarded its landscape in a wholly different way. As John Michell observed in his *New View Over Atlantis*:

It amazed the Chinese that materially advanced Europeans should be quite ignorant of the geomantic science, and so culturally retarded that they could see no further than the visible surface of the landscape. Many believed that the foreigners knew feng-shui, but for some reason were keeping their knowledge secret. It was noted that a grove of trees planted to give shade to a Hong Kong hospital, had been placed according to the best geomantic principles, and that the richest foreigners had built their houses in a most favourable position below the finest dragon hill in the colony. Yet at other times foreigners seemed truly ignorant and gullible. They would accept as concessions the most inauspicious land in the country, flat, angular and featureless, where predictably they were subjected to flood, drought, attacks by white ants and other plagues and disasters. Moreover their doomed proposals to build railways through dragon lines seemed blatantly perverse.

Some experts in feng shui have examined the success of Hong Kong under the British Government, before it was handed back to China, and have made a link with the auspicious placement of Government House atop the island's peak. More than a hundred years ago E.J. Eitel described the irony:

> Why, they say, there is a Government House, occupying the very best spot on the northern side of the island, screened at the back by high trees and gently-shelving terraces, skirted right and left by roads with graceful curves, and the whole situation combining everything that Feng Shui would prescribe – how is it possible that foreigners pretend to know nothing of Feng Shui?

Perhaps, then, the understanding between East and West has been in place for longer than we might have thought, but has merely remained hidden below the surface. If this is true, the time seems to have arrived for feng shui to come out in the open. When the new headquarters of the Hong Kong Shanghai Bank were designed in the 1970s the task was given to the European architect Sir Norman Foster. He was, however, required to incorporate the advice of one of Hong Kong's foremost feng shui masters Koo Pak Ling throughout the design and implementation of the project.

It was Koo who initially determined the most favourable direction from which to enter the building – angled to one side, rather than directly from the front. He also oversaw the siting of some of the key interior functions, including the imposing escalators. He determined that a key piece of land between the building and the sea needed to be purchased by the bank to ensure the company's continued prosperity. Even much of the fine detail in the new building was decided on by the feng shui man – Koo determined the siting of furniture and pot plants in key executives' offices. Interested observers, like journalist Suzanne Green of United Press International, have watched the bank's fortunes continue to rise since the new building was completed on the site of the original headquarters:

> The site itself was not, of course, of his choosing, but it has proved itself (to the believer's eye at least) by the success of the Bank over so many years of operation from the same address. It stands in a direct line between the Government House and the harbour, so it has a very powerful protective Black Tortoise composed of the Peak and the Governor. In front of it are the waters of the harbour, and water which cannot be seen to flow away is indicative of wealth in Feng Shui terms. Across the water are the Nine Dragon Hills of Kowloon, permanent markers of good fortune and a stately presence. To the east and to the west, White Tiger and Azure Dragon ridges sweep down to the harbour, cradling the Bank's site. No road points arrow-like at the building, for in front of it is the Statue Square, and the main pedestrian way to the Bank runs along the Square and only then disgorges people at an angle towards the carefully aligned escalators.

The Chinese vocabulary of feng shui does not always sit happily with Western culture. However, as many Western companies have found out: when in Asia, do as the Asians do – even though the different cultures may perceive events very differently. As Sarah Rossbach describes in her book, *Feng Shui*, when Dow Chemical opened a new plant in Asia, they were surprised at the interpretation of events:

> At Dow Chemical, a feng shui expert held the opening ceremony of a plant during a week of pouring rain. A threatening deluge held off until after the outdoor extrava-

ganza for 300 guests. The executive who organised the event, Dean Wakefield, the marketing communications director, was congratulated by Chinese executives – not for avoiding soaked dignitaries but for the downpour that followed. The rain signified that 'the money can't wait to pour down on you'. Mr Wakefield said that the venture has been successful beyond the company's expectations.

The consequences of Westerners ignoring the demands of feng shui can be both tragic and very expensive, as one British architect working in Hong Kong discovered. As part of the Hong Kong Shanghai Bank's in-house architectural team, Roger Williams was asked to design a pair of houses in Hong Kong's New Territories. The two houses were to be built on the side of a mountain known as 'The White Dragon', the location giving spectacular views over another mountain called 'The Azure Dragon'. Williams had designed a swimming pool into the project, which was reached via a set of white steps leading down the hill and through a round gateway.

Soon after the building work on the houses was complete, Hong Kong was hit by hurricane Wanda. Homes were destroyed and many people killed. The local *tong*, or ruling family, which had been devastated by the death of many members, blamed Roger Williams and the new houses he had built. They said the cause of the tragedy for their family had been Williams' failure to build on 'the Azure Dragon', while building on 'the White Dragon'. This had caused imbalance. Also, they claimed, 'the White Dragon' had angered 'the Azure Dragon' by baring its teeth – in the form of white steps – and opening its mouth – as demonstrated by the round gateway. In this way, the *tong* asserted, the Western architect had caused the storm to kill their family. So who won the case? Williams' employers, the Hong Kong Shanghai Bank, were ordered to pay one million Hong Kong dollars to the aggrieved *tong*. The architects were also ordered to remove the steps and gateway that had 'caused' the terrible tragedy.

*

While some feng shui ideas are becoming integrated into mainstream practice, it remains hard for the Western mind to understand its apparently more sinister practices. Feng shui practitioners who have been brought up in traditional ancient ways possess an armoury of rituals, some of which seem to border on witchcraft. Typical of these rituals is the *Tun Fu* ceremony, a popular spirit-calming ceremony often used on an area of land prior to the start of any new building work. A *Tun Fu* ceremony, carried out by a feng shui master (here referred to as a *geomancer*) named Cheung Yuen Chong on 17 January 1960, at Pak Wai village in Hong Kong's New Territories, was reported by a G.C.W. Grout, a government officer:

He started by placing the incense, the cups and the rice bowl and red packet on a table ... The incense was then lit and water placed in the rice bowl. Two pieces of joss paper were then lit, placed in the rice bowl of water, and the nail put into it. He then took up one of the pieces of wet bamboo, passed it over the burning incense and wrote certain inscriptions on it, copying out of the book, and passed it over the incense again, the written side down ...

After about five minutes of prayer he seized the young live cockerel by the head in his left hand, and taking hold of the nail from the rice bowl, plunged it into the cockerel's eye. On the impact the young cockerel almost struggled free, fighting it so hard that the geomancer had to tighten his grip and to push it into the cockerel's eye once more. With a crunching noise he pierced the nail right through the cockerel's head and out of the other eye. Thereupon, the cockerel ceased struggling and lay limp, as if dead ... The limp cockerel was placed on the ground and the geomancer then filled his mouth with water from the rice bowl and blew on the cockerel twice, hitting it on the rump at the same time. Surprisingly enough, the cockerel got up and started staggering about, not knowing where to go, as it was still dazed and couldn't see.

260

... Lastly, the geomancer declared that work could start in three days' time and said the ceremonies were over.

The fact that the feng shui master is referred to in this report as a geomancer is significant. Geomancy – the search for harmony between man and earth – has a long history in the West, and is the closest equivalent we have to the East's feng shui. The practice of geomancy has long been the source of inspiration for the creators of sacred buildings – cathedrals, mosques and other temples. Since early civilization these have been designed and built around principles of sacred geometry – the use of archetypal shapes and number systems to convey subconscious yet powerful meaning. Writer Nigel Pennick has described the role of the geomancer throughout history:

Like the animal kingdom, early man was integrated with the environment, occupying his niche in a completely natural and unconscious manner. His life was controlled by the passage of the seasons, his nomadic wanderings on the face of the globe directed by necessity. The faculty now known as intuition was his guiding principle. It led him to find water, nourishment and shelter. It enabled him to sense the presence of danger and to avoid it. His symbiotic relationship with the 'ecosystem' was not yet broken. Possessing intelligence, he recognised his dependence upon Mother Earth, who had brought him into being and sustained him. She was the universal deity. Each part of her was therefore sacred, suffusing her with spirit and manifest in differing forms according to the place. The various powers present in rocks, hills, trees, springs and rivers were operative and available at the appropriate times.

While Pennick proposes this sensitivity as a lost art, there are those who believe this 'natural' ability to sense energies and use them to create harmony can be rediscovered by those with the desire and persistence. A growing number of modern, Western practitioners are now widening the appeal and application of feng shui and geomancy. One of these is the

British woman Karen Kingston who stresses the need for people to clean the energies in their homes, as well as simply doing the hoovering. She recommends a number of different 'space clearing' techniques such as the burning of specific herbs, playing bells and drums, clapping and visualizing light in and around the home. She claims to combine her natural psychic senses with geomantic techniques gleaned from different cultures. Karen Kingston says that her techniques have evolved from a number of key experiences that helped to demonstrate her own sensitivity – a sensitivity which she claims we can all develop:

One evening in 1978, I was driving over to visit a couple of friends who had just moved into a new flat when an idea occurred to me which – but I did not know it – was to change the course of my life.

I arrived on their doorstep and explained to them what I had in mind. Rather than have them show me around their new home, I asked them to allow me to explore their place blindfolded . . .

They were as interested as I was to try this little experiment, so they hunted out a thick black silk scarf and tied it tightly around my eyes. Then, starting at the front door, we began our journey around the flat, following the inside perimeter of the space . . .

The first thing I discovered was that I could mostly tell which pieces of furniture belonged to my friends and which belonged to the landlord. The pieces belonging to my friends had a warm, familiar energy to them, whereas those belonging to the landlord had a duller, more ponderous vibration.

. . . One very strong signal was what I could only describe at the time as 'mental hardness'. I also registered painful aches in my bones, especially my finger joints.

. . . A week later I got an excited phone call to tell me that they had checked with the landlord and discovered that the previous tenant had lived there for twenty years and had been a very stubborn old man with severe arthritis, especially in his hands!

... As my ability to read energies in buildings developed, I began to realise that a lot of it was unsavoury and undesirable. In particular, I wanted my own home to be as free from other influences as possible. It was therefore a natural progression to learn ways to cleanse and clear the energy of buildings, and I called these techniques 'Space Clearing'.

William Spear, another modern Western expert in feng shui, is also keen to demystify what can appear to be an impenetrable system of belief and superstition. 'If you like, it's just good and bad vibes.'

Perhaps the clearest expression of the great ideal, the profound aim behind feng shui, is expressed by a famous Chinese proverb: 'If there is harmony in the home, there will be order in the nation. If there is order in the nation there will be peace in the world.'

DOWSING

Dowsing has a long and mostly hidden history. There is evidence that dowsing was used by Ancient Egyptians: wall pictures show people carrying a forked stick held out in front of them. In China there is a statue image of Emperor Kwang Su from around 2200 BC with an identical implement. The human need for water and the knowledge that it is always 'down there somewhere' have married in the simple idea that some, if not all of us, have a sympathetic sense of where to find it. Unsophisticated man, more in touch with the elements and energies of the earth, may have been more naturally sensitive to the signals that indicate water. Whether we believe in the efficacy of dowsing, and whether it is *always* successful, its documented history is filled with many triumphant reports, and not just in the search for water. Today there are dowsers who search for minerals, precious stones, missing people, criminals, dead bodies, illnesses in humans and animals, remedies for ailments, earth energies, ley-lines, 'geopathic stress' ... the list continues to grow, and the number of different tools the dowser uses also increases. Where once upon a time the only tool was a forked stick, there are now straight rods, angle rods, wands, pendulums, and forked implements made from many different materials.

It certainly was not like this in 1661, when the basics of dowsing were first observed by scientist Robert Boyle. Boyle, perhaps the greatest chemist of the modern scientific era, was well aware of dowsing's potential, and even tried it himself in a search for valuable metals for his chemical experiments. While he was personally unsuccessful he was open to the genuineness of the dowser's art:

A forked hazel twig is held by its horns, one in each hand, the holder walking with it over places where mineral lodes may be suspected, and it is said that the fork dipping down will discover the place where the ore is to be found. Many eminent authors, amongst others our distinguished countryman Gabriel Plat, ascribe much to this detecting wand, far from credulous or ignorant, have as eye-witnesses spoken of its value. When visiting the lead-mines of Somersetshire I saw its use, and one gentleman who employed it declared that it moved without his will, and I saw it bend so strongly as to break in his hand. It will only succeed in some men's hands, and those who have seen it may much more readily believe than those who have not.

Still the most common use of dowsing is in finding, or 'divining', water. In an age of mains water it is very hard to imagine a time when the building of a house brought with it the challenge of digging a well to supply its needs. In his famous book of 1822, *The Confessions of an English Opium-Eater*, Thomas de Quincey describes the work of the Somerset water diviners, who, in this extract, are referred to as 'rhabdomantists', from the Greek meaning divining by the use of a rod:

> In Somersetshire, which is a county the most ill-watered of all
> in England, upon building a house, there arises uniformly a
> difficulty in selecting a proper spot for a well. The remedy is to
> call in a set of local *rhabdomantists*. These men traverse the
> adjacent ground, holding the willow wand horizontally: wher-
> ever that dips, or inclines itself spontaneously to the ground,
> there will be found water. I have myself not only seen the
> process tried with success, but have witnessed the enormous
> trouble, delay, and expense, accruing to those of the opposite
> faction who refused to benefit by this art.

Perhaps the most successful water diviner in British history
was a Victorian named John Mullins, who was born in 1838.
When 21, Mullins was employed to help build a large new
house on the Ashwick Estate in Gloucestershire, owned by Sir
John Ould. Sir John had already employed a dowser from
Cornwall to find a source of water for the new house. This
dowser had identified a line on which, he said, water could be
found. Sir John decided on an experiment: he asked the few
people present to try the same with the dowser's rod. In his
daughter's hands the response was so extreme that she could
not hold on to the rod, and let it drop. Workmen dug at the
spot, and a substantial cache of water was found. Some days
later Sir John decided to expand the experiment to the
workmen working on the new house – 150 in all including
John Mullins. When Mullins stepped up and tried, the dowsing
rod moved so violently, it snapped. Sir John was so impressed
that he asked Mullins to find a source of water at one of his
local farmhouses. Mullins was spectacularly successful: not
only did he find a source some 85 feet below ground, but it
produced a very useful 200 gallons an hour.

It was to be the first of more than 5,000 water sources that
Mullins located throughout his long dowsing career. Despite
his success, though, Mullins continued to work as a building

mason for the next 20 years or so, only becoming a full-time water diviner and well-sinker in 1882 at the age of 44. His business ethics meant that he only charged for his work when he was successful. This may have been a deciding factor in his employment by a Sir Henry Harben of Warnham Lodge in Sussex. Sir Henry had already paid out more than a thousand pounds on three abortive attempts to find water on his land. Despite his scepticism, Sir Henry decided to call in Mullins for one last try, even meeting him at the railway station to make sure that the dowser could gain no prior local knowledge of his property.

As they walked over Sir Henry's land, Mullins had a reaction from the dowsing rod. They were over a small underground stream, Mullins told Sir Henry, but it would not provide sufficient for his needs. Sceptics might question this as a typical hoaxer's trick, but it is worth pursuing the story to the end. Mullins pinpointed two more sites on higher ground, as well as other sites on the opposite side of the road, close to where Sir Henry owned cottages. To test Mullins' accuracy Sir Henry decided to sink wells at all the sites that had been pinpointed. Every one produced significant and useful amounts of water. A visiting geologist described Mullins' achievement as 'supernatural'.

Colonel Kenneth Merrylees was another British Victorian diviner, born over a hundred years ago in 1896. He became particularly famous for his ability to dowse for unexploded bombs during and after the Second World War. As part of a bomb disposal team he would use his skills to locate the position and depth of bombs with delayed action fuses which had penetrated deep into the ground. He was reputed to be able to detect bombs as far as 50 feet below the surface. In one case he located and defused a 500-pound bomb which had 'burrowed' under the swimming pool at Buckingham Palace in September 1940.

Merrylees, who later became the chairman of the British Society of Dowsers, was equally famous for his ability to find water. While in the Middle East and India, his talents at finding water in remote, or barren regions earned him the title: 'God of the water'. In the Indian district of Rawalpindi, a borehole for a hospital ran dry, but when Merrylees dowsed the area he found another source some 50 yards away. That source is still believed to be running today. He normally worked with hazel twigs and whalebone dowsing rods, but was also, apparently, able to demonstrate his ability to locate water from a map. Merrylees was, however, always modest about his talents:

> I am not exceptional among 'sensitives' in that I am, after a short time, acutely uncomfortable if I stay on the lines of a fair-sized flow, and I know from experience it's impossible for me to sleep over one. I found it impossible to accept a purely physical explanation of the dowser's ability. I am forced therefore to look beyond the limitations of orthodox physics and the five senses ... [there is] a connection by the dowser's mind with some sort of knowledge beyond all physical existence limits.

As the nature of war has changed, the need to locate unexploded bombs and land mines by dowsing has increased. In 1967, a *New York Times* article entitled 'Dowsers Detect Enemy Tunnels' lifted the lid on a US Marine project to use dowsing to detect enemy artcfacts in Vietnam. In this apparently successful experiment, the potentially lethal technique of wandering around minefields with a forked twig was replaced by the seemingly miraculous method of 'map dowsing'. With map dowsing the dowser works remotely – moving his or her finger or a pointer over the map of an area and noting the responses of the pendulum or rod that he or she is holding in the other hand.

Uri Geller, the well-known psychokineticist and metal bender, earns much of his living from his map dowsing and divining skills. He commands large fees for helping exploration companies locate oil and other minerals hidden in the ground. In this field of dowsing, he is said by many to be the

UNEXPLAINED NATURAL PHENOMENA

man with the golden touch – the 'King Midas of the late 20th century' – and is keen to bring dowsing out into the open as a respectable way of locating valuable resources: 'It's rumoured that many countries and companies have used dowsing over the centuries as a means of exploration, but have kept quiet for fear of ridicule,' Geller claims.

Working intially with maps of potentially fruitful areas, Geller says he can 'sense' promising locations. He then flies over these selected locations in order to pinpoint positive reactions more accurately. Whether or not people believe him, he has, by mineral explortion standards, been remarkably successful:

> Out of 11 clients that have used my services so far, four have struck big, another four did very respectably and only three had lacklustre results. You will be amazed at how much money some of the mining companies waste by throwing away huge sums on unnecessary exploration. Our challenge to them is this: why spend $100 million a year to find nothing, when for little more than 1 per cent of that budget you can hire our services and have a much higher chance of a strike.

There have been a number of reports in the UK's *Financial Times* about the very large fees that Geller's dowsing work has commanded. When asked about an alleged 'standard' advance fee of £1 million Geller went somewhat further:

> That's right. In fact the *Financial Times* was also right when it said of the 11 projects I have undertaken in the past 10 years, four have been big successes where the royalties went way beyond the original £1 million advance. I'm not prepared to say more than that, other than the rewards from my mining consultancy have enabled me to enjoy an excellent lifestyle.

Despite this endorsement from the corporate sector, there is actually very little scientific evidence that dowsing works. Indeed scientific study of dowsing has been remarkably unsuccessful. Well-known dowser Tom Graves has explained this by saying that the reliability of dowsing is very dependent on the participant's 'need' to be successful. If there is a great need for water in a remote region, for instance, he or she may have a better chance of success. Such a theory would make any scientific testing very difficult, since the essence of any scientific test is its ability to be repeated under synthetic laboratory conditions.

In his 1987 book *Psychic Breakthroughs Today*, D. Scott Rogo reported on a research project that challenged a dowser to forecast the winners of horse-races. Unknown to the dowser there were two other psychology students attempting to do the same. One of these students was a racing 'buff', who was experienced at trying to pick winners, the other was completely inexperienced. Over a period of two weeks, the three of them were given 80 horse-races to forecast. The inexperienced student, who we might call the 'control' subject in this experiment, picked 14 winners – a 17.5 per cent strike rate. The horse-racing expert picked 23 winners – close to a 29 per cent strike rate. The dowser was disappointed: on her best day she 'only' managed four out of eight correct. Out of the 80 races she picked a total of 32 winners – an impressive 40 per cent success rate overall. While the samples are too small to be significant, and including the fact that the experiment is likely to have very variable results, it is, nevertheless, worth noting. If we were to proceed with Tom Graves' theory that the success levels of dowsing are related to the 'need' for success, we might conclude that a dowser in dire financial straits is more likely to succeed at money-making strategies than a financially comfortable dowser. Whether Uri Geller would agree with this theory is not yet clear.

No account of dowsing encounters would be complete without mention of the world's most famous and multi-talented dowser the Abbé Alexis Mermet. Mermet was a priest who spent most of his life in France and Switzerland during the early part of the 20th century. He was probably most at home as a medical dowser, or practitioner of *radiesthesia*, using a pendulum to locate and diagnose specific medical problems. Nevertheless he was also renowned for his ability to find water with extraordinary precision, whether on site, or by map dowsing. In the autumn of 1933, however, it was Mermet's ability to locate missing persons that was called upon when a six-year-old boy disappeared from the village of Valais in Switzerland.

The villagers had already searched the village and surrounding countryside without finding any sign of the small child. It was the town's mayor who contacted the Abbé and asked for his assistance in this distressing case. Mermet used his pendulum and came to an almost unbelievable conclusion: the boy had been captured by an eagle, and carried off into the mountains. He also reported that the bird, which had a very large wingspan, had dropped the child at two locations, while it recovered its strength to fly on.

Monsieur Baloz, the child's father, searched the first location without finding any evidence of the child having been there. When a fall of snow covered the second location mentioned by Mermet, the villagers started to believe that the infallible Mermet had led them astray. Two weeks later the snow melted. At the second location that Mermet had identified, a group of woodcutters stumbled on the body of the little boy. He had been badly torn apart by something, even though his clothes and shoes were clean, and showed no signs that he had walked anywhere. The evidence certainly fitted with Mermet's conclusions. The boy's father wrote the Abbé Mermet a letter on 18 March 1934:

Now that the body of my poor boy has been recovered, it is our duty to thank you for so kindly helping us and giving us such precise information. Everything has been confirmed. It is now certain, as you said in your letter, that the poor boy was carried away by an eagle which did not stop in its flight until it reached the mountain heights at the two places you had indicated, and where the body was eventually found. We also observed that the boy's clothes were as clean as they were on the morning of the disappearance. You were the only person who really knew and understood what had taken place. Please forgive us if we appeared to be very doubtful about your indications. Several eyewitnesses in Sierre declared having seen, on the same day, an enormous eagle flying north. Again thanking you, L. Baloz.

LANDSCAPE ZODIACS

In 1929 a sculptor named Katharine Maltwood published the extraordinary theory that the features of the landscape around Glastonbury in south-west England formed a 'terrestrial zodiac'. In other words, a map of the 12 astrological symbols had been projected onto a ten-mile-diameter circle of land. There are, she claimed, at least 12 complete figures and animals formed from hills, roads, tracks, rivers and ponds and other natural and man-made phenomena, exactly as they appear in the heavens.

Initial reactions to such an idea were, and still are, inevitably disbelieving. How could our ancestors have achieved such a massive effort of engineering? For what purpose? Is this not just the imagination of an artist projecting what she wished to see in the randomness of natural landscape? Yet despite opposition to such an unlikely idea, a number of 'earth mystery' researchers have picked up the theory and developed it. Mary Caine, author of *The Glastonbury Giants*, and perhaps the Zodiac's foremost proponent, addresses the fundamental criticism:

Preposterous? Maybe, but there on the map are the twelve signs of the zodiac in correct order in a circle ... all five miles long. Can this be chance? It has been calculated that if the odds against two signs being right with each other are two to one, the odds against twelve being in the correct relationship are nearly 480 million. And if we study their exact form the odds get even longer. Thirteen heads for instance face west; the winter signs are to the cold north, the summer signs to the sunny south, and when the planisphere is superimposed to scale on the map, *the zodiacal constellations fit over their earthly counterparts.*

Some of the astrological figures described by the Glastonbury Zodiac are not those we would currently identify with the star signs we know. Aquarius, for instance, at the centre of the Zodiac, is meant to portray a bird, possibly a phoenix. Cancer is shown as a ship, drawn from straight lines. However, the figure of Taurus the bull has pronounced horns, and one of the Gemini twin appears to have visible ribs, formed from terraced fields, and his hair is still a flourishing woodland. Some say the Zodiac contains some convincing coincidences.

Katharine Maltwood's 'discovery' of the zodiac occurred when she was asked to do illustrations for a new translation of a book on the Arthurian quest for the Holy Grail. In the end it turned out to be her own 'grail quest'. Legend has it that Joseph of Arimathea brought the Holy Grail – the chalice from which Jesus and his disciples drank at the Last Supper – to Glastonbury in Somerset, England. On landing at the Isle of Avalon, he thrust his thorn-wood staff into the ground where it took root and grew, flowering every Easter and Christmas until today (except for a hiccup when a religious puritan cut it down, blinding himself with a wood-chip in the process). Arviragus, the then ruler of the region, granted Joseph and his companions '12 hides of land' around Glastonbury to sustain themselves. Mary Caine maintains that these 12 'hides' of land – an ancient measurement of area – were, in fact, the 12 figures of the Glastonbury Zodiac.

In the Arthurian myth, the search for the Holy Grail starts from Camelot – now believed to be Cadbury Castle near Glastonbury. As Maltwood followed the Grail Quest around Avalon for her illustrations, she started to see patterns emerging. Mary Caine describes what happened:

She had been asked to draw a map of the itinerary of the Arthurian Grail Quest round Avalon, and, as she tracked a knightly encounter with a lion to Somerton on the six-inch Ordnance Survey map, Leo himself leapt out at her with a roar, his underside entirely drawn by the river Cary, his back outlined by ancient Somerton Lane, his mane tangled by woods in *Cat*sash Hundred. Then she saw a giant baby modelled by Dundon and Lollover Hills nearby. Too much! The Vale of Avalon, she knew, had long been haunted by a lion and a giant. From their relative positions an astrologer friend suggested a zodiac, and soon the whole grand constortium was carefully uncovered.

In fact Katharine Maltwood was not the first to have put forward the idea that there was a zodiac focused on Glastonbury. Queen Elizabeth I's astrologer, John Dee, and his mediumistic partner Edward Kelley are reputed to have discovered the Glastonbury Zodiac in the 16th century, although it is not clear whether Maltwood, or her astrologer friend, were aware of this. John Dee stated that the Glastonbury Zodiac showed

... the starres which agree with their reproductions on the ground do lye onlie on the celestial path of the Sonne, moon and planets, with the notable exception of Orion and Hercules ... all the greater starres of Sagittarius fall in the hinde quarters of the horse, while Altiar, Tarazed and Alschain from Auilla do fall on its cheste ... astrologie and astronomie carefullie and exactly married and measured in a scientific reconstruction of the heavens which shows that the ancients understode all which today the learned know to be factes.

If there really are 12 astrological figures laid out over a ten-mile circle across Somerset, in exactly the same positions that they occupy in the night sky, it would certainly show an incredible effort on behalf of an earlier civilization. It would also demonstrate a miraculous ability to shape and adapt the existing landscape to reflect the myths and archetypes of human consciousness. Since it is only properly visible from the air, it would also indicate an extraordinary grasp of surveying techniques.

Katharine Maltwood believed that the Glastonbury Zodiac was unique. She believed, also, that it had been laid out over 4,700 years ago. Its later ties to the mystical Arthurian legend made it, for her, both special and particular. For her the Zodiac was the Round Table of Arthur placed at the heart of the mythical Avalon. Since her initial discovery in the 1920s, though, there are now claims for more than six further terrestrial zodiacs in the English, Welsh, Irish and even French landscapes. By location they are at: Kingston on Thames; Nuthampstead in Hertfordshire; Ongar in Essex; Stanley, near Durham; Holderness in Yorkshire; Bury St Edmunds in Suffolk; Pumpsaint and Preseli in Wales; and Verdon in France. If they are to be believed, the majority occur in the south of England and Wales and four of them are on the same latitude – 52 degrees North. They appear to be precisely sited, in the manner of Stonehenge, and would seem to be the result of very careful surveying. Some experts now believe that the whole of the British Isles was divided into 'geomantic provinces', each of which contained its own zodiac. This system, they say, was replaced in Christian times by dioceses watched over by bishops. It would appear that the zodiacs fall very neatly into these dioceses – indicating that the Christian Church may have adopted an earlier, pagan system of territorial division.

Can all these zodiacs really have been created by the hand of man? Or are they merely the improvement of natural forms that existed already? Whichever is true, Professor Robert Lord is convinced of their importance:

The precise purpose of the British terrestrial zodiacs we may never be able to rediscover. But with further accumulation of knowledge, it should be possible within a few years from now to build up a general theory of their significance. This will be particularly so if prejudices against their acceptance can be

274

overcome. It will be especially significant if zodiacs are found in parts of Europe where detailed recorded histories go back further than in Britain. One thing we can be certain of is that the construction of these zodiacs was no passing whim of a semi-primitive people. To project sophisticated drawings onto a landscape, to arrange them in a particular order, and to incorporate natural features such as rivers and streams, would require very considerable surveying skill, a degree of skill that would make much modern surveying seem mere child's play. Some then must have taken several generations to complete; and the dedication and ingenuity put into them cannot have been surpassed even by the cathedral builders of medieval times.

John Michell, the earth-mysteries expert and author of *The New View Over Atlantis*, has posited the bold theory that landscaping on a massive scale has been practised in many other cultures:

In China until recently, as long ago in Britain, every building, every stone and wood, was placed in the landscape in accordance with a magic system by which the laws of mathematics and music were expressed in the geometry of the earth's surface. The striking beauty and harmony of every part of China, which all travellers have remarked, was not produced by chance. Every feature was contrived. The main paths of planetary influence, determined by thousands of years of astronomy, were discovered in the landscape, the smaller lines that ran between them reproduced in the crags and fissures of the earth. These were the lines of dragon current or *lung-mei*. The various parts of the earth each fell under a particular planetary influence passed down through the lines which ran above them ... Even the shape of hills should conform to their astrological position ... Where nature had placed two hills in discord, Chinese geomancers had the shape of one altered. The top of the peak would be cut off or the rounded hill sharpened with an earthwork or flattened in to a high plateau. In this way the paths of the various influences across the country were visibly defined, the very bones of the landscape altered to reflect the celestial symmetry ... The whole of China south of the Great Wall was formed to a single design, in which the topographical features of the landscape were artificially moulded to produce their conformity with the required pattern.

Already we wonder at the miraculous achievements of the medieval cathedral builders. If true, here is a construction much more remarkable. What though would have made our ancestors carry out works on such a scale? What would have justified such a work? The absence of a reason presents a problem to Colin Wilson, writer on the occult:

I have to confess that I am by no means wholly convinced. As far as I am concerned one vital piece of evidence is missing ... I find it very hard to imagine how Glastonbury's Temple of the Stars could have been used in any practical way. I am willing, I should add, to be convinced. But for me the mere demonstration that various configurations of the land could be the signs of the zodiac is no convincing proof. I would need to be told precisely how the worshippers used the Zodiac in their religious ceremonies.

This whole idea of 'as above, so below' is very tempting, but for many it remains in the realms of fantasy. Is it just an example of psychological projection, rather than any more physical form of projection? Perhaps though, if further evidence of zodiacs were verified, we might have more reason to believe that there may, indeed, be a kind of heaven on earth. Mary Caine, for one, is already convinced: 'The zodiac pattern is written not only in the stars, but on human form and character, on animals, plants and even minerals. It is also, it seems, inscribed on the very face of the earth itself – perhaps all over the world.'

CROP CIRCLES

The first crop circle of the modern era seems to have appeared near a town called Tully, in Queensland, Australia, on 19 January 1966. Tractor driver George Pedley was driving through a neighbour's cane farm, when he saw a 'spaceship' fly out of Horseshoe Lagoon, a small swamp some 30 yards ahead of him. The ship was bluish-grey, about 25 feet wide, and 9 feet high: 'It spun at a terrific rate as it rose vertically to about 60 feet, then made a shallow dive and rose sharply. Travelling at a fantastic speed, it headed off in a southwesterly direction. It was out of sight in seconds.' When Pedley found the spot where the craft had been, he saw that a 30-foot circle of reeds had been swirled flat. Within the circle, 'the reeds were without exception bent below water level, dead and swirled around in a clockwise manner, as if they had been subjected to some terrific rotary force.' Two more circles were found in which the plants had been ripped from the sodden soil. It was not long before supernatural investigators were arriving and stories of the UFO 'nests' began to circulate the globe. Whether anyone realized it at the time, the crop-circle phenomenon had begun.

It was not until August 1980, though, that the phenomenon found its natural habitat in the fields of southern England. One morning a Wiltshire farmer named John Scull discovered a strange circle in one of his oat fields: it was about 60 feet in diameter and seemed to have been swirled flat with some force. When the local press published a report it soon attracted the attention of Wiltshire's many local UFO enthusiasts. Very quickly stories of giant craft landing in the fields of southern England were the talk of the area.

With each year that passed, ever-increasing circles appeared in the fields of Wiltshire and Hampshire – an area well known for its ancient sites: Avebury, Silbury Hill and Stonehenge. In some years as many as 50 circles would manifest – and in seemingly every case without the presence of witnesses. Researchers from every area of science and the paranormal became embroiled in a struggle for a modern-day Holy Grail. Theories abounded: whirlwinds, tornadoes, hedgehogs, RAF jets, hoaxers, MI5, CIA, UFOs, alien energy beams. Nothing was impossible.

Digging in the archives revealed that this might not be a new phenomenon after all. The earliest report of a circle in a corn field appears to have been in Assen in Holland in 1590. In the 17th century an English scientist named Robert Plot suggested that circular patterns in fields might be caused by rapidly descending blasts of air: an idea that would be picked up on by at least one 20th-century researcher.

When one circle appeared in the 17th century its appearance was attributed to a 'mowing devil'. A contemporary report revealed the reasoning behind the attribution:

> [The Mowing Devil: or Strange News out of Hartford-shire]
> Being a True Relation of a Farmer, who Bargaining with a Poor Mower, about the Cutting down Three Half Acres of Oats: upon the Mower's asking too much, the Farmer swore That the Devil should Mow it rather than He. And so it fell out, that every Night, the Crop of Oat shew'd as if it had been all of a Flame: but next Morning appear'd so neatly mow'd by the Devil or some Infernal Spirit, that no Mortal Man was able to do the like.

Back in the fields of Wiltshire the research continued and certain characters emerged to play their parts in the unfolding drama. As a scientist, Terence Meaden would certainly never have countenanced a supernatural explanation for the evolving phenomenon. Nevertheless the crop circles found this ex-Oxford physicist rubbing shoulders with more ufologists, dowsers, psychics and healers than most scientists meet in a good few lifetimes. Meaden's experience of weather phenomena led him initially to believe that the crop circles were formed by whirlwinds or mini-tornadoes. But as new, more complex, circles formed, Meaden was forced to 'adapt' his theory to fit the facts: the atmospheric agent was now a 'plasma vortex', a spinning whorl of ionized gas which discharges partly or completely on contact with the fields.

By the mid-1980s two UFO writers named Pat Delgado and Colin Andrews had arrived very firmly on the crop-circle scene. As UFO enthusiasts, their focus was on the theory that intelligent extra-terrestrial life was creating the increasingly complex forms. With their pilot friend Busty Taylor, Delgado and Andrews flew over every crop formation they could find taking aerial shots of the striking images. From the early 'plain' circles, circles with satellites, circles with rings, circles linked by other shapes, to the elaborate pictograms and insectograms of the late 1980s, Delgado and Andrews tirelessly recorded whatever they could. They dowsed the circles for mysterious energies. They recounted stories of powerful effects, of healings, of television camera breakdowns and electric phenomena. Meaden's theory was struggling as the circles became more complex, more apparently 'intelligent'. 'Explain that with your plasma balls' came the message from the UFO camp with every strange new addition to the pictogram gallery.

Researchers flew in from around the world, armed with an impressive array of measurement instruments. At the same time reports of circles from around the world began to multiply. Countries as far afield as Brazil, Japan, India, Canada and Switzerland were now reporting the appearance of circles. What had started in the Wiltshire fields had become a global phenomenon within ten years.

With the dawn of the 1990s the controversy intensified. In his struggle for the very soul of science, Terence Meaden brought together some impressive eye-witness accounts to support his basic theory that crop circles were the result of atmospheric phenomena. In August 1990 a couple named Gary and Vivienne Tomlinson claimed to witness the birth of a crop circle:

It was about 9pm and we were returning from our walk across the cornfields out at Hambledon. Half way, we stopped to watch the wind blowing on the corn, sending wave after wave of ripples right across the corn, making it appear like a golden brown sea. I have always held a fascination for wind and sound, and can lose myself watching it. Suddenly there was a change in wind pattern, it appeared to be pushing from both directions. At the centre point the wind gathered force pushing forward sending strong waves in the corn. The whistling grew stronger in the corn, almost like a high pitched pan-pipe flute sound.

We both looked up to see if there was a helicopter above us. There was none, it felt strange. Suddenly there was a gush of strong wind pushing against us. The wind circled round us, looking down, we noticed corn being pushed down. It started with one large whirlwind. This broke into another one, pushing the offset one into the side, whirling away pushing down the corn.

The circle we were in was fast becoming interesting. Miniature whirlwinds were appearing one after another, rapidly whirling around the corn in small bunches, then gently falling down.

We stood watching in amazement, the corn swirled and then gently laid down. There was no feel of wind now or sound. It felt strange watching these ever-fast gathering whirlwinds. They just seemed to increase; they were enveloping around quickly. I panicked, grabbed my husband's hand and pulled him out of the circle.

It felt strange, perhaps because of the unknown answers that lay in the balance. I believe the answer lies in the current build-up of wind and force.

Meaden's case was also strengthened by more accounts that predated the current controversy, and confirmed that simple circles had been appearing for many years. Another eye-witness report was sent to the *Sunday Express* in 1990 by Kathleen Skin of Cambridge:

I witnessed a corn circle being formed in 1934. I was gazing over a field of corn waiting to be harvested when I heard a crackling like fire and saw a whirlwind in the centre of the field, spinning stalks, seeds and dust up into the air for about 100 or more feet.

I found a perfect circle of flattened corn, the stalks interlaced and their ears lying on each other (some even plaited) on the periphery. The circle was hot to the touch. There was nothing to be seen in the sky – no wind, and no sound. Maybe on a windless day the corn stalks form an electric current which attracts an electric force in the atmosphere meeting with such pressure that the corn is pressed hard on to the ground in a circular motion. A sort of miniature tornado.

The high-profile argument with Meaden on the one side and Andrews and Delgado on the other was just the kind of story that the UK media loved. It was originally Pat Delgado's pushing that had involved the national press in the contro-versy, but by 1990 the situation seemed out of control: hyped witness stories, prizes offered to circlemakers, hoaxers paid to fool other newspapers. The whole crop-circle phenomenon was threatening to melt down from the heat of the confusion. For many, though, the worst was yet to come.

It was September 1991 when the crop-circle world was thrown into turmoil by two retired artists named Doug Bower and Dave Chorley. 'Doug and Dave', as they became known in popular mythology, confessed to the hoaxing of hundreds of circles going back as far as 1978. They even claimed to have been inspired by the Australian UFO nest circles wit-nessed by George Pedley in 1966. Ironically they were both interested in UFO phenomena. At the time of the revelation it was portrayed that Doug and Dave were claiming to have created them all. The two men knew this was not true. They were in touch with other crop-circle artists who, they admit-ted, had performed equally cunning stunts.

After this blow many crop-circle enthusiasts who had believed in a supernatural explanation faced a crisis of faith.

Some deserted the fold, disappearing from view to lick their wounds. A hard core remained despite the new popular perception that all circles were hoaxes. In a further irony, Doug and Dave's revelation seemed to strengthen the position of Dr Terence Meaden, whose plasma vortex theory was now revived to explain the simple circles for which there were first-hand witnesses.

As the 1990s progressed there was no let up in the creativity behind the images. With every year they became more and more exotic, incorporating mathematical and geometrical symbolism. Circlemakers became more public about their activities: they were not hoaxers, rather they were anonymous artists working on vast cereal canvases. Ironically many of these 'cereal artists' still believe that there is a real phenomenon involved in some of the crop circles. A number of them claim to have had supernatural experiences while they were actually creating circles:

> We drove to another field that we had previously chosen as a potential circles site. This time everything ran smoothly and the formation was soon underway. Part-way through the construction of the formation there was a powerful burst of light; we all stopped, looked around, and after a bit of head scratching continued the formation. This was followed soon afterwards by an identical burst of light. I later described the experience as analogous to having a flash gun let off in my face, with the light momentarily blinding.

In 1996 many people thought the hunt for the cause of 'real' crop circles had been solved when a video appeared showing the formation of a crop circle. In the video, taken at Oliver's Castle in Wiltshire, England, two small balls of light are shown moving together in circular, almost intelligent, movements over a field of wheat. As their movement progresses, a formation of circles appears in the field beneath them, before they leave the area, disappearing over a hedge. Here at last was the evidence that everyone in the crop-circle 'field' had been looking for.

The video had been brought to Colin Andrews one evening by a man calling himself 'John Wheyleigh'. But when Wheyleigh failed to arrive at further meetings Andrews became suspicious. Other facts about the man did not check out. Andrews issued a press release a month later, stating that the video was almost certainly a hoax, perpetrated by a television or video company in an effort to entrap him. If true it would follow a well-established pattern in the history of crop circles: phenomenon first, supernatural theories next, hoaxers claim credit last. Such is the confusion, subterfuge and suspicion that now surrounds crop circles that an area of research that was once filled with an air of excitement and enthusiasm has become tainted with rancour and bitterness. Polarization between the 'all crop circles are hoaxes' camp and the 'crop circles are the result of supernatural forces' camp is still as great as when the first crop circles appeared in the early 1980s. Now the warfare goes on over the Internet as competing websites offer information and disinformation aimed at discrediting the opposite parties. One site operated by the 'Circlemakers' – a group who delight in demonstrating their creative and artistic endeavours in the night-time corn – published some of the hate mail they receive from a group called Black Watch:

> Friend. If you value your health and well being you will end
> your criminal activities in the fields of England, now!
> Do not take this warning lightly. We are many.
> Black Watch.

Presumably the motivations of groups such as Black Watch are to leave the fields free for genuine phenomena. Whether their strategy is likely to be successful remains to be seen.

On 7 July 1996 a startling configuration appeared in a field within sight of Stonehenge, Wiltshire's timeless megalith. Consisting of 149 separate circles making up a curling pattern, the pictogram was a simplified rendering of a fractal, geometric shape known to mathematicians as 'the Julia Set'. Soon this image was known as the Stonehenge Julia Set, and within weeks was appearing on websites, T-shirts and coffee mugs around the world. What struck most observers was the intense complexity of the image: how could hoaxing humans have created such an intricate and accurate 'agriglyph' in the dead of night? It simply must be the creation of a superior intelligence. Colin Andrews again put his neck on the line: 'If these Julia Sets can be proven to be made by humans, then we can all pack our bags and go home. If these are human-made, I won't be giving speeches on this subject next year.'

One journalist, James Hockney, described the level of disbelief in the scientific camp: 'Even Terence Meaden, a physicist and sceptic was lost for words on how such complicated formations could have been made. His explanation was that the formation was constructed by 30–100 people working all day on it with the permission of the farmer.' How indeed could such a vast image have appeared in a time window that had originally been estimated as a matter of 45 minutes, without any evidence of human intervention? One answer came from cereal artist Rod Dickinson. In an interview now published on the Internet, Dickinson claimed that he knew who had done it and how it was done. A group of three people, he claimed, had constructed the Julia Set at night in less than three hours. He described the working method in detail:

> You start with the large central circle, which is placed right next to a tram line (the narrow avenues created by tractor/ sprayers). People asked why it had the large central circle, which is a little out of place in a Julia Set. Simple. To avoid damaging surrounding crops, you have to have a large central area already laid down, from which you can measure out diameters to other parts of the formation.

Challenged to demonstrate the making of such a circle Dickinson declined: 'All it would really prove is that people

CAN make these extraordinary formations. That does not eliminate the possibility of something paranormal someplace else, but it would suggest that we have to be much more careful and rigorous before we label any of these formations anomalous.' Dickinson, in common with many of the circle-makers, is not completely antagonistic to the idea that there are real circles. Indeed he admits to having had his own inexplicable experiences with brilliant flashes of light in the midst of his circle art. He also has his own position about which of the circles are 'real': 'I can definitely account for most of the major pictograms from 1991 on. I myself made several dozen of them . . . Some of the simple circles could be the real thing. I really don't know.'

A new strand has emerged in the thinking of some circle-makers. They are not there to create hoaxes, they say. They are making genuine circles, genuine art. Some also claim that they can now create the energetic patterns in the circles that dowsers would expect from 'real' circles. They are creating temporary sacred spaces with their own powerful, and in some cases, healing energies. One anonymous circlemaker describes the cross-over between 'hoax' and the paranormal: 'Our work generates response, often from other circlemakers, and can sometimes act to catalyse a wide range of paranormal events. I still believe there is a genuine phenomenon, but I now also believe that we're a part of it.'

SOURCES

1. POWERS OF THE MIND

Levitation

Lewis, David, tr., *Saint Teresa: Life*, International Catholic Truth Society, Brooklyn, NY

Thurston, Herbert, *The Physical Phenomena of Mysticism*, Henry Regnery Company, Chicago, 1952

Psychokinesis

Fairley, John and Welfare, Simon, *Arthur C. Clarke's World of Strange Powers*, Guild Publishing/William Collins Sons & Co., Glasgow, 1984

Jahn, Professor Robert, *The Margins of Reality*, Harcourt Brace & Co., London

McKenna, Paul, *The Paranormal World of Paul McKenna*, Faber & Faber, London, 1997

Thoughtography

Eisenbud, Jule, *The World of Ted Serios*, Jonathan Cape, London, 1968

Psychometry

Robinson, Chris, with Boot, Andy, *Dream Detective*, Warner Books, London, 1996

Memories of Past Lives

Bernstein, Morey, *The Search for Bridey Murphy*, Pocket Books, New York, 1978

Guirdham, Dr Arthur, *The Cathars and Reincarnation*, CW Daniel, Saffron Walden, 1990

Telepathy
Fairley, John and Welfare, Simon, *Arthur C. Clarke's World of Strange Powers*, Guild Publishing/William Collins Sons & Co., Glasgow, 1984

Dreams
Holbeche, Soozi, *The Power of Your Dreams*, Piatkus Books, London, 1991

Precognition
Robinson, Chris with Boot, Andy, *Dream Detective*, Warner Books, London, 1996

Psychic Detectives
Robinson, Chris with Boot, Andy, *Dream Detective*, Warner Books, London, 1996

Spiritual Healing
Grad, B., Cadoret, R.J. & Paul, G.I., 'The Influence of an Unorthodox Method of Treatment on Wound Healing of Mice', *International Journal of Parapsychology* 3: 5, 1961
Grad, B., 'A Telekinetic Effect on Plant Growth', *International Journal of Parapsychology* 6:473, 1964
Holbeche, Soozi, *The Power of Your Dreams*, Piatkus Books, London, 1991
Myss, Caroline, *Anatomy of the Spirit*, copyright © 1996 by Caroline Myss. Reprinted by permission of Harmony Books, a division of Crown Publishers, Inc., NY
Randles, J., *Strange But True Casebook*, Piatkus Books, London, 1995

Near-Death Experiences
Moody, R.A. Jr., M.D., *Life After Life*, Bantam Books, London, 1975, copyright © MMB Inc., St Simons Island, Georgia
Swedenborg, Emanuel, *Compendium of the Theological and Spiritual Writings of Emanuel Swedenborg*, Crosby and Nichols, Boston, 1853

Powers of Heat and Cold
David-Neel, Alexandra, *Magic and Mystery in Tibet*, Penguin Books, London, 1971

Freedom Long, Max, *The Secret Science of Miracles*, DeVorss & Co, California, 1981

2. MYSTERIOUS BEINGS

Sea Monsters
Ridgeway, John and Blyth, Chay, *A Fighting Chance*, J.B. Lippincott Company, Philadelphia, 1967

Bigfoot
Green, John, *The Sasquatch File*, Cheam Publishing, Aggassiz, B.C., Canada, 1973
Napier, John, *Bigfoot, the Yeti and Sasquatch in Myth and Reality*, Jonathan Cape, London, 1973

Yeti
Bord, Colin and Janet, *Alien Animals*, Granada Publishing, London, 1980
Heuvelmans, Bernard, *On the Track of Unknown Animals*, tr. Garnett, Richard, Hill & Wang, New York, 1959
Napier, John, *Bigfoot, the Yeti and Sasquatch in Myth and Reality*, Jonathan Cape, London, 1973
Sanderson, Ivan, *Abominable Snowmen*, Chilton Book Company, Radnor, Philadelphia, 1961

The Loch Ness Monster
Witchell, Nicholas, *The Loch Ness Story*, Terence Dalton, Suffolk, 1974

Lake Monsters Worldwide
Bord, Colin and Janet, *Alien Animals*, Granada Publishing, London, 1980

The Chinese Wildman
International Wildlife, 11:18–19, January–February 1981
New York Times, 5 January 1980
Pursuit, 14: 64–66, Second Quarter 1981

Alien Big Cats
Fate magazine, May 1985
McRae, Toni, '"Buderim Beast" Made Man Shake', *Queensland Sunday Mail*, 28 August 1995

Vampires
Webb, Chris, 'Uri Geller's Encounters', *The Vampire*, December 1995

Werewolves
Baring Gould, Sabine, *The Book of Werewolves*, Senate Publications, London, 1995

Zombies
Godwin, John, *Unsolved: The World of the Unknown*, Doubleday & Company, Garden City, NY, 1976

Angels
Anon, 'On a White Horse: St George and Phantom Army,' *The Universe*, 30 April 1915
Anon, 'The Angel of Mons', *Parish Magazine, All Saints*, Clifton, E. Austin & Son, 1916
Gibbs, Nancy, *Time Magazine*, 27 December 1993
Grant, Robert J., *Are We Listening to Angels?* ARE Press, Virginia Beach, 1994
Israel, Martin, *Angels: Messengers of Grace*, by permission of the publishers: The Society for Promoting Christian Knowledge, London, 1994
Price, Hope, *Angels: True Stories of How They Touch Our Lives*, Pan Books, London, 1993
Taylor, Terry Lynn, 'Creating With the Angels', copyright © 1993 by Terry Lynn Taylor. Extract reprinted by permission of H.J. Kramer, P.O. Box 1082, Tiburon, CA 94920. All rights reserved.

Nature Spirits and Fairies
Andrews, Ted, *Enchantment of the Faerie Realm*, Llewellyn Publications, St. Paul, MN, 1993
Evans–Wentz, W.Y., *The Fairy Faith in Celtic Countries*, H. Frowde, London, 1911; Lemma Pub. Corp., New York, 1973

Hawken, Paul, *The Magic of Findhorn*, Souvenir Press, London, 1975

Lawson, John Cuthbert, *Modern Greek Folklore and Ancient Greek Religion: A Study in Survivals*, 1911

Maclean, Dorothy, *To Hear the Angels Sing*, used by permission of Lindisfarne Books, Hudson, NY 12534, 1975

Treadgold, Mary, 'Correspondence', *Journal of the Society of Psychical Research* 48: 765 September 1975

Wright, Machaelle Small, *Behaving As If The God In All Life Mattered*, Perelandra Press, Warrenton VA, 1997

Psychic Animals

Bardens, Dennis, *Psychic Animals*, Capall Bann Publishing, Chieveley, Berks, 1987

Maeterlinck, Morris, *The Unknown Guest*, Methuen, London, 1914

McElroy, Susan Chernak, *Animals as Teachers and Healers*, copyright © 1997 by Susan Chernak McElroy, reprinted by permission of Ballantine Books, a Division of Random House Inc., NY

Wild Children

Singh, Joseph, and Zingg, Robert M., *Wolf Children and Feral Man*, Harper and Brothers, New York, 1942

3. INCREDIBLE HAPPENINGS

Synchronicity and Coincidence

Bach, Richard, *Nothing By Chance*, William Morrow and Company, NY, 1969

Jung, C.G. and Pauli, W., *The Interpretation of Nature and the Psyche*, Pantheon Books, New York, 1955

Vaughan, Alan, *Incredible Coincidences*, J.B. Lippincott Company, NY, 1979

Sunday Times, London, 5 May 1974

The Face on Mars

Fate magazine, quoted in McKenna, Paul, *The Paranormal World of Paul McKenna*, Faber & Faber, London, 1997

Ball Lightning
Weather, May 1949
Science, 153: 1213–20, 9 September 1966

Spontaneous Human Combustion
American Medicine, 9:657–8, 22 April 1905

Strange Rains
The Marine Observer, October 1963
Weather, 4:121–22, April 1949

Anomalous Archaeology
Leeds Mercury, 8 April 1865
The Zoologist, 1851

Earth Energics
Barber, Chris and Williams, John G., *Ancient Stones of Wales*, Blorenge Press, Abergavenny, 1989
Walter, from Eugene Victor, *Placeways*, University of North Carolina Press, 1988
Graves, Tom, *Needles of Stone*, Gothic Image Publications, Glastonbury, 1978
Lethbridge, Tom, *The Legend of the Sons of God*, RKP, London, 1972
Mountford, Charles, *Winbaraku and the Myth of Jarapiri*, Rigby, Adelaide, 1978
Richards, John, *But Deliver Us From Evil*, published and copyright 1984 by Darton, Longman, Todd Ltd., and used by permission of the publishers.
Watkins, Alfred, *Early British Trackways*, Garnstone Press, London, 1972
Watkins, Allen, *Alfred Watkins of Hereford*, Garnstone Press, London, 1972

Feng Shui
Baker, Hugh D.R., 'Fung Shui – Applied Ecology Chinese Style' [sic], *Building Projects*, 3: 160–161
Eitel, E.J., *Feng-Shui, or the Rudiments of Natural Science in China*, Hong Kong, 1873; reprinted by Graham Brash (Pte), Singapore, 1973

Kingston, Karen, *Creating Sacred Space with Feng Shui*, Piatkus, London, 1996

Mitchell, John, *The New View Over Atlantis*, Thames and Hudson, London, 1983

Pennick, Nigel, *The Ancient Science of Geomancy*, Thames and Hudson, London, 1979

Rossbach, Sarah *Feng Shui*, Hutchinson & Co. Ltd., London, 1983

Dowsing

Boyle, Robert, 'Second Essay on Unsucceeding Experiments', quoted in Spence, Lewis, *An Encyclopaedia of Occultism*, George Routledge and Sons Ltd., London, 1920; reprinted by The Citadel Press, Secaucus, N.J. 1960

De Quincey, Thomas, *The Confessions of an English Opium-Eater*, The Folio Society, London, 1948

Letter to Abbé Mermet, quoted in Nielsen, Greg and Polansky, Joseph, *Pendulum Power*, Aquarian Press, London, 1986

Webster, Jonathan B., 'Uri Geller's Hidden Agenda', *Livewire Magazine*, April/May 1997

Landscape Zodiacs

Caine, Mary, 'The Glastonbury Giants or Zodiac', from *Glastonbury – Ancient Avalon, New Jerusalem*, ed. Andrew Roberts, Rider Books, London, 1978

Lord, Professor Robert, 'Terrestrial Zodiacs in Britain', (proceedings of the First Cambridge Geomancy Symposium, 1977), quoted in Pennick, Nigel, *The Ancient Science of Geomancy*, Thames and Hudson, London, 1979

Michell, John, *The New View Over Atlantis*, Thames and Hudson, London, 1983

Wilson, Colin, 'Afterword', from *Glastonbury – Ancient Avalon, New Jerusalem*, ed. Andrew Roberts, Rider Books, London 1978

Crop Circles

Circlemakers website, (see Further Selected Reading for internet address)

FURTHER SELECTED READING

1. POWERS OF THE MIND

Levitation

Home, Daniel Dunglas, *Lights and Shadows of Spiritualism*, Virtue, London, 1877

Picknett, Lynn, *Flights of Fancy*, Ward Lock, London, 1987

Psychokinesis

Rhine, J.B., *Extra-Sensory Perception*, Faber & Faber, London, 1938

Thoughtography

Randles, Jenny, *The Paranormal Source Book*, Piatkus, London, 1996

Watson, Lyall, *Supernature*, Coronet, London, 1973

Memories of Past Lives

Cockell, Jenny, *Yesterday's Children*, Piatkus, London, 1993

Guirdham, Arthur, *We Are One Another*, Turnstone Press, Wellingborough, 1974

Roberts, Jane, *The Seth Material*, Bantam Books, New York, 1981

Steiner, Rudolf, *Reincarnation and Karma*, Rudolf Steiner Press, London, 1977

Stevenson, MD, Ian, *Twenty Cases Suggestive of Reincarnation*, American Society for Psychical Research, New York, 1966

Wambach, Helen, *Life Before Life*, Bantam Books, New York, 1979

Whitton, PhD, Dr Joel and Fisher, Joe, *Life Between Life*, Grafton, London, 1987

Telepathy

McMoneagle, Joseph, *Mind Trek*, Hampton Roads, 1996

Rhine, J.B., *Extra-Sensory Perception*, Faber & Faber, London, 1938

Dreams

Jung, Carl, *Dreams*, tr. Hull, R.F.C., Routledge and Kegan Paul, London, 1974

Jung, Carl, *Memories, Dreams, Reflections*, tr. Hull, R.F.C., Routledge and Kegan Paul, London, 1971

Precognition

Ouspensky, P. D., *The Strange Life of Ivan Osokin*, Arkana, London, 1992

Psychic Detectives

Wilson, Colin, *The Psychic Detectives*, Pan Books, London,1984

Spiritual Healing

Brennan, Barbara Ann, *Hands of Light: A Guide to Healing Through the Human Energy Field*, Bantam Books, New York, 1987

Cayce, Edgar, (compiled by B. Ernest Frejer), *The Edgar Cayce Companion*, ARE Press, Virginia Beach, 1995

Manning, Matthew, *The Link*, Colin Smythe, Gerrards Cross, 1974

Watson, Lyall, *Supernature*, Coronet, London, 1973

Psychic Surgery

Fuller, J.G., *Arigo – The Surgeon of the Rusty Knife*, Thomas Y. Crowell Publishers, NY, 1974

Near-Death Experiences

Evans-Wentz, W.Y., (ed.) *The Tibetan Book of the Dead*, Oxford University Press, New York, 1957

Kubler-Ross, Elizabeth, *On Death and Dying*, Macmillan, New York, 1969

Kubler-Ross, Elizabeth, *Death is of Vital Importance*, Station Hill, New York, 1995

Rinpoche, Sogyal, *The Tibetan Book of Living and Dying*, Rider Books, London, 1992

Vincent, Ken R., *Visions of God*, Larson, New York, 1994

Wilson, Colin, *Afterlife – An Investigation of the Evidence for Life After Death*, Grafton Books, London, 1985

2. MYSTERIOUS BEINGS

Sea Monsters
Heuvelmans, Bernard. *In the Wake of the Sea Serpents*, tr. Garnett, Richard, Hill and Wang, New York, 1968

Bigfoot
Bord, Colin and Janet, *The Evidence for Bigfoot and Other Man-beasts*, Aquarian Press, London, 1984
Green, John, *On the Track of the Sasquatch*, Cheam Publishing, Aggassiz, B.C., 1968

The Loch Ness Monster
Dinsdale, Tim, *Loch Ness Monster*, Routledge and Kegan Paul, London, 1972
Mackal, Roy, *The Monsters of Loch Ness*, MacDonald, London, 1970

Lake Monsters Worldwide
Costello, Peter, *In Search of Lake Monsters*, Coward, McCann & Geoghegan, New York, 1974
Dinsdale, Tim, *Monster Hunt*, Acropolis Books, Washington D.C., 1972
Mackal, Roy P., *Searching for Hidden Animals*, Doubleday and Company, Garden City, NY, 1980
Meurger, Michael, *Lake Monster Traditions*, Fortean Tomes, London, 1988

The Chinese Wildman
Clark, Jerome, *Unexplained*, Visible Pen

Alien Big Cats
Fortean Times, various issues

Vampires
McNally, Raymond T., *In Search of Dracula*, Robson Books, London, 1994

Zombies
Cavendish, Richard, ed., *Man, Myth and Magic*, Marshall Cavendish Corporation, New York, 1973
Metraux, Alfred, *Voodoo in Haiti*, tr. Hugo Charteris, Sphere Books, London, 1974

Seabrook, William B., *The Magic Island*, Harcourt, Brace & Co., New York, 1929

Angels

McLure, Kevin, *Visions of Angels and Bowmen*, Kevin McLure, Harrogate, 1996

Nature Spirits and Fairies

Bettelheim, Bruno, *The Uses of Enchantment*, Alfred A. Knopf, New York, 1976

Briggs, Katharine, *The Fairies in Tradition and Literature*, Routledge and Kegan Paul, London, 1978

Kirk, Robert, *The Secret Common-Wealth*, ed. Stewart Sanderson, D.S. Brewer, Suffolk, 1976

Psychic Animals

Watson, Lyall, *Supernature*, Coronet, London, 1978

Wild Children

Bettelheim, Bruno, *The Uses of Enchantment*, Alfred A. Knopf, New York, 1976

Dudley, Edward, and Novak, Maximilian, eds, *The Wild Man Within: An Image in Western Thought From the Renaissance to Romanticism*, University of Pittsburgh Press, Pittsburgh, 1972

3. INCREDIBLE HAPPENINGS

Synchronicity and Coincidence

Koestler, Arthur, *The Roots of Coincidence*, Random House, New York, 1972

The Face on Mars

McMoneagle, Joseph, *Mind Trek*, Hampton Roads

Hoagland, Richard, *The Monuments on Mars*, North Atlantic Books, Berkeley, CA, 1987

Ball Lightning

Barry, J.D., *Ball Lightning and Bead Lightning*, Plenum Press, New York, 1980

Meaden, Terence, ed., *The Journal of Meteorology*, Bradford-on-Avon, Wilts.

Spontaneous Human Combustion
Gaddis, Vincent H., *Mysterious Fires and Lights*, David McKay Company, New York, 1967
Harrison, Michael, *Fire From Heaven: A Study of Spontaneous Human Combustion*, Pan Books, London, 1976
Randles, Jenny and Hough, Peter, *Spontaneous Human Combustion*, Robert Hale, London 1993

Strange Rains
Michell, John, and Rickard, Robert J.M., *Phenomena: A Book of Wonders*, Thames and Hudson, London, 1977

Anomalous Archaeology
Brennan, J.H., *Time Travel – A New Perspective*, Llewellyn Publications, St Paul, MN, 1997

Earth Energies
Broadhurst, Paul and Miller, Hamish, *The Sun and the Serpent*, Pendragon Press, Launceston, Cornwall, 1989
Devereux, Paul, and Thomson, Ian, *The Ley Hunter's Companion*, Thames and Hudson, London, 1979
Watkins, Alfred, *The Old Straight Track*, Abacus, London, 1974

Dowsing
Bird, Christopher, *The Divining Hand*, E.P. Dutton, New York, 1979
Graves, Tom, *Discover Dowsing*, Aquarian Press, London, 1993
Lethbridge, T.C., *The Power of the Pendulum*, Routledge and Kegan Paul, New York, 1976
Nielsen, Greg and Polansky, Joseph, *Pendulum Power*, Aquarian Press, London, 1986
Rogo, D. Scott, *Psychic Breakthroughs Today*, Aquarian Press, London, 1987

Landscape Zodiacs
Pennick, Nigel, *The Ancient Science of Geomancy*, Thames and Hudson, London, 1979

Roberts, Andrew, ed., *Glastonbury – Ancient Avalon, New Jerusalem*, Rider Books, London, 1978

Crop Circles
Andrews, Colin and Delgado, Pat, *Circular Evidence*, Bloomsbury, London, 1989
Circlemakers Website: http://www.hrc.wmin.ac.uk/circlemakers
Schnabel, Jim, *Round in Circles*, Hamish Hamilton, London, 1993

INDEX

USA Networks' *Sci-Fi Channel* is available in millions of homes worldwide and features a mix of original and classic science fiction, science fact, fantasy and horror. For further information, visit the *Sci-Fi Channel*'s web site – The Dominion – at http://www.scifi.com.